Sport in the Global Society

General Editor: J.A. Mangan

SOCCER IN SOUTH ASIA

SPORT IN THE GLOBAL SOCIETY

General Editor: J.A. Mangan

The interest in sports studies around the world is growing and will continue to do so. This unique series combines aspects of the expanding study of *sport in the global society*, providing comprehensiveness and comparison under one editorial umbrella. It is particularly timely, with studies in the cultural, economic, ethnographic, geographical, political, social, anthropological, sociological and aesthetic elements of sport proliferating in institutions of higher education.

Eric Hobsbawm once called sport one of the most significant practices of the late nineteenth century. Its significance was even more marked in the late twentieth century and will continue to grow in importance into the new millennium as the world develops into a 'global village' sharing the English language, technology and sport.

Other Titles in the Series

SOCCER IN SOUTH ASIA

Empire, Nation, Diaspora

Editors

PAUL DIMEO
University College Northampton

and

JAMES MILLS
University of Strathclyde

FRANK CASS

LONDON • PORTLAND, OR

First published in 2001 in Great Britain by
FRANK CASS PUBLISHERS
Crown House, 47 Chase Side
London N14 5BP

and in the United States of America by
FRANK CASS PUBLISHERS
c/o ISBS, 5824 N.E. Hassalo Street
Portland, Oregon 97213-3644

Copyright © 2001 Frank Cass & Co. Ltd.

Website: www.frankcass.com

British Library Cataloguing in Publication Data

Soccer in South Asia: empire, nation, diaspora. – (Sport
in the global society; no. 29)
1. Soccer – South Asia
I. Dimeo, Paul II. Mills, James
796.3´34´0954

ISBN 0-7146-5146-X (cloth)
ISBN 0-7146-8170-9 (paper)
ISSN 1368-9789

Library of Congress Cataloging-in-Publication Data

Soccer in South Asia: empire, nation, diaspora/editors, Paul Dimeo
and James Mills.
p. cm. — (Sport in the global society; no. 29)
"This group of studies first appeared as a special issue of Soccer
and society (ISSN 1466-0970), Vol. 2, No. 2, Summer 2001, published by
Frank Cass" – T.p. verso.
Includes bibliographical references and index.
ISBN 0-7146-5146-X (cloth) – ISBN 0-7146-8170-9 (paper)
1. Soccer–South Asia–History. I. Dimeo, Paul, 1971-. II.
Mills, James, 1970-. III. Soccer and society. Vol. 2, no. 2. IV.
Cass series–sport in the global society; 29.
GV944.S643 S63 2001
796.334´092–dc21   2001002914

This group of studies first appeared as a special issue of *Soccer and Society*
(ISSN 1466-0970), Vol.2, No.2, Summer 2001, published by Frank Cass

Printed in Great Britain by Antony Rowe Ltd., Chippenham, Wilts

Contents

List of Photographs

All photographs are reproduced courtesy of Mohammed Shafiq.

Acknowledgements

The editors thank a range of individuals and organizations for their help in putting together this volume. The book grew out of the conference 'Football India: the Past, Present and Future' that they hosted at University College Northampton in July 2000. It was at this event that the necessity of bringing together papers on football in south Asia became obvious, and so the staff at UCN who helped to organize the day and ensure its success are chief among those that ought to be thanked. Penny Hubbard was absolutely indispensable as she thought of all the important details that were missed by the editors, such as the need to book rooms, arrange parking, feed delegates and so on. She then made sure that these details were attended to as the editors could in no way be relied upon to do this themselves. All of the staff in the administration and support services at UCN that Penny persuaded to help or who succumbed to the pleading of the editors spared no effort and made the event look well-planned and effortless. We gratefully acknowledge their assistance.

Among the delegates at the event were a number of individuals whose enthusiasm for many of the issues discussed here convinced the editors that it was a significant project. The editors are grateful for the contributions of Chima Okorie, Jas Bains and Arunava Chaudhuri at the event and for the insights of Kash Taank and Salim Siddat. The editors hope that this volume will be just one of the ways of putting the energy generated at the event into practice. The sponsors of the event were important since they ensured that delegates from India could attend and, as such, thanks are due to ForIndia.com and the Marketing Department at UCN. FIFA, the 'Kick It Out' campaign and the English Football Association are also to be thanked for their contributions to the day. On this note the editors would like to acknowledge funding from the British Academy, the Carnegie Trust for the Universities of Scotland and the University of Strathclyde, who have met the costs of research trips to India on which the ideas behind this compilation first took a hold.

Our trips to India have been made all the more enjoyable and profitable thanks to a number of individuals who offered their time, advice and resources with generosity. We especially thank Sharda Ugra, Sanchita Sen, Amitabha das Sharma, Anthony and Jyoti Botelho, Alberto Colaco, Arnab Ghosh and Sabanayakan. However, one man stands out as making a singular contribution: Brahmanand Shankwalker took us to our first Indian match at the Fatorda Stadium in Margao in Goa, in May 1995. We are grateful for this kind invitation and his continued influence on our work.

This collection of papers has been brought together, been put through several stages of editing and revision, and then has been peer-reviewed and finally published in little over a year since the original conference. The editors express their gratitude for the professionalism of the contributors who have met every deadline and promptly responded to every query no matter how trivial. We would also like to thank Jon Manley at Frank Cass who has been excellent to work with.

Foreword

The FIFA records, like most statistics, tell only half the story. The fact is that the All India Football Federation (AIFF) was founded in 1937 and joined FIFA 11 years later – quite late, one might think, for a country with such particular British connections. After all, those ubiquitous British merchants, sailors and assorted missionaries had successfully exported the game and implanted it in South America and other less colonial corners of the globe almost a century earlier.

The reasons for the delay in the formal establishment of the game in India are many and invariably more complex than the self-evident, secondary role the sport had traditionally played – and, without doubt, still does – to that of cricket. Also, the formal date of affiliation to the world body masks the fact that the AIFF had in the Indian Football Association (West Bengal) a forerunner that dates back, somewhat more plausibly and still very proudly, to 1893.

No doubt the authoritative contributors to the following pages will trace many of the factors dictating the course of development of Indian football from a political and sociological point of view. But generally it may be said that this evolution from foundation to the present has seldom been easy. In consequence, there is still a temptation to classify this, the world's second most populous nation, in the familiar category popularly and vaguely known as 'sleeping giants'. The term has been applied, with varying degrees of justification, to many other countries, especially to those in Africa, where the giant has woken and has startled others into doing so. In China, to take another example, the giant appears to be awake but is seemingly incapable of getting out of bed.

The Indian colossus remains mostly in slumber, despite intermittent bouts of insomnia, reacting to the occasional attempts to rouse it. But such awakenings have seldom had sufficient effect as to transcend regional frontiers.

While the domestic game has, of course, mobilized millions at one time or another, especially in isolated hotbeds such as Calcutta, Bombay or Goa, neither India nor, for that matter, any of its neighbours in the subcontinent has ever made any impact of note on international competition. This sobering record of under-achievement applies to the game at all levels, from junior to senior, not to mention the very specific conditions that apply to women's football.

Invited to take part in the 1950 World Cup, India declined the opportunity to travel to Brazil for the first post-war tournament because its players were not allowed (under FIFA regulations) to play without boots or shoes. The invitation – in retrospect, a once in a lifetime opportunity – was never repeated and since then no team from the subcontinent has ever made it through the regional qualifying process to the finals of any FIFA world competition.

For many countries elsewhere participation in the FIFA competitions has proved to be an essential element in the development of the game. Exposure to competition at the highest level educates and motivates. Africa's youth players (particularly in Nigeria, Ghana and Cameroon) are striking examples of this reality.

Another reflection of modest accomplishments may be found in the FIFA World Ranking, introduced in 1993, where the best position ever achieved by India is 94th in 1996. Bangladesh's best is 111th in 1996, Sri Lanka's 122nd in 1998, Nepal's 124th in 1994 and Pakistan's is 141st in 1994.

FIFA cannot be fairly said to have neglected India and its neighbours over the past quarter of a century. During this time, for example, different development courses have been held in the subcontinent as elsewhere in the world. Scores of countries and hundreds of thousands of individuals in all continents have benefited from this scheme, not only players and coaches but also referees, administrators and sports doctors. Again, the direct comparison with Africa is unavoidable: there is justification in attributing a large part of the several African countries' World Cup success to the concerted coaching work done under the umbrella of these FIFA programmes.

The reason why the success rate has not been the same in both regions may be the subject of a more detailed study. But the impression is sometimes inescapable that Indian football does not always recognize the value of such programmes, as appeared to be the case with the cancellation of a course scheduled for India in June 2000. Such cancellations by the host nation are as regrettable and incomprehensible as they are rare, for the recipients are customarily only too grateful to be offered assistance of this kind.

But FIFA's assistance to India and other countries continues on other levels. There is, for example, the straightforward financial aid programme that sees one million dollars put at the association's disposal over a four-year period, such funds being made available in response to coherent and approved plans and budgets, to avoid wastage or misappropriation.

In addition, the new *Goal* project is set to benefit countries in this as in other regions, the particular characteristic of the *Goal* approach being to provide countries with tailor-made assistance according to their own specific needs. Nepal, for example, has already benefited, and there is no reason why India should not do so in the near future.

These remarks should not fail to mention another important way in which FIFA is currently involved in India, and, indeed, also in neighbouring Pakistan. In early 1977 FIFA co-sponsored the Atlanta Agreement, which laid the basis for a concerted programme to eliminate the exploitation of child labour from the football-producing industry in these two countries. The programme brings together the big names of the sporting goods industry, chambers of commerce, trade unions, the International Labour Office and children's organizations such as UNICEF and Save the Children. It aims systematically to abolish child labour in sweatshops and to provide educational opportunities instead. This is not an easy programme to implement, for it encompasses not only labour but also sociological and cultural aspects, but it is one to which FIFA, and the sport of football in general, remains committed.

FIFA is also, of course, highly conscious of the situation of Asians living in Britain who are confronted with social barriers to the full enjoyment and participation in football. Applying the word as well as the spirit of the FIFA Statutes, which clearly reject any form of discrimination on racial or any other basis, is an undertaking fraught with all manner of complications. But the will remains to achieve this, ideally through the co-ordination of practical actions based upon experience – much of the latter, sadly, bitter.

FIFA's slogan, 'For the Good of the Game', is sometimes considered a little trite. Most slogans are. But it reflects a genuine ambition to improve the game on a global scale, and the Indian subcontinent and its people, at home or abroad, remain a priority target for these efforts. In helping south Asian football to develop, however, FIFA needs unequivocal signs that these nations are also anxious to help themselves.

KEITH COOPER
Director of Communications, FIFA

Series Editor's Foreword

J.A. MANGAN

In November 2000, *The Daily Telegraph* ran a story on an Englishman, Tim Grandage, former Rugby schoolboy and Calcutta Hong Kong Bank executive, his Indian Future Hope school and his street children internationals at the first Asian Rugby Championships in Sri Lanka. For these hugely disadvantaged children, under the compassionate Grandage and with the unostentatious support of the Harlequins Rugby Club, 'a previous alien sport [had] become the cornerstone of their lives'.[1] The lambent spirit of Cecil Earle Tyndale-Biscoe, the earlier English humanitarian schoolmaster, clearly remains alive and well on the Sub-continent.[2]

In one sense, Grandage is the past; his boys are the future. Unquestionably innovatory, *Soccer in South Asia* is both the present and the future, while future volumes in Sport and the Global Society on Asia will represent an important aspect of the future. *Soccer in South Asia* is a 'stepping stone' over a hitherto, sometimes occasionally polluted, historical stream. It is a link between European comment on Asia and Asian comment on Asia.

A triadic approach is overdue: Western voices on Asia, Asian voices on Asia, Eastern and Western voices on Asia. This is fully recognized here by the volume editors and Series Editor.

In *Europe: A History*, published in 1996, which incidentally does scant justice to the significance of sport in recent European cultures, Norman Davies was briefly concerned about Eurocentrism in historical writing. He defined as a matter of attitude, not content, the traditional tendency of European authors to regard their civilization as superior and self-contained, and to neglect the need for 'taking non-European viewpoints into consideration'.[3] The editors of *Soccer in South Asia*, of course, know better than to do this and have put this dated approach[4] behind them, and the series Sport in the Global Society can, and will, go further in due course. Gathering corn in foreign fields, as is made clear in *Soccer in South Asia*, is a thing of the past. In the future the harvest will be shared.

In *The Search for Africa: A History in the Making* published in 1994, Basil Davidson wrote hopefully of future African history:

> In this new epoch, perhaps, 'their' reality and 'ours' – again from whichever side you take it – may begin to converge: not in the singularities of culture, remaining as these will as richly various as human nature, but in their ever more evident requirement of conjoint acceptance. 'They' will begin to be 'there' as much as 'we' are – from whichever way you come in forms and intensities never before possible in consciousness

and he added, optimistically, that,

> As they take shape there, and as we begin to see them in their reality and all the lineaments of their condition, and as the same perception arises in reverse, so in that measure can we and they approach and stand on common ground and in doing that, find the synthesis which can realize conjoint potentials.[5]

This gentle blast on a neoteric post-imperial trumpet has loud resonances for an adjoining continent to the east. Davidson, who has devoted all his professional life to the 'task of recovering and reinstalling Africa within the equalities of world consciousness',[6] stated also in 1994 that the task was by no means near its end. All this is true of Asia now.

In its combination of European and Asian analysts on the Indian subcontinent, with contributions at once original and illuminating, *Soccer in South Asia* brings together Western and Eastern perspectives that jointly enrich our understanding of an Eastern world too often in the past viewed from a narrow Eurocentric angle. They step out of the dark into the light.

Forthcoming publications in Sport in the Global Society will add a further 'stepping stone' over what once was sometimes a less than limpid historical stream – thus three judiciously placed 'stepping stones' will be in place ensuring breadth and depth of analysis – European, European and Asian, and Asian.

With specific reference to Asia, D.G.E. Hall, in *A History of South-East Asia*, in the fourth edition published in 1981, observed that 'the work that has been done by European scholars in the discovery of South East Asian history is beyond praise'.[7] Much the same can be said with regard to this importantly innovative study of soccer in South Asia, especially in view of the editors' action in bringing together analysts of East and West.

Hall went on to remark that the 1980s witnessed 'signs of dissatisfaction on the part of European scholars with their previous approach to the subject, which, it is felt, has been too much influenced by certain preconceptions inherent in their own training and outlook'.[8] He added that it was appropriate that the revolutionary change that characterized South-East Asia after 1945 had led inexorably 'to much reexamination of the other conceptions of its history, and to attempts at a re-orientation of outlook'.[9] This re-orientation is a pleasing feature of *Soccer in South Asia*. In Western sports studies, which have come late to the Asian historical field, this radicalism *should* be built on, and this is the intention of this Series.

Hall also stated something that the initiated know only too well, that the literatures[10] of the peoples of South-East Asia 'abound in writings which are ... or connected with historical events! Their number is legion ... Relatively few have as yet been used by historical writers. The great majority still await exploration and comparative study.'[11] My visit to Chengdu University Sports Institute in Sechuan Province in the mid-1990s brought this home to me dramatically. The impressive large library filled with Chinese monographs, collections and journals produced in me a post-imperial missionary impulse not to take the West to the East but to bring the East to the West – through the mediums of English and Cass. Sport in the Global Society will ensure that Asian academics will be encouraged not only to contribute to, but to edit and author books on history, sociology and other disciplines, in the Series in the future – to the benefit of East and West. They have the cultural and linguistic tools to ensure a valuable balance to European perspectives.[12]

This makes good sense. Asian voices in English on modern sport are still in too short supply in academia. Both this ground-breaking volume on Asian soccer, and in particular its sub-continental contributors, are therefore especially welcome. The editors are to be congratulated on their perspicacity in this regard. And in pursuit of what Davidson has called the 'essence of purposive study', as mentioned briefly above, Sport in the Global Society will shortly ensure then that the voices of Asians themselves are heard more fully and not only as contributors to collections, but as editors and authors. A start will be made soon with the innovative collections, *Sport in Asian Society: Past and Present* and *Confronting Conservatism: Women, Sport, Asia*, and the seminal monograph *Women, Sport and Society in New China: Holding up More than Half the Sky*.[13]

Simultaneously, a triadic approach, therefore, will characterize the Series; the analytic approach will be multicultural; balance, breadth and depth will be the ambition; completeness of perspective will be the aim.

Regional involvement, of course, has been the sensible policy in earlier Series volumes on the Nordic world, the Australasian world and the Latin American world and it will continue to be the policy for future volumes involving other world regions, including shortly North America and Eastern Europe.[14]

Thus with *Soccer in South Asia* an invaluable start has been made, a 'stepping stone' has been put in place, and more 'stones' will soon be set down. In Sport in the Global Society in the new millennium, the East will increasingly come to the West; Eastern voices will speak for themselves; Eastern commentators will advance Western perspectives on Asia.[15] Thus with three 'stepping stones' spanning what in the past has been a sometimes less than crystal clear historical stream[16] Rudyard Kipling's well-known 'Eurocentric' couplet:

> Oh, East is East, and West is West,
> and never the twain shall meet
> Till Earth and Sky stand presently
> at God's great Judgment Seat.[17]

will prove to be an ever more dated vision of events – temporal and celestial!

J.A. MANGAN
*International Research Centre
for Sport, Socialisation and Society
University of Strathclyde*
July 2001

NOTES

1. B. Gallagher, 'Rugby Hope', *Daily Telegraph* (Sport), 25 Nov. 2000, 1.
2. See J.A. Mangan, *The Games Ethic and Imperialism: Aspects of the Diffusion of an Ideal* originally published by Penguin/Viking in 1986 and recently republished by Frank Cass in 1999. Note especially Chapter Seven which deals in more detail than *Soccer in South Asia* in which he also appears, with Cecil Earle Tyndale-Biscoe who in 1895 took English games to Kashmir in the interests of its youth. There were many others of his ilk, most not quite so determined, including notably Alexander G. Fraser, who made an outstanding contribution to Trinity College in Kandy, Ceylon, now, of course, Sri Lanka, a little later. Equally fascinating in his way, he will be the subject of a chapter in the forthcoming *Sport in Asian Society: Past and Present* to be published in the Series Sport in the Global Society, and edited by J.A. Mangan and Fan Hong.
3. N. Davies, *Europe: A History* (Oxford: Oxford University Press, 1996), p.16.
4. For an Asian pointed and forceful criticism of a particularly inadequate Eurocentric approach, in marked contrast to the approach in *Soccer in South Asia*, see Fan Hong, 'Two Roads to China: The Inadequate and the Adequate', *International Journal of the History of Sport*, 18, 2 (June, 2001), 148–67.
5. B. Davidson, *The Search for Africa: A History in the Making* (London: James Currey, 1994), p.14.
6. Ibid., p.8.
7. D.G.E. Hall, *A History of South East Asia* (fourth edition) in the Macmillan Asian History Series (London: Macmillan, 1981), p.xxviii.
8. Ibid., p.x.
9. Ibid.
10. Ibid.
11. Ibid.
12. For an excellent example of this, see Fan Hong, 'Two Roads to China', passim.
13. Reference has already been made above to *Sport in Asian Society: Past and Present. Confronting Conservatism: Women, Sport, Asia* will be edited by Keiko Ikeda, Dong Jinxia and J.A. Mangan and *Women, Sport and Society in New China: Holding up More than Half the Sky* will be authored by Dong Jinxia.
14. See H. Meinander and J.A. Mangan (eds.), *The Nordic World: Sport and Society* (London and Portland, OR: Frank Cass, 1998), J.A. Mangan and J. Nauright, *Sport and Australasian Society: Past and Present* (London and Portland, OR: Frank Cass, 2000), *Sport and Latin American Society: Past and Present* (London and Portland, OR: Frank Cass, 2001) and the Cass volumes in preparation. V. Girginov and J.A. Mangan, *Sport in Eastern European Society: Past and Present* and J.A. Mangan and M. Dyreson, *Sport in North American Society: Past and Present*.
15. Of course, Fan Hong's *Footbinding, Freedom and Feminism: The Liberation of Women's Body in Modern China* (London and Portland, OR: Frank Cass, 1998) provided a firm footing on the bank of the 'stream' a little while ago.
16. For evidence of this see, for example, Hall, *A History of South East Asia*, p.xxviii and his reference there to the self-confident savant, F.W. Stapel's 'ponderous five-volume *Geschredenis van Nederlandsch Indie*, in which the 'Hindu period' of Indonesian history is treated as if it were a sort of prelude or introduction to the history of Dutch activities'. Immediately afterwards, Hall provides a valuable caveat, however, when he writes caustically of those Indian writers, who may be accused of an Indian-centric approach! We all need to be sensitive to the need for balance.
17. Quoted in Davies, *Europe*, p.17.

Introduction: Empire, Nation, Diaspora

JAMES MILLS and PAUL DIMEO

Football is, almost without question, the most popular game in India.[1]

In 1911 over 60,000 Indians thronged to the Calcutta Maidan to witness an Indian team beat a British regimental eleven to win the IFA Shield. During the 1930s Muslims travelled across the country to watch Mohammedan Sporting during the period in which they won the Calcutta League five times in a row. The British presence on the FIFA committee deliberately obstructed the invitation of the Indian national football team to the World Cup of 1950.[2] By the 1990s a brewery owned all of the top Calcutta clubs and a TV company had bought its own team in the National Football League.

Football and the historical changes that have shaped modern south Asia have been closely related for over a century. Football and society in parts of the region are also intimately linked. While the major clubs were founded by the English-speaking elite, an observer could declare by 1959 that 'soccer in India is a poor man's game'[3] and that, as such,

> if a vote were to be taken among all the millions of Indians from all parts of the land who have any interest in or connection with sport, I feel certain that football would easily top the list of their preferences.[4]

An interest in the game often becomes a passion in south Asia that has broader social implications that affect even the minutiae of behaviour. For example, the game can determine the diet of its supporters so that in Calcutta Mohun Bagan fans always eat prawns, known as *chingri*, when they beat their local rivals East Bengal, whose own fans will consume only the local river fish, the *hilsa*, when their team has triumphed. This passion can fuel extreme personal and social behaviour. For example, a teenage fan in Calcutta in the 1970s committed suicide as his club slumped to another defeat by local rivals. By the end of the decade a riot at a derby match had resulted in the death of 16 supporters.

This volume will provide a comprehensive introduction to these stories from south Asian football and to a range of figures, moments and events in the history and recent development of the sport in India.[5] However, as the paragraphs above suggest, football in south Asia has been closely linked to the processes that have shaped the societies and histories of the region since the nineteenth century. Colonialism, the rise of nationalism and communalism, the establishment of nationhood in a post-colonial world, the challenge of the regions and the effects of globalization and economic liberalization have all left their mark on the development of the game. At the same time, however, football has often had an important role to play in the emergence and impact of these processes and has been a powerful vector for those forces. Quite simply, south Asian history and society have transformed football in the region while simultaneously the game has shaped the history and society of south Asia. This volume will therefore not simply act as an encyclopaedia of football in the region, it will instead begin to analyse these relationships and will draw conclusions both about the history and the sociology of football and about the histories and societies of the region.

THE HISTORIOGRAPHY OF SOUTH ASIAN SPORT

Since football has been embedded in south Asian society and history for over a century it comes as a surprise that the game in particular and, indeed, sport in general in the region have not received sustained academic analysis to date. Serious social historians of south Asia, who should know better than to ignore evidence of any sort, prefer to dismiss the game even where it is central to the events that they are analysing, 'already during pre-riot days there were instances of self-mobilization along communal lines over trivial issues. For example, reverses suffered by the Mohammedan Sporting Club in football matches enraged Muslim feelings which were expressed in sporadic violence against the Hindus.'[6]

The suspicion lingers that sport and football have been neglected as they are viewed with apprehension as 'western' or 'un-Asian' activities. Of course, sports such as football were introduced by Europeans, but they have long been indigenized. Indeed, any assumption that such activities are not enjoyed by, and practised with considerable skill by, south Asians is a curious echo of the attitudes of the colonial period when the British constructed Indians as non-sporting as part of an Orientalist strategy to represent them as moral and racial inferiors.[7]

Studies of indigenous sports and games are few and chief among these is J. Alter's *The Wrestler's Body* published in 1992. This book takes an anthropological approach to *Bharatiya kushti* or Indian wrestling in north India, an activity that is a fusion of Hindu sporting traditions dating back to the eleventh century and Persian martial skills introduced by the Mogul armies of the sixteenth century. His concern in examining the activities of the wrestlers is, in part, the concern of this volume too, to step outside of the conventional categories preferred by south Asian studies, which he identifies as 'caste, economics, politics, agriculture, land tenure, marriage, kinship, ritual and religion'.[8] None of these, so often studied in isolation from one another, satisfactorily acts as a tool of analysis for wrestling, which, he observes, 'transcends the categories that anthropologists and others have traditionally used to interpret Indian society and culture. It is a sport, but it is also an elaborate way of life involving general prescriptions of physical culture, diet, health, ethics and morality.'[9] The importance of the sport lies in its providing an arena for Indians to challenge, ignore and reinterpret the rules of social and moral engagement, and Alter concludes that 'wrestling only contingently reaffirms pervasive cultural themes such as rank and status; more significantly, it opens up the stage for a protean, maverick revision of these themes'.[10]

His study of the Indian game *kabaddi* offers a contrasting example to that of wrestling.[11] Both have been used as sites for the construction of ideological myths about 'Indian-ness', but the history of each sport highlights the different versions of 'Indian-ness' that various nationalist groups were using indigenous games to construct. Wrestling, based on individual commitment and development, on Indian spiritual exercises and on an Indian diet, was used to represent 'anti-modern' Indian-ness. This was a version of the nation manufactured by proponents that rejected modernity and saw India as quintessentially non-modern. *Kabaddi* could also be presented as authentically Indian, but at the same time it had many of the aspects of 'modern' sports, especially in its focus on team discipline and coordination. It therefore appealed to such groups as the Rashtriya Swayamsevak Sangh (RSS),[12] the Hindu extremist political organization, which was eager to promote a version of Indian-ness that emphasized modernity and mobilization. The different histories of the two games in the twentieth century – wrestling remains obscure while *kabbadi* has been exhibited at the Olympics – reflect their selection as emblems of two very different ideological articulations of India's national essence.

By far the most research completed on sports in India, however, has been that which has focused on the games introduced by the British during their period of colonial rule. Much of this work has dealt with cricket since it is widely believed to be the most popular game in the region.[13] Some of these studies detail the colonial introduction of the game[14] and argue that it was self-consciously employed by the British with colonizing objectives in mind. The aim of introducing the sport at the public schools opened for the Indian elite was to inculcate in them a moral system and a unity of experience. Within the Victorian moral system characteristics such as patience, persistence and *esprit de corps* were considered virtues by the British who were eager to have their Indian collaborators incorporate such values into their behaviour. Sports were seen as an ideal means of transmitting these virtues, and 'cricket, of course, was the pre-eminent instrument of moral training'.[15] The game was also promoted as a means of providing all Indians with a common interest and Guttmann has concluded of officials such as Lord Harris, the Governor of Bombay in the 1890s, that his hope in promoting cricket in the local community was that it 'might bond together India's religiously, linguistically and ethnically diverse population'.[16] Importantly, however, Guttmann does identify a more complex relationship between cricket and imperialism. He points out that, while many such as Harris actively promoted the game, 'the average member of the officers' club in Madras or Calcutta' was more likely to hinder its spread amongst the Indian population. In other words, the British colonizers were not united in the ways that they used sport in their empire. On the one hand there were those that chose to use it as a means of inculcating outlooks and attitudes in the local population in order to draw it closer to the colonizer in terms of interests and loyalties. On the other, however, there were those who used the game to emphasize their separateness from and superiority to Indians through the opening of exclusively European clubs and the belittling of Indian players.[17]

However, it would be wrong to assume that Indians took to cricket simply because the British willed it and, in fact, a lot of attention has been paid to the processes by which cricket was adopted and adapted by Indians and the reasons for its indigenization. Ramachandra Guha examines the way in which the sport was first used as a vehicle for expressing anti-colonial and nationalist emotions[18] and then points out that the game developed as a site for the development of communalist (Muslim and Hindu) identities during the 1930s and the 1940s.[19] Writers such as Ashis Nandy, Arjun Appadurai and Ian McDonald have examined the theme of the indigenization of the game in the post-colonial period and point to its central place in a range of emerging positions and identities in the years after Independence in 1947. Nandy has argued that the underlying rhythms and mythic structures of the game make it profoundly Indian and that it is therefore consistent that the game should be most enthusiastically appropriated by those from south Asian cultures.[20]

Appadurai and McDonald have instead argued that post-colonial politics and culture explain the rise of cricket in India to the status of popular sport. Appadurai points to state support and commercialization as the driving forces behind the promotion of the game to the masses. The latter adopted the game as 'it became an emblem of Indian nationhood at the same time that it became inscribed, as practice, into the Indian (male) body'.[21] In other words, to post-colonial generations of men cricket became a means of developing a national and a masculine identity. The appropriation of the game has been a self-consciously anti-colonial process, argues Appadurai, who concludes that 'cricket gives ... the sense of having hijacked the game from its English habitus into the colonies at the level of language, body, and agency as well as competition, finance and spectacle.'[22]

McDonald similarly finds that cricket has been a vehicle for the articulation and invention of post-colonial identities, but insists that these are less national and more communal in nature. He points to the range of social and economic forces that have swept India in the 1990s and argues that there has been the emergence of a 'lumpen middle class'[23] that wishes to express its new wealth and power in extreme Hindu politics. These afford them identities by which they can assert themselves over minority groups within India and by which they can challenge others on the international stage. Cricket, as a 'national' sport, is something that they wish to dominate and control in order to demonstrate their power, 'due to its place in civil society and as a significant element of popular culture, international one-day and test cricket offers fertile terrain for the articulation of Hindu chauvinist and communalist ideologies.'[24]

Studies made of football in India locate the origins of the game alongside cricket in the projects of colonialism. In *The Games Ethic and Imperialism* J.A.

Mangan found football with cricket in the programmes of the public schools and mission colleges established by the Raj to mould young Indians into loyal servants of the Empire. At Mayo College, for example, the school boasted by 1907 'three cricket and football elevens, each with a capital ground',[25] and at Bannu School in the North-West Frontier Province the headmaster could claim that as a result of his exertions, 'the simpler native games are gradually giving place to the superior attractions of cricket and football'.[26] Football, like cricket, was thought to be more than a recreation or a useful component of a fitness regime. The moral purpose behind the introduction of the sport was frankly stated by the biographer of Theodore Leighton Pendell, the headmaster of Bannu, 'Pennell combined work and education by playing with the boys at both cricket and football, showing them how to "play the game" in a bigger and nobler sense.'[27]

In his study of football in Calcutta Tony Mason similarly identifies the schools established by the British as important centres for the teaching of football to the local Indian elite. Indeed, he goes on to suggest that their involvement with the game continued after their schooldays and that they were responsible for the foundation of the first Indian football clubs in the city in the 1880s, 'we do not know much about the social origins of the players, but it seems likely that they came from the educated lower-middle and middle classes'.[28] He also points to the role of the military in Calcutta in introducing the sport to India. Football was one of the many games encouraged among both British and Indian soldiers by their officers in order to promote fitness, discipline and to avert boredom[29] and it was regimental teams that contributed towards the formation of the early leagues which they commonly dominated.

Richard Holt covers much of the same ground in his *Sport and the British: A Modern History* and uses Mangan's examples to point to the role of schools in promoting football among the Indian elite. His chapter is useful, however, as it begins to consider the issue of resistance to the sporting programmes of the British and to the moral designs that lay behind them. He argues that 'nationalist opposition to Anglo-Saxon sports ... was limited and ineffective' because 'the native elite mostly rejected their own culture and tried to win the respect of the Raj through sport'.[30] While Holt is useful for flagging up the important issue of resistance, he is limited and simplistic in the way that he deals with it.

The reason for this is that he seems entirely ignorant of the work of theorists of resistance that have made it clear since 1982 that Asian reactions to modernizing forces fall outside the simple dichotomy of collaboration or rejection. The theoretical approaches of historians such as the Subaltern Studies writers[31] and of anthropologists such as James Scott are important here as they focus attention on the independent agendas of Indian groups in their dealings with colonial states and also demand that recognition be granted to 'everyday' forms of resistance such as 'foot dragging, dissimulation, false compliance, pilfering, feigned ignorance, slander, arson, sabotage and so forth'.[32] They assert that members of subjected groups have complex and autonomous agendas and strategies of their own.[33] These often lead to resistance to state designs, but not necessarily to the spectacular resistance of a revolt or a riot.[34] Rather it is resistance through the cost–benefit analysed and unspectacular methods of avoidance, feigned compliance or mimicry.[35]

Feigned compliance and mimicry are especially important ideas when identifying the limitations of Holt's approach to the issue of resistance to sport. Feigned compliance on the part of Indians participating in the games of Europeans would be difficult to detect in historical documents but nevertheless remains a possibility that would disrupt his naive conclusion that those playing simply craved the 'respect' of the colonizers. Similarly, the idea of 'mimicry', the deliberately incomplete and disrupted imitation of designated ideas and roles which has been called 'the logic of inappropriate appropriation',[36] would problematize his assertions. If those playing football were doing so in ways, and for reasons, that would be unrecognized by Europeans then the hegemony of the latter is shattered and what at first appears to be collaboration is instead a challenge. Quite simply then, these historians and anthropologists point out that to find evidence of resistance agendas among subjected groups it is important to avoid simply looking for violent reactions and rejections. Rather, it is necessary to seek out the subversive but often covert actions of those who at first appear to be in subject positions.

This volume aims to address the range of themes raised within this historiography and also to highlight new ways of looking at sport in south Asia. In doing this it hopes to be multi-disciplinary in as much as it is informed both by conclusions reached by sports historians and sociologists and by the theoretical perspectives of south Asian studies writers. The often contradictory imperial objectives of those who first introduced 'modern' sports into south Asia will be examined, as will the whole range of agendas of and impacts on the societies and cultures of the regions that chose to interact with the European games. However, the intention is to emphasize that the British had stopped being a significant presence in Indian football by the 1930s and that Indians had adopted the game and played amongst themselves since they had first picked it up in the nineteenth century. In other words, the British are only a small part of the story of Indian football and one of the reasons for the chronological breadth of the volume is to put them in their place. This is a particular concern since most of the writing on Indian football to date tends to emphasize British involvement.[37] The interests of this volume are to show that, from the first time that a Bengali kicked a ball to the most recent examples of Indian corporations buying long-established clubs, south Asians have had complex reasons for engaging with football and have had unique and particular impacts on it. It is these reasons for engaging and those impacts on the game that explain the relationship between football, society and history in south Asia.

SOCCER IN SOUTH ASIA

The key issues to be considered from these perspectives fall into the loose categories of the past, the present and the future. In considering the history of south Asian football five contributors deal with the themes identified in the historiography above but have also sought to extend the conceptual framework through which the game there has been approached.

Novy Kapadia's chapter acts as a broad introduction to the key moments and to some of the most influential figures in the history of football in south Asia. The study is intended to provide an accessible account for readers who are unfamiliar with the game in the region. It gives an introduction to the clubs, to the competitions and to the lore of the game in order to lay the foundations for the more analytical chapters that follow. In other words, it was felt that before launching into discussions of such issues as the significance of Mohammedan Sporting's successes or the industrial heritage of SC Salgaocar it would be helpful to give readers a sense of who and what Mohammedan Sporting and SC Salgaocar are.

Kapadia, a TV commentator and popular writer on Indian football, provides a version of events which focuses on the twin themes of success and failure in the south Asian game and shows that the sport has had a decent share of both. Highlights of the history of Indian football include the 1911 triumph of Mohun Bagan over the East Yorkshire Regiment which has been discussed elsewhere,[38] but the importance of Kapadia's paper is that he does not allow this event to dominate the history of Indian football as other writers have been prone to do.[39] Instead, he explores other less well known but no less important Indian club achievements, such as the Rovers Cup triumphs of the Bangalore Muslims club in the 1930s and the victory in the Ashe Cup of 1943 of the 'City Afghans' over the Royal Air Force team that included Denis Compton. Kapadia is also careful to show that India's international team has a rich heritage, from the first outing at the London Olympics of 1948 to the 1962 Gold Medal triumph at the Asian Games, and he traces the fate of the national side up to the 2000 tour of England.

He also covers the major clubs in Indian football today and traces their disparate origins. Clubs such as Mohun Bagan and Mohammedan Sporting have histories that lead back to the nineteenth century while others such as FC Kochin are little more than five years old and are the result of the modern forces of commercialization and professionalization that have swept Indian football. The essay also identifies the key players of the modern era such as I.M. Vijayan and Baichung Bhutia, while remembering those who were considered the outstanding members of previous generations, such as Jarnail Singh and Neville D'Souza.

J.A. Mangan extends his earlier investigations of the dissemination of football on the very edges of British India[40] into a full account of the introduction of football in Kashmir and the North-West Frontier Province in the 1890s. The emphasis here is on one of the key themes already identified, that of sport as a tool of empire. He demonstrates that football and the other activities introduced by spirited schoolmasters and missionaries had a number of objectives all of which had explicitly disciplinary functions. Mangan first focuses on the work of Theodore Leighton Pennell among the fractious Pathan and Afghan tribes of the North-West Frontier Province. He reproduces evidence from Pennell's diaries that shows how football was at the intersection of the several projects of colonial discipline, military, educational and spatial, through which the British were trying to impose their authority and control the region,

> This time we are in a large grassy sward between Bannu city and the cantonments. There is a crowd, as before, of some thousands of spectators, but the football goal-posts and flags show that the game is something different. It is the day of the provincial tournament of all the schools of the province ... the referee, an English officer from the garrison, has blown his whistle, and the youthful champions come out.[41]

The complexity of interpreting indigenous responses to these projects is also a concern of Mangan's. His study of the impact of the missionary and headmaster Cecil Earle Tyndale-Biscoe in Kashmir provides an example that spans almost a hundred years and as such muddies the waters of the collaboration/resistance dichotomy preferred by Holt. Tyndale-Biscoe literally used force to introduce football to the students of the region as their cultural aversion to contact with leather necessitated their being herded together and beaten until they kicked the balls. Here is an obvious example of colonial force and resistance. Yet by the 1930s it was possible to say that 'not only is football played by the school boys, but the general public have taken to it with enthusiasm. They have a football league of various teams'.[42] Indeed, by the 1990s the boys of the school actively recreate the episode when their ancestors were herded and beaten as a celebration of the moment that football was introduced by the founder of their school. Mangan is certainly correct when he concludes that soccer is a form of cultural encounter between the superordinate and the subordinate and as such offers a fascinating opportunity to place the grand projects of colonial control in the context of their often partial and ironic realizations.

Paul Dimeo's chapter begins a series of three regional studies that highlight the diverse histories of football in south Asia. These bear out Mangan's broader thematic observations about the importance of schools and missions in the introduction of the sport in colonial India and about the complexity of indigenous reactions. However, what they also do is colour in much of the rest of the picture of how the game actually developed in these regions and what other groups and agencies were involved. They also trace a range of responses, accommodations and refusals that demonstrate the multiplicity of possibilities when south Asian societies were confronted with football.

Bengal is the focus of the Dimeo study which looks at the politics of football in Calcutta. The capital of the British Empire in India until 1911, this port has produced three of south Asia's oldest clubs which are still among the most successful and wealthy in modern India. He argues that the city and the region have emerged as the traditional powerhouse of football in India because the game and its institutions became a potent vehicle for the energies that emerged during the history of the period from the 1880s to 1947.

Football was in the first place shaped by the paradoxes of colonialism in late nineteenth century Bengal. On the one hand, cultural imperialists saw in the game a way of inculcating values in the Indian elites that would guarantee their loyalty and Dimeo produces fresh evidence that the sport was deliberately and consciously nurtured as a tool of empire. However, he finds that this impulse to spread football among the local elites often ran counter to a British urge to separate European from Asian. The sport was once again a tool of empire at the will of this urge to divide and the game was used to draw racial lines as Indians were excluded from clubs, cups and competitions because of their colour. Football was a site for inclusion and for exclusion then, as the game was shaped by the often contradictory forces of colonialism. While certain administrators saw the game as a means of drawing the Indian elite to the British, those who sought to exclude Indian players were setting the game up as a theatre for resistance.

Dimeo argues that football became this during the period after 1900 as Bengal became the centre of nationalist resistance in India. The most famous instance of this was in 1911 when thousands of Indians watched Mohun Bagan beat the East Yorkshire Regiment to win the IFA Shield for the first time. Newspapers celebrated this win as more than a football victory and preferred to see it as a vindication of the independence struggle. Dimeo again identifies a paradox at the heart of these appropriations of football: he points out that the nationalist portrayal of the triumph as a repudiation of racist discourses of Indian physical frailty was still painted in the very British idiom of masculinity and competition.

Alongside colonialism and nationalism a third force that shaped Bengali society and for which football became a vehicle was communalism. Dimeo concludes by pointing to the popularity of Mohammedan Sporting both in Bengal and across India during the 1930s. He implicates this in the development of Muslim identity and of separatist nationalism during this period as Mohammedan Sporting was a self-consciously communalist football club that enjoyed unprecedented success in the Calcutta league in this period. In short, Dimeo argues that soccer in Bengal is embedded in the culture of the state and that the region remains the centre of Indian football precisely because the game has been so intertwined with local history.

In focusing on football in Goa and on the game in Tibet, James Mills and Alex McKay examine very different colonial contexts for the development of Indian soccer from those explored by Mangan and Dimeo. Goa is a contrasting example as it was a Portuguese rather than a British colony and, indeed, did not achieve independence until 1961 (14 years after the rest of India was freed from British rule). Mills looks at the unique features of Goan history that were a result of this separate experience of European imperialism. He argues along the lines of Dimeo that football in this particular region is so popular because it quickly became implicated in the broader historical processes of local society. He identifies five of these processes in Goa: the activities of an indigenized Catholic church, a history of emigration, a forced industrialization, the politics of decolonization, and the search for a means of protecting the difference of a Goa that found itself immersed in the Indian Union after 1961.

The first point of contrast between the Goan experience and that of British India is in the place of religious institutions in the propagation of football. The British missionaries who took football with them as a weapon of moral instruction were a self-evidently foreign presence which often needed to use force to impose its sports. The Catholic church was similarly the means by which football was introduced into Goa and by which it was spread through its seminaries and by its priests. Yet by the nineteenth century, when the game first reached the west coast of India, the Catholic church in Goa was a fully indigenized institution, and the majority both of its functionaries and the local population were Indian. While football in both British and Portuguese India was introduced by the Christian churches, the churches and their place in local communities were very different.

Having been introduced into Goa, the game spread rapidly through its educational institutions, both Christian and Hindu, so that by the 1920s, when large sections of the young male population were leaving the region to work in British India, they took the game with them. Mills shows that the Goan experience of diaspora, a theme in the society of the region that is still important today, is tied up with football as clubs were established wherever Goans settled in numbers and, indeed, these teams were sent back to the home towns and villages. Football thus became a means of maintaining Goan contacts and identities for expatriate communities and also an important means of communicating messages about wealth and success to those that had stayed at home.

The game was consciously promoted by Portuguese politicians in the 1950s as a populist effort at maintaining their hold on the area and Benfica played exhibition games there towards the end of the decade. The failure of this project meant that Goa was incorporated into India in 1961 and became involved in a struggle to defend its separate status and identity in the face of the determination of neighbouring regions to take responsibility for it. Mills shows that football became a site for the articulation of this struggle and he concludes that, once the state had succeeded in maintaining its independence the game, became a means of celebrating and promoting Goan difference from the rest of India. The unique history of Goa in south Asia has been consistently played out in the realm of football.

Alex McKay considers the historical relationship between football and India from a different perspective than that of the authors mentioned so far. Their studies look at the region as a receptor of the game from Europe, but McKay, in looking at the way in which football arrived in Tibet, demonstrates that India has also been a point of transmission for soccer in Asia. He shows how British colonial officials and the Indian soldiers that accompanied them made their way from India to the Tibetan kingdom in order to maintain a diplomatic presence on the borders of the British Empire. They took football with them, but the game was more than simply a means of passing the time. It was deliberately propagated by European officials as a means of attracting the locals to the British mission. He also argues that some officers had other ambitions still for football and promoted it as a means of trying to build a modern sense of 'nation' among local groups. Their objective in doing this was to stiffen the resolve of Tibetans to maintain their independence in the face of a perceived threat from Russia, a threat which explained the British presence in the first place. Interestingly, McKay argues that the British were not the only foreign presence that attempted to use games in order to pursue their objectives. The Chinese diplomatic mission to Tibet similarly encouraged the playing of *Mah-jong* amongst the communities of the cities in order to promote their cause.

The case study of Tibet, however, offers far more than an example of India acting as a vector rather than simply as a receptor for football. McKay studies the reactions of the Tibetan elite to the game brought by the British from India and shows how contingent responses to football could be. The elite comprised the senior generation of monks from within the Tibetan religious system, which was made up of monasteries that dominated the society and the culture of the region. The 13th Dalai Lama at the head of this system at first seemed curious about and even supportive of football and his bodyguard had its own team while British officials in Tibet recorded that he received the results from local competitions. However, by the 1920s there was a backlash against perceived forces of modernity and football was one of the activities banned as representing a corrosive foreign influence. The ban was effective and, despite the apparent attraction of the local population to the game, it quickly withered under the force of the religious edict. Here then is an example of the failure of British cultural imperialism in the face of a determined elite with the power to resist European colonial designs. As such, it is an interesting contrast to the Indian example, where the existence of a more heterogeneous society in which cultural and social power were far less centralized meant that there was never such a concerted approach to the game.

While the first five contributors outline and analyse the history and origins of football in south Asia, the final three consider current issues in the game in India and begin to examine its possible futures. It should be made clear that, while the first five papers do concern themselves with issues in the history of the game in south Asia in general, the final three have a more specific focus on modern India. Although it would be important to include analyses of developments in the game in the other modern south Asian states, it is currently the case that the research is simply not available for a similarly detailed study of the sport in any of those countries.

Mario Rodrigues uses his experience as a writer on Indian sports for almost two decades to begin outlining the major challenges to the game in the 1990s and argues that the last ten years of the sport in India have witnessed a series of major changes. He identifies three new forces and shows how these have come to dominate the game and to determine the possibilities for the future. The first of these has to a certain extent opened up Indian football to the other two so that commercialization brought with it professionalization and globalization. In 1990s India economic liberalization bred a new aggression in corporations operating in south Asia and these saw in football, and more specifically in the newly founded National Football League, a means of promoting their brands. Major international players such as Philips and Coca-Cola and the most significant Indian companies such as Tatas and United Breweries all became involved either as sponsors, club owners or founders of football academies and the major TV networks Star-ESPN and Doordarshan signed contracts with the AIFF for coverage.

The sudden focus on football and the large amounts of money that entered the game had immediate impacts. Until the 1990s the Indian footballer had most commonly joined a club in return for a job for life. Many of the larger clubs such as SC Salgaocar or Mahindras were the sporting clubs of large companies so players were set up with posts within them in return for playing for the team. After retirement from the game they stayed on the staff and worked in another capacity. Other clubs such as East Bengal were not officially affiliated to any particular enterprise but they carried enough clout to secure jobs with local companies for their players. This was immediately affected as money flowed into the Indian game, with players changing hands on an annual basis and pocketing transfer fees in return for sacrificing the job-for-life security of the old system. Indian clubs also began looking abroad for players now that they were offering lucrative contracts and Indian players found themselves in competition with African, Central Asian and Arabian players. Commercialization brought professionalization and globalization with it into Indian football.

However, Rodrigues again raises the question about impacts that was a theme in the historical considerations of football and colonialism. Powerful though the forces of commercialization, professionalization and globalization have been, the structures and politics of Indian society have ensured that they have met with a range of obstacles that have meant that they have failed to entirely reshape the game. An amusing instance would be the fate of Coca-Cola's bottling plant in Goa which found itself without water after the company declined the invitation of the state's chief minister to sponsor his team. More serious is the withdrawal of companies such as Coca-Cola and Philips from sponsorship of Indian football, which they explained as the result of disappointment with the administration of the game. The AIFF, with its amateur status and its regional structure still intact from its foundation during British rule, is often cited as a barrier to the 'development' of the game in the country and a recent challenge to its control of football was launched by the clubs which saw it as having failed in its dealings with major sponsors and TV companies.[43] Rodrigues concludes then that the 1990s may have seen the rise of commercialization, professionalization and globalization in the Indian game but that these forces have not swept all before them because of the ability of local institutions and individuals to resist or to divert them. It is this meeting of the broad processes that have changed football globally with the specific organizations and conditions of the Indian game that will continue to shape football in the country into the twenty-first century.

Bill Adams and John Hammond bring their own experiences in football administration and development to the debate about the current state of and possible futures of the Indian game. The focus in these essays is on youth participation in football and on the identification and development of the best of these young footballers for the professional game. Adams first of all considers the problems faced by Indian children who wish to play football. He suggests that they may be loosely separated into three main categories: those who do not attend school at all but are at the same time not full-time members of the workforce; those who do attend state or low-cost private schools; and those who are educated at the elite institutions of India. Each group faces its own set of difficulties in developing as footballers. Those who receive no education at all, while not employed full time, are often expected to be the most flexible members of the family unit and so the demands on their time are unpredictable, which can interfere with planned leisure activities. This group is most likely to be in the poorest sections of society, and in the cities this means little access to the space necessary for football. Similar problems face those children who do receive a basic schooling in the insufficiently financed education sector since they are still expected to work with their families and live in the overcrowded cities. Being at school gives them no significant advantage as the facilities of their institutions are likely to be limited.

Even that tiny minority of children at the country's elite and expensive educational facilities face a number of obstacles to their playing football. The schools do include the game in their annual calendar but they attempt to cram so many other activities into the physical education slots that little time is spent on soccer. In addition to this, coaches tend to be poorly trained and have to work with outdated syllabuses. The pressure on these coaches to ensure that the school is successful in competition means that they often resort to underhand methods such as including over-age players in teams. They can get away with this because there is no single body to oversee youth football and the bodies that do see soccer at that level as their concern rarely manage to cooperate or to pool their resources.

Adams begins then to analyse exactly what the obstacles are to Indian children playing sport in general and football in particular. Having done so, however, he also provides a number of examples that demonstrate that Indians of all socio-economic groups readily involve themselves with football when they are given the opportunity and he concludes that, despite the obstacles that he has outlined, there is an interest in engaging with the game. He argues that rather than focus on expensive but high-profile football academies, which is the model adopted by a number of Indian agencies, small-scale programmes aimed at all ability levels tend to have more lasting results. With a new organization such as the embryonic

Indian Youth Soccer Association to coordinate these activities independently of existing organizations, he argues that many of the obstacles both to mass participation and to the development of the most talented can be overcome.

Hammond examines a case study of a country where similar problems were identified and assesses the effectiveness of a planned and centrally coordinated nationwide response. In providing examples from Australia, he makes the point that it is possible for a country to use a long-term, youth-orientated policy to improve its standing in world football. This is an important and pertinent comparative example since football has to compete with other sports such as cricket in Australia as with India. Hammond also emphasizes that policy in Australia took root despite poor pre-existing youth football structures.

Hammond underlines the problems with alternative approaches, and warns of the quick-fix approach of simply grafting an academy system on to a poorly organized feeder network or of simply appointing an expensive foreign manager. Instead, he outlines the model used in Australia, where coaching the coaches was the first step so that a well-trained cadre of organizers was available to work in the localities. These men could reorganize school and club-level football so that the brightest prospects could be spotted and assessed objectively. A well-planned feeder system based around the localities could then develop, leading to regional training camps and squads from which the most talented could then progress to the academy network.

After 25 years of the system Australia now produces major talents such as Mark Viduka and Harry Kewell. The international side just missed qualification for the 1998 World Cup but has proved in such performances as the recent 2–0 win over Scotland at Hampden that Australia can now compete at the highest level. Indeed, these successes will continue as the system is designed to be self-perpetuating as graduates from the academies pay back the cost of their training and education.

The model is a useful one to conclude the book on as it suggests that Indian football, with its long and eventful history but with its current crop of problems, could turn to the experience of other countries in order to point it to a promising future. The Australian example shows that a political will, a willingness to bear initial financial outlays and a determination on the part of all involved to achieve a series of footballing objectives can really make a difference and lift a nation's game out of its existing state. Read in conjunction with the Adams paper, which ends on a note of optimism in pointing to the growing dissatisfaction with existing football bodies together with financial commitments by corporate groups eager to promote soccer, these two papers begin to explore the possible futures of the Indian game.

The volume is the first comprehensive study of Indian football and brings together academics, journalists, football coaches and administrators in order to make accessible a broad range of knowledge and experiences. It introduces the history of football in south Asia and in the several academic analyses of aspects of this history it begins to consider the thematic and theoretical approaches to be adopted when looking at the origins of the game in India. It also looks at the recent state of the sport and the issues that most concern observers of football in India today. In doing this it also starts to consider and suggest potential futures for the game, and, indeed, offers one comparative case study as a means of understanding some of the ways in which it is possible to begin to think of the game developing. In short, this volume might not cover all of the relevant issues in the subject, and it is doubtful whether it would be possible to do this in just one book. However, the book does make available the most up to date research and the full range of knowledge of some of the most experienced observers of the Indian game.

NOTES

1. A. de Mello, *Portrait of Indian Sport* (London: Macmillan, 1959), p.183. The date of this statement is important as it demonstrates that the game had thrived in the post-colonial period and before the so-called globalization of football of recent times. Football in India was therefore reliant neither on colonial patronage nor on the marketing strategies of contemporary international sports organizations and their corporate partners.
2. AIFF to FIFA, 10 Jan. 1950. From correspondence supplied by FIFA Communications to the authors.
3. de Mello, *Portrait*, p.9.
4. Ibid., p.183.
5. India rather than south Asia is the focus of considerations of the recent developments and the future of football since there is a lack of research available for the game in the other countries of the region.
6. S. Das, *Communal Riots in Bengal, 1905–1947* (Delhi: Oxford University Press, 1993), p.170.
7. The authors have a number of experiences of south Asian studies sociologists expressing ignorance of the fact that football is such a popular game in India with a long history and of being questioned as to why the analysis of the game could possibly be important for an understanding of south Asia.
8. J. Alter, *The Wrestler's Body: Identity and Ideology in North India* (Berkeley, CA: University of California Press, 1992), p.4.
9. Ibid., p.5.
10. Ibid., p.6.
11. J. Alter, 'Kabaddi, a National Sport of India: The Internationalism of Nationalism and the Foreignness of Indianness', in N. Dyck (ed.), *Games, Sports and Cultures* (Oxford: Berg, 2000).
12. For other considerations of the RSS and sport see I. McDonald, 'Physiological Patriots? The Politics of Physical Nationalism and Hindu Nationalism in India', *International Review for the Sociology of Sport*, 34 (1999), 343–58.
13. It is far from clear that cricket has ever been the most popular game or has the hold on the country now that it is thought to have. For the latter point see M. Rodrigues in this volume. As for the former assertion, 'soccer ... is a game which most boys around the country play at one time or another – at school or on the "maidan", which is the equivalent of the English village green. Thus, there is a nationwide understanding of, and liking for, soccer, stronger than that for cricket, which has until now tended to be more a game for the rich man' (de Mello, *Portrait*, pp. 9–10). M. Bose has confirmed this observation, 'logically after independence, football should have become India's number one sport. It ... certainly permeated greater layers of Indian society, even down to the semi-rural areas' (M. Bose, *A Maidan View: The Magic of Indian Cricket* (London: Allen & Unwin, 1986), p.35).
14. For narrative introductions to the origins of the game see E. Docker, *History of Indian Cricket* (Delhi: Macmillan, 1977), M. Bose, *The History of Indian Cricket* (London: Andre Deutsch, 1990), R. Cashman, *Patrons, Players and the Crowd: The Phenomenon of Indian Cricket* (Delhi: Longman, 1980).
15. J.A. Mangan, *The Games Ethic and Imperialism: Aspects of the Diffusion of an Ideal* (Harmondsworth: Viking, 1985), p.134.
16. A. Guttmann, *Games and Empires: Modern Sports and Cultural Imperialism* (New York, NY: Columbia University Press, 1994), p.33.

17. Ibid., pp. 32–3.
18. R. Guha, 'Cricket and Politics in Colonial India', *Past and Present*, 161 (1998), 165–9.
19. Ibid., 175–90.
20. A. Nandy, *The Tao of Cricket: On Games of Destiny and the Destiny of Games* (New York: Oxford University Press, 1989).
21. A. Appadurai, 'Playing with Modernity: The Decolonization of Indian Cricket', in C.A. Breckenridge (ed.), *Consuming Modernity: Public Culture in a South Asian World* (Minneapolis: University of Minnesota Press 1995), p.45.
22. Ibid., p.46.
23. I. McDonald, 'Between Saleem and Shiva: the Politics of Cricket Nationalism in "Globalising" India', in J. Sugden and A. Bairner (eds), *Sport in Divided Societies* (Aachen: Meyer and Meyer, 1999), p.231.
24. Ibid., p.232.
25. I. Malcolm, quoted in J.A. Mangan, *Games Ethic and Imperialism*, p.136.
26. T. Leighton Pendell quoted, ibid., p.176.
27. E. Hayes quoted, ibid., p.176.
28. T. Mason, 'Football on the Maidan: Cultural Imperialism in Calcutta', *International Journal of the History of Sport*, 12, 1 (1990), 87.
29. Ibid., p.85.
30. R. Holt, *Sport and the British: A Modern History* (Oxford: Clarendon Press, 1989).
31. R. Guha (ed.), *Subaltern Studies I* (Delhi: Oxford University Press, 1982).
32. J. Scott, *Weapons of the Weak* (London: Yale University Press, 1985), p.29.
33. Guha, *Subaltern Studies I*, p.4.
34. Scott, *Weapons of the Weak*, pp.31–2.
35. For more detail on this term and its implications see H. Bhabha, *The Location of Culture* (London: Routledge, 1994).
36. L. Gandhi, *Postcolonial Theory: A Critical Introduction* (New Delhi: Oxford University Press, 1999), p.150.
37. Where Mason, Holt and Guttmann deal with football in India the British are always included in the picture. The suspicion remains that this entails a privileging of the British role above that of other groups. This may be because of the reliance of these authors on English language sources. It may also be due to an ethnocentrism evident in such statements as 'Calcutta is a place not usually synonymous with football passion' (Mason, 'Football on the Maidan', 85). In India, Calcutta *is* synonymous with football passion, so what the author of this statement means is that Calcutta is not usually synonymous with football passion where he comes from – Britain.
38. Mason, 'Football on the Maidan', 85–96.
39. J. Bains and R. Patel, *Asians Can't Play Football* (Solihull: Asian Social Development Agency, 1996).
40. Mangan, *Games Ethic and Imperialism*, pp.178–92.
41. T.L. Pennell, *Among the Wild Tribes of the Afghan Frontier* (London: Seeley, 1909), p.155.
42. E.D. Tyndale-Biscoe, *Fifty Years against the Stream* (Mysore: Wesleyan Missionary Press, 1930), p.20.
43. For example, see 'IPFA Unlikely to Participate in NFL', *Times of India*, 28 Nov. 2000. See also N. Kapadia in this volume.

1

Triumphs and Disasters: The Story of Indian Football, 1889–2000

NOVY KAPADIA

Football in India has a continuous history that stretches back into the nineteenth century. Many clubs can trace their origins back to the 1880s and competitions still exist that have been contested ever since that period. This study will act as an introduction to this history and aims to outline the key events and figures in the story of football in India.

DOMESTIC FOOTBALL: THE GLORIES OF THE INDIAN GAME

Football was introduced to India by British regimental teams and missionaries during the period of colonial rule. As Calcutta was at the time the capital of the British government in India, the game became popular in this eastern metropolis and the first clubs in the country were formed there in the 1880s and two of them are still the most famous clubs in India: Mohammedan Sporting and Mohun Bagan. The exact date when Mohammedan Sporting was founded is unknown but it is believed to be around 1891. However, Mohun (meaning 'sweet') Bagan (meaning 'group') was formed in 1889. Mohun Bagan is the only Indian club that has won every major domestic tournament and in 1989, as part of centenary celebrations, it was declared the National Club of India and special postage stamps were released on the occasion by the government.[1]

Since its inception, Mohun Bagan has not just been a club but an institution in Bengal. It was formed to develop the competitive ethos and fighting spirit among the youth of Bengal (in undivided India) by playing football and other games as recreation.[2] To this day, Mohun Bagan runs football teams (senior and junior) as well as cricket, hockey and athletic squads. For years there was a special ethos about Mohun Bagan and the youth of Bengal aspired to play for this elite, prestigious club. The intelligentsia and aristocrats of Bengal all supported Mohun Bagan financially and emotionally. The aim of the club was to produce strong but principled athletes. A player who failed in a school or college examination was not allowed to play for Mohun Bagan and smoking and drinking were forbidden in the clubhouse.[3] Mohammedan Sporting was formed with the same principles but most of their players were young Muslims. In those days players received only their expenses and playing kit but no monetary reward.

Many of the players started as college students and later the clubs helped them to get jobs which gave them time off to play football.

Both these clubs, along with some others now defunct, started playing competitive football with British regimental teams in the Calcutta League (held in the summer months) and contested the three major domestic tournaments: the Indian Football Association (IFA) Shield in Calcutta, the Rovers Cup in Bombay (now Mumbai) and the Durand Cup in Simla. Of these, the last is the oldest in India. It was started in 1888 and is the third oldest football tournament in the world after the FA Cups in England and Scotland. British football lovers in Bombay and Calcutta started the Rovers Cup in 1891 and the IFA Shield was founded in 1893. This trio of tournaments is still held annually. For a little over a century they were the mainstay of Indian football and provided adequate competition and exposure to clubs from all over the country. To win the Triple Crown – the Durand, Rovers and IFA Shield (known as the Blue Riband tournaments) in one season – was the ultimate aim and only Mohun Bagan in 1977 and East Bengal (formed in Calcutta in 1924 by football fans from that region) in 1990 have achieved this feat.

A critical moment in Indian football came in 1911 when Mohun Bagan (playing barefoot) won the IFA Shield, beating the East Yorkshire Regiment 2–1 in the final in Calcutta. A crowd of over 60,000 assembled on the Maidan to witness the final. Special trains were organized for it and people also came by ferry and ship from nearby East Bengal (now Bangladesh). Many who witnessed this match barely saw any action since there were no proper stands. People in the front rows communicated the score by flying kites and sending messages tied to the toes of pigeons.[4]

This win by Bagan on 29 July was a significant sporting triumph. It was the first time an Indian team had overcome a renowned British regimental side to win such an important tournament. The win was hailed even in the British media. The *Manchester Guardian* on 4 August wrote,

> A team of Bengalis won the IFA Shield in India after defeating a crack British regimental team. There is no reason, of course, to be surprised. Victory in association football goes to the side with the greatest physical fitness, quickest eye and the keenest intellect.[5]

However, the victory had wider implications. Since the protest movement against the Partition of Bengal in 1905 and the organization of the *swadeshi* campaign,[6] Calcutta had been the centre of the growing Indian nationalist movement that had as its ultimate objective to overthrow British rule. The IFA Shield triumph therefore took on political significance, as an inspirational symbolic victory for the oppressed over their oppressors. It also challenged fundamental views on the racial superiority of white Europeans over south Asians. Legend has it that some supporters certainly saw the victory in the context of the freedom struggle. The triumphant Mohun Bagan players were leaving the ground when a well-dressed supporter tugged at Sudhir's sleeve and, pointing to the East Yorkshires' colours and the Union flag aloft on nearby Fort William, said, 'This one you have done but what about that?'[7]

Besides Calcutta, other regions where football developed in British India were the garrison towns of Madras (now Chennai), Bangalore, Hyderabad, Ambala, Delhi, Peshawar and Dacca. The last two cities were then part of undivided India. Bangalore, then capital of Mysore state, produced some exceptional talents. The Bangalore Muslims club was the first Indian team to win the Rovers Cup in 1937 and repeated the feat in 1938. In 1937 in an all-India final they upset Mohammedan Sporting 1–0, and the following year beat the Argyll and Sutherland Highlanders 3–2. By the 1940s players from Mysore dominated the international team and the 1948 Olympics team had six players from this region. They were K.V. Varadraj, S.A. Basheer, B.N. Vajravelu, Ahmed Khan, Dhanraj and S. Raman.[8] However, the best players from the city tended to be lured to the big clubs of Calcutta so players such as Ahmed Khan played for East Bengal or Mohun Bagan rather than stay in Bangalore. As such, the area never developed as a rival regional power to Calcutta and Bengal. Nowadays Bangalore football is dominated by institutional sides such as Indian Telephone Industries (ITI), Chief of Inspectorate Lines (CIL) and Hindustan Aeronautics Limited (HAL), and the popularity of the game has declined.

It was in the city of the Nizams, Hyderabad, that football really took off in the 1920s. Football there received the patronage of royalty, especially of the Nawab of Tarband and the Maharajas of Kakinada and Rajmandri.[9] The Hyderabad FA was formed in 1939 and the famous coach S.A. Rahim, who guided India to two Asian Games gold medals, was the secretary from 1943 until his death in June 1963.[10]

The most famous team to emerge from this city was the black and yellow shirted Hyderabad City Police. They were known as the 'City Afghans', the name of the police force during the reign of the Nizam of Hyderabad.[11] The team had a string of triumphs in the pre-Independence era. One famous game, which established Hyderabad City Police's reputation, was the Ashe Gold Cup final in Bangalore in 1943. They won 2–1 against the Royal Air Force, a team that included England's double international Denis Compton. The City Afghans trailed by a single goal for much of the game but rallied to win with two late penalties by the defender Norbert Andrew Fruvall.

It was the 1950 Durand football tournament final, the first after Independence in 1947, that established Hyderabad City Police as a legend in Indian football. In that memorable final they trailed Mohun Bagan 0–2 until ten minutes before the final whistle but equalized through Laiq in the last seconds. This dramatic fightback won the hearts of the crowd. Thousands of fans invaded the ground and mobbed and chaired Laiq. Some enthusiastic fans even kissed him and an over-exuberant one in his eagerness to congratulate his hero bit him on the cheek. Poor Laiq reached the dressing room with blood flowing down his face. The wound meant that he missed the replay which his team went on to win 1–0.[12] The club won the Rovers Cup for five years in a row, from 1950 to 1955, and the state league championships for 11 consecutive years. In 1950, 1957 and 1959 Hyderabad City Police participated in 12 national tournaments and won all of them, playing in the 2–3–5 system.

N.A. Fruvall, as captain of the Hyderabad City Police, began to shape the club in the 1940s. At that time teams in Hyderabad did not have coaches, so it was the responsibility of the captain to mould his players into a coherent unit. It was Fruvall who helped to recruit star players such as Noor Mohammed, Laiq and Susaih Jr. By the time of his retirement in 1951 he had moulded Hyderabad City Police into one of best teams in the country. Syed Abdul Rahim took over from Fruvall and continued to develop the squad. A teacher by profession, he was a great tactician, motivator and disciplinarian. Above all he will be remembered for popularizing football in Hyderabad by his innovative coaching methods,

> He used to organize non-dribbling tournaments so that teams could improve one-touch passing and combination. There were also weaker leg tournaments where a player was only allowed to kick and tackle with his weaker foot. This enabled players to become two footed. For juniors he organized height restricted tournaments, five a side and seven a side games in local parks. Thus the flow of talent in Hyderabad football was consistent for over three decades.[13]

Rahim ensured that his players' conduct on the field and dedication were exemplary. Jamal, Aziz, Susaih Jr and Noor Mohammed did not miss even a single match for five long years. Noor and Jamal even played a match for their team on the same afternoon that their mother died.[14] The team was also renowned for its discipline, cohesion, team spirit and never-say-die attitude. The players were the epitome of sportsmanship and never questioned a referee's verdict even in the midst of a tense match.

The team was an institutional side and players got no monetary rewards. The late Noor Mohammed, who played in every national match between 1950 and 1958, once said, 'Often at practice we had just one football and for refreshments afterwards just a cup of tea but our hard practice, will to succeed and excellent coaching from the late Rahim Saheb, enabled us to become a successful team.'[15] Playing with exemplary manners and receiving few rewards for their performances, the club was popular all over India and came to be identified as the team of the common man, in opposition to the elite clubs of Calcutta. In the period just after Independence, Hyderabad City Police came to symbolize the ethos and spirit of the age, the will to sacrifice, overcome odds and work for great ideals and their popularity transcended regional and religious identities.

Until India started a semi-professional National League in the 1996–97 season the Durand Cup was the most prestigious tournament on the Indian circuit. The winners received three trophies, the Durand Cup, the Viceroy's trophy (after Independence called the President's Cup) and the Simla trophy (donated by citizens of Simla when the competition was held there in the days of the British). The Durand tournament is conducted annually by a special society nominated by the Services Sports Control Board of India. In 1987 they were the first to introduce prize money in Indian football. The winning team was then presented with Rs150,000 (about £7,500 by the exchange rates of 1987), the runners up received Rs100,000 (£5,000) and the top goal scorer and best player were rewarded with Rs5,000 (£250) each. In 1997 the winners of the Durand tournament were FC Kochin of Kerala (India's first professional club) and they received Rs500,000 (about £8,300 by 1997 exchange rates) together with an Ambassador car for each player. In the 2000 season the AB Electrolux Company sponsored the Durand tournament and Alwyn was the title sponsor. The winning team won Rs400,000 (£6,600), the runners-up Rs200,000 (£3,300) and the defeated semi-finalists Rs100,000 each (£1,600).[16]

The Durand tournament has always been held at the seat of government, so since India's Independence it has been played at Delhi. Between 1941 and 1949 the Durand football tournament was not played due to the Second World War, the struggle for Independence and the Partition riots. During British rule the Viceroy himself always presented the trophies. After Independence the President of India carried on this tradition until the threat from terrorists in the 1980s made it too dangerous. The far-sighted Durand committee was also the first to introduce an age-group football tournament in India, when they started the Subroto Mukherjee Cup in 1960 for champion school teams from each state and the union territory of India.

The first Indian team to win the prestigious Durand tournament was Mohammedan Sporting in 1940 when they beat the Royal Warwickshire Regiment 2–1 in Delhi. Centre forward Hafiz Rashid and inside left Saboo scored the goals for the winners. One hundred thousand people witnessed the final, with seating on only one side of the ground. Eminent Muslim politicians flew in from far off cities such as Calcutta, Dacca, Hyderabad and Bhopal for the match and people came in trains from across India. This victory by a team consisting of 11 Muslim players was a massive boost to the Muslims' separatist movement.[17]

The final was played on 12 December at the Irwin amphitheatre, supervised for the first time by an Indian referee Capt Harnam Singh. He was a civilian sergeant in the Army Office in the Delhi Cantonment. Recalling that special day, Singh remembered that he had a police escort from his house in the Cantonment area to the National Stadium. Upon arriving at the ground, he was dismayed to find that there was a major problem. The British linesmen, Warrant Officers Oliphant and Greene, refused to officiate as they said it was below their dignity to be linesmen under a comparatively junior referee such as Singh. They felt slighted and threatened to back out from the match. The Durand Society organizers tried in vain to persuade the recalcitrant duo. The Viceroy, then Lord Linlithgow, arrived at the Stadium to inaugurate and attend the final. When informed of the crisis, Linlithgow let it be known that he would court-martial Oliphant and

Greene if they continued to behave in such a way. The pair suddenly decided that they could work with the Indian referee after all. Musing on the incident, Singh said, 'This tension only added to my pre-match nervousness. I felt better when Maj Porter gave me a hot cup of cocoa laced with brandy.' The match went off smoothly and Harnam recalled, 'I must say that the British linesmen, once they had agreed, did a competent job and gave me full cooperation.'[18]

The victory in the Durand tournament was the culmination of a memorable decade for Mohammedan Sporting. They won the Calcutta league for five years in a row in the mid 1930s (a record which remained unsurpassed until East Bengal won the same title for six years in a row from 1970 to 1975). Their successes led to mass support and Muslims in every city of undivided India were fans of the team. They had an abundance of money and were the first Indian team to play with boots and to focus on a proper diet and physical fitness for their players. Due to their widespread support, Mohammedan Sporting was the first to attract talent to Calcutta from all over India. Full backs Juma Khan and Bachi Khan came from Peshawar and Quetta in the North-West Frontier Province. Goalkeeper Usman Jan was from Delhi and the ace centre forward Rashid hailed from Ajmer in Rajasthan.

In 1924 East Bengal football club was formed by fans who had come to Calcutta for work from the region that is now Bangladesh. The East Bengal club became a social, political and geographical rival of Mohun Bagan. The older and more established club, Bagan was supported by the original inhabitants of West Bengal and the club had an elitist, middle-class ethos. East Bengal received dedicated support from people who came from the eastern region of Bengal, as well as from the lower-middle and the working class. Through the years immense rivalry has developed between Mohun Bagan and East Bengal akin to that between Rangers and Celtic in Glasgow as the basis of the relationship is a fierce clash of identities and loyalties. Any game between these Calcutta giants arouses immense passions. When Mohun Bagan failed to beat East Bengal for six years (1970 to 1975) a teenage fan of the former club committed suicide as a sacrifice to the gods to change the club's fortunes. The fans of Mohun Bagan celebrate a victory over their traditional rivals by eating prawns (known as *chingri*). Similarly East Bengal fans celebrate a win over Mohun Bagan by eating a river fish *hilsa*, which is a symbol of their club. It is also a tradition that the fans of the club that has lost go to bed hungry on the evening of their defeat. East Bengal supporters also celebrate victory by lighting paper torches and swinging them in the air. These paper torches are known as *mashals* and they are a part of the East Bengal flag. East Bengal supporters first used this method of celebration in the 1970 IFA Shield final, after their historic 1–0 win over Pas Club of Iran.[19]

In the post-Independence era East Bengal club has achieved some of the most memorable results in Indian football. It is the only club with more wins than losses against foreign clubs in home matches.[20] The most famous triumphs were the win against Pas Club, mentioned above, the 3–1 victory against Pyongyang

City Club of North Korea in the 1973 IFA Shield final and the win over the Dok Ro Gang club of North Korea in the 1973 DCM final.

In the early 1970s the North Koreans were regarded as the best in Asia due to their 1966 World Cup success, when they beat Italy 1–0, and reached the quarter-finals, when they led Portugal 3–0 before conceding six goals. The North Korean club that contested the DCM tournament final against East Bengal in Delhi in 1973 had six players that took part in the 1966 World Cup. However, East Bengal, cleverly coached by the astute motivator P.K. Banerjee, out-thought the North Koreans by using a flexible 4–5–1 system. Mohammed Akbar was the lone forward and East Bengal's packed midfield enabled them to dominate play. The North Koreans were so impressed with East Bengal's display that their embassy in Delhi made recordings of the Calcutta team's matches and sent them back to Pyongyang for careful study and analysis. The North Koreans feared that India, with six East Bengal players in their ranks, would be their most dangerous opponents in the 1974 Asian Games. However, India fared poorly and lost 4–1.

INTERNATIONAL FOOTBALL: GOLD MEDALS AND GOLDEN OPPORTUNITIES

Indian teams started touring Malaysia, Singapore, China and Japan in the late 1930s. The 1948 London Olympics was India's first major international tournament outing. A predominantly barefooted Indian team played on a wet and cold surface in London and lost 2–1 to France. India created more scoring chances but because of the cold conditions the forwards could not shoot properly and Raman and Parab missed a penalty each. 'After the match was over, hundreds of appreciative spectators congratulated the Indian players on their sporting manner on the field and regretted that the better team had lost.'[21] At the 1952 Helsinki Olympics the Indian team froze in the cold and were trounced 10–1 by Yugoslavia, a team that had won the silver medal in the 1948 Olympics and would go on to win it again in that year's tournament. One result of this was that the All India Football Federation (AIFF) thereafter made the wearing of boots compulsory for all Indian players.[22]

India qualified regularly for the Olympics until 1960, and in 1956 at Melbourne India finished a respectable fourth. They lost in the semi-finals to eventual runners-up, Yugoslavia, after leading 1–0 until the final ten minutes. In the same tournament they beat the hosts Australia 4–2 in the quarter-finals with centre forward Neville D'Souza scoring a hat-trick.[23] India's performance in the 1956 Melbourne Olympics should be evaluated within the standing of Asian football during that time. The other two Asian countries made no impression in these Olympics: Japan lost in the first round 0–2 to Australia and Thailand was routed 1–9 by the United Kingdom. Compared with other Asian nations, India performed creditably and coach Rahim fielded the team in an embryonic 4–2–4 formation. Renowned soccer critics and officials such as Dr Willy Meisel and Sir

Stanley Rous appreciated India's performance and congratulated the coach for making his team play modern football.[24] In the 1960 Rome Olympics India again performed creditably, losing 2–1 to powerful Hungary, drawing 1–1 with France and losing 1–3 to Peru. Both Hungary and Peru scored the match-winning goals in the closing stages of their games. France also equalized just five minutes before the final whistle. Domestic matches in India in those days were still limited to 70 minutes and so the players were not used to playing a full 90 minutes.[25] Since the 1960 Olympics, however, India has failed to qualify for the football tournament.

India also qualified for the 1950 World Cup at Brazil. However, a lack of foreign exchange, the long sea journey and the problem of barefooted players forced India to pull out of this tournament. This was a major setback. Until the mid 1960s India was considered to be one of the top three in Asian football. In both the 1951 Asian Games at Delhi and the 1962 Asian Games at Jakarta India won the gold medal in football. In a regional competition known as the Quadrangular tournament, India were unbeaten champions for five successive years. Rahim took his successful experience with Hyderabad Police on to the international stage as India's coach. Due to his prowess, India was one of the first Asian countries to play in the then modern 4–2–4 formation. In the inaugural 1964 Asia Cup at Tel Aviv India finished runners-up, narrowly losing 1–0 to Israel in the final. In the mid 1960s four Indian players (goalkeeper Peter Thangaraj, centre back Jarnail Singh, left back Altaf Ahmed and roving midfielder Yusuf Khan) figured in the Asian All Stars XI that played Leicester City in exhibition matches at Malaysia and Hong Kong. After this period international successes were limited. In the 1970 Asian Games India won a bronze medal when Syed Nayeemuddin, who went on to coach the national side, was the captain. The team was then coached by G.M.H. Basha and P.K. Banerjee. In the 1974 Asian Junior tournament India, coached by the former Olympians M.A. Salaam and Arun Ghosh, were joint champions with Iran.

The 1962 Asian Games gold medal remains one of the greatest achievements of Indian football because of the difficult circumstances in which it was won. The head of the Indian contingent G.L. Sondhi had criticized the hosts, Indonesia, for excluding both Israel and Taiwan for political reasons. As a result, the crowds were hostile to India.[26] The late Jarnail Singh, India's ace defender, who also captained the Asian All Stars XI in 1966 and 1967, experienced the atmosphere of hostility in Jakarta. As a devout Sikh, Jarnail always wore a turban which made him conspicuous. To avoid the attention of the passionate crowds, Jarnail always had to travel sitting on the floor in the team bus. Recalling the final against South Korea Jarnail said,

> The capacity crowd of over 100,000 booed us and did not even pay respect to our national anthem. When the ball came in our half, such was the din that the referee's whistle was not audible. When we attacked there was pin-drop silence. As most of the Indian contingent had returned home, we had

limited support. We were grateful to the Pakistan hockey team [they had beaten India 2–0 in the final the day before], which cheered for us throughout the match.[27]

The Indian team showed remarkable dedication and adaptability to win the final 2–1 against the favourites South Korea. Because of injuries, coach Rahim improvised with the playing 11 for the final. Jarnail, the centre back, had a bandaged forehead and so was not used in his favourite position. Rahim experimented by using him as a bustling centre forward to harass the Korean defence into errors. The ploy was successful as Jarnail scored in the first half. Right winger P.K. Banerjee scored the other goal and, while the Koreans pulled one back, India managed to hang on to win the Asian Games football gold medal for the second time.

The players were so motivated that some of them overcame sickness and injuries to play in the final. Goalkeeper Peter Thangaraj had barely recovered from a bout of influenza but played because coach Rahim felt that his height gave India a psychological advantage. Trilok Singh, the right back, was in pain because of a cut toenail but played with grit and courage. Towards the end of the match, Jarnail was again bleeding at the forehead but refused to come off. The team had left Calcutta for Jakarta on Independence Day, 15 August, 1962. Many of them considered this to be a good omen. Rahim's clever tactics of using Yusuf Khan as a withdrawn forward and playing the 3–3–4 system also bemused opponents who favoured the traditional 2–3–5 system.[28]

To provide international exposure for Indian players, the AIFF started the Jawaharlal Nehru International Tournament in 1982. Uruguay, Argentina, the USSR, Yugoslavia, Hungary and Poland are some of the major nations to have participated in this competition. Uruguay won the inaugural Nehru Cup in 1982 and their team included Enzo Francescoli. In 1984 Argentina had Burruchaga and Nery Pumpido in theirs and the Polish one, the champions that year, had several World Cup stars such as Smolorak and Wajeicki. The USSR, champions from 1985 to 1988, had stars such as Rinat Dessaiyev, Vassily Rats, Oleg Blokhin and Alexei Mikhailchenko in their team. In the 1990s the AIFF's lack of foreign currency, the disintegration of the Soviet Union and the fall of communism in eastern Europe are factors that have caused the Nehru Tournament to become a biennial event. Previously India had cultural exchange agreements with the socialist governments of eastern Europe and so football teams from there participated without demanding payment in dollars.

From 1982 (the year the Asian Games were held in Delhi) to 1996 India experimented with five different eastern European coaches. Dietmar Pfiefer, who came from East Germany, Milovan Ciric, who was a Yugoslav who had also coached Red Star Belgrade, Josef Gelei of Hungary, who had played as goalkeeper in the 1966 World Cup, Jiri Pesek of the Czech Republic and Rustam Akhramov of Uzbekistan. None achieved notable success. There have been foreign coaches for the age group level teams also. Ivo Sajih-Scheich of Slovenia was coach of the India Under-21 team at the third Rajiv Gandhi International Tournament (U-21 years) at Goa in 1998, but heavy defeats saw his contract terminated after the tournament. Islam Akhmedov of Uzbekistan was appointed coach for the India sub junior (U-16 years) team in April 2000. However, he was unable to guide India to the final rounds of the Asian championships.

In 1997 India's most successful club coach of the 1990s Syed Nayeemuddin was appointed national coach until the conclusion of the 1998 Bangkok Asiad. Nayeemuddin, a stern disciplinarian, developed a physically fit, tactically alert and confident national team that dominated regional competitions. India beat the Maldives 5–1 in the 1997 South Asian Football Federation (SAFF) Championship final and won $50,000, their highest ever prize money. In the same year they reached the semi-finals of the Nehru Cup International Tournament for the first time. Nayeemuddin was succeeded by Sukhwinder Singh, who was also the coach of JCT Phagwara. Under his guidance, India retained the SAFF championships in Goa in April 1999, beating Bangladesh 2–0 in the final.

RECENT HISTORY AND THE CHANGING INDIAN GAME

The more recent history of Indian football has been one of change and this section will review many of the recent developments, further analysis of which appears elsewhere.[29] Until the 1996–97 season there was no national league in India. In the decades after Independence the game was popularized by state leagues and a range of tournaments in which teams from several states in India were invited to participate. These tournaments often overlapped. The AIFF officials in the early 1990s felt that the standard of the national team was declining since playing excessive domestic tournaments fatigued players. They thus restricted each tournament to a fortnight with the limited participation of just 12 teams.

Concerned at India's declining standing in international football, FIFA sent a three-member committee in February 1995 to investigate and suggest methods of improvement. One suggestion that was implemented within a year was the establishment of a semi-professional National League. This started in the 1996–97 season and eight teams participated in the inaugural National Football League (NFL) sponsored by Philips. JCT Phagwara (Punjab) were the champions and Churchill Brothers (Goa) finished as runners-up. In 1997 the Philips League was expanded to include ten teams. Matches were played on a home and away basis from December 1997 to March 1998. Mohun Bagan emerged champions and received Rs5 million as prize money (£83,000). They also got a share of the gate money collected in home matches and so in total earned about nearly Rs5.5 million. East Bengal finished runners up and Salgaocar finished third. Prize money was given to the top six teams. However, each participating team got Rs750,000 (£12,500) as preparation money before the league started.

In 1998 a second division of the NFL was also started but without a sponsor. In order to cut costs, the second division was played at three centres: Bangalore, Guwahati and Cuttack. Indian Telephone Industries (ITI) Bangalore and Tollygunge Agragami (Calcutta) were promoted to the first division. Since then the second division has been held in the same fashion.

Philips ended their sponsorship of the NFL after two seasons and for the following two Coca-Cola were the sponsors. As sponsorship from Coca-Cola was reduced for the 1999 NFL, the format was changed to cut costs. The 12 participating teams were divided into two equal groups and matches were played on a league basis. The top three from each group played a double leg final round held in Goa and Calcutta. Salgaocar from Goa emerged as champions with East Bengal runners-up. Salgaocar, formed in 1956, were the first club from Goa to win the NFL. In the last few years Salgaocar have become one of the best clubs in India. Their results have been very consistent. They won the KBL-Federation Cup in 1997, beating East Bengal 2–1 in Calcutta. They also became the first club from Goa to win the Durand-Rovers double crown in one season in 1999.

Mohun Bagan's win in the 2000 Coca-Cola NFL was the greatest comeback in the history of Indian football. Before the start of NFL 2000 the club was not even tipped to finish among the top six (who were entitled to prize money ranging from Rs4 million [£66,600] to Rs500,000 [£8,300]). Yet they won the league by the widest margin to date. They finished with 47 points from 22 matches and the runners-up, Churchill Brothers (also runners up in the inaugural 1997 NFL), with 41 points. In the three previous NFL competitions the favourites always emerged victorious. In the 1997 Philips National League JCT Mills had a team full of the superstars of Indian football, Baichung Bhutia, I.M. Vijayan, Jo Paul Ancheri and Carlton Chapman along with five talented foreigners. As overwhelming favourites they duly won. In the next year Mohun Bagan, with the Nigerian Chima Okorie in sparkling form, were the best in the country and also won the league. In 1999 Salgaocar were favourites and carried off the championship.

Before the start of the 1999–2000 NFL Salgaocar (winners of both the Durand and the Rovers Cup), East Bengal and Churchill Brothers were highly fancied. The Goa clubs finished second and third, respectively, but East Bengal came seventh their worst performance ever. With their success in the NFL in 2000 Mohun Bagan established itself once more as Indian football's premier club. In 1911 they were the first Indian team to win a major domestic tournament, and in the new millennium they are again trendsetters: the first to have won the NFL twice, and the winners of the first major domestic tournament of the new century.

There were three factors behind Mohun Bagan's triumph. The first was the successful recruitment of four talented foreign players, left back Dusit Chaiersman of Thailand (who played for Asian All Stars), striker Igor Skhvirin of Uzbekistan (who won the Asiad 1994 gold medal), winger Stephen Abarowei of Nigeria (who played for his country's age group teams) and Jose Ramirez Baretto of Brazil. The foreigners scored 22 of the club's 36 goals and Skhvirin was top scorer with 11 goals in 14 matches. A settled midfield that included R.P. Singh, the player of the 1999–2000 NFL, was a second contributing factor. Finally, the emergence of goalkeeper Sandip Nandy helped to bolster Mohun Bagan's fragile defence. The squad has several players who have won the NFL both in 1998 and in 2000. They are the goalkeeper Hemanta Dora, left back Lolendra Singh, midfielders Satyajit Chatterjee, R.P. Singh, Debjit Ghosh and Basudev Mondal and winger Abdul Khalique. Stephen Abarowei is the only foreigner to have won the NFL twice, with JCT in 1997 and Bagan in 2000.[30]

The AIFF had started the Federation Cup in 1977 as an annual tournament for the leading dozen clubs of India. This tournament was expanded to an all-India knock-out competition in the 1996–97 season with the advent of sponsorship. It was sponsored by the makers of a prominent brand of Indian whisky and was called the Kalyani Black Label or KBL-Federation Cup. The winners were East Bengal in 1996, Salgaocar in 1997 and Mohun Bagan in 1998. Since 1999 this tournament has not been played due to the withdrawal of the sponsors. The winners received Rs1.5 million (£25,000) and the runners-up Rs1 million (£16,600). In the semi-final of the 1997 KBL Federation Cup tournament a crowd of over 131,000 turned out at the Salt Lake stadium at Calcutta to watch the clash between arch rivals East Bengal and Mohun Bagan.[31]

In 1996 the AIFF signed a ten-year agreement with Rupert Murdoch's satellite TV channel in Asia Star TV, for the sole telecast rights of the Philips League, KBL Federation Cup and India's international matches. The deal was negotiated by IMG who collaborated with Leisure Sports Management (LSM) who were the marketing agents for the AIFF. Trans World International (TWI) was the production company for Star Sports. The deal was worth $1 million per year to the AIFF. IMG had also procured the sponsors Philips and KBL for the league and the knock-out tournament. However, due to the government's stringent licensing laws, Star TV was unable to get uplinking facilities for live telecasts of the matches. The deal was broken off by the AIFF in January 1998. At present the AIFF has a contract with the national terrestrial television network Doordarshan. According to the terms of this contract, Doordarshan pays the AIFF Rs500,000 (£8,300) for a stipulated number of domestic matches per annum. In this manner many of the national football league matches get televised live on Doordarshan's Sports Channel, known as DD Sports.

Though professionalism in Indian football is still embryonic, 'under the table' payments to players have been common for almost 50 years, primarily in Calcutta and more recently in Goa. This has usually been tolerated by the authorities. Until the 1980s institutional clubs such as Salgaocar or JCT hired players by offering them jobs for life with the company but now it is more common for players to be put on annual football contracts. East Bengal's brilliant quintet of forwards in the 1950s, Venkatesh, Appa Rao, Dhanraj, Saleh and Ahmed Khan, played for the small sum of Rs3,000–5,000 per season. The Asian All Star defender Jarnail Singh moved to Mohun Bagan from Rajasthan Club for just

Rs6,000. Mohammed Habib, who played for the Calcutta clubs from 1966 to 1984 and was hailed as the 'King of Kings' by India's most successful domestic coach P.K. Banerjee, similarly never received large sums of money. At his peak he was paid Rs40,000 for the season.

The first player to receive Rs50,000 per season was Shyam Thapa when he left East Bengal for Mohun Bagan in 1977. The first to get Rs100,000 was the Iranian international Majid Bhaskar (who played in the 1978 World Cup for his country) when he came to study in India and ended by joining East Bengal in 1980. He was paid this sum for the 1981 season. The burly Nigerian striker Chima Okorie received the then record payment of Rs300,000 per season when he left Mohammedan Sporting and joined East Bengal in 1987. He managed to beat this when he moved from East Bengal to Mohun Bagan for Rs500,000 in 1992.[32] This transfer was also historic for other reasons. Mohun Bagan followed traditions similar to those of the Yorkshire County Cricket Club or Athletico Bilbao as they had previously only ever recruited Indian players.[33] During the Second World War, Denis Compton was posted to Calcutta and appeared as a guest player for Mohun Bagan, but they had never actually signed a non-Indian player. By completing the 1992 transfer Okorie became the first foreign player to be signed by the club.

With the advent of TV coverage and increased sponsorship, transfer fees have rocketed. In the 1997–98 season the highest paid player was the young striker Baichung Bhutia, who received Rs1.5 million (£25,000) for switching from JCT to East Bengal. In the 1998–99 season Mohun Bagan signed India's ace striker I.M. Vijayan (who holds the Indian record of 31 goals for his country) for the handsome sum of Rs2.7 million (£45,000).[34] The entire fee goes to the player and clubs do not receive any compensation for their loss.

In Indian football there have thus been several rags-to-riches stories, but the most remarkable is that of I.M. Vijayan. He was born in a mud hut in Thrissur in Kerala and could not afford a pair of shoes until he was 12 years old. His father died when he was young and his mother worked as a floor cleaner in nearby houses to support the family. To supplement the family's income, Vijayan sold bottles of soda water at the nearby football stadium. Watching matches there he developed an interest in the game, practised barefoot and developed into a skilful player. At the age of 15 he enrolled in the three-year football camp in Kerala. There his skills were spotted and he joined Kerala Police and throughout the 1990s established himself as one of India's most successful forwards. He has played for the leading clubs Mohun Bagan, JCT and FC Kochin and to date is the only Indian with two hat-tricks in international football.

Such is his fame that a 35-mm colour documentary drama entitled *Kalo-Hirin* (The Black Stag) was made about his life. In the film the story of his remarkable career is recounted in the form of a ballad accompanied by the popular folk dances *Thoukalli* and *Vattakalli*. Directed by Cherian Joseph, the 30-minute film cost Rs500,000 and took eight months to make. Vijayan's first coach T.K.

Chatunni and friend Chima Okorie also made cameo appearances.[35] He is now acting in the Malayalam film *Shantham* directed by Jayarajan. Vijayan plays the role of an innocent youngster (Velayudhan) who is haunted by feelings of guilt after committing a chance murder.[36]

While Vijayan is a rags-to-riches icon, Baichung Bhutia is the middle-class hero of Indian football. Born in a small village in Tinkitam (five hours' drive from Gangtok, the capital of Sikkim) Baichung was spotted as a rare talent at the age of 16 when East Bengal signed him. Initially he was used sparingly but his quicksilver reflexes have made him India's most feared striker. Articulate and smart, Baichung is the first Indian footballer to attract sponsors and have an all-India corporate image. Reebok are among his backers and he has advertised products for brands such as McDowell's whisky and Coca-Cola. Baichung's desire to improve his game by playing abroad sets him apart from other Indian players. He made several attempts to get a contract with a club in either England or Major League Soccer in the USA. He had trials with Fulham and West Bromwich Albion in 1999 and in September became the first Indian to play in the English league when second division Bury FC signed him.[37] His contract has been renewed for the 2000–01 season.

The money earned by top level football players in India is considerably higher than the national average of Rs5,000 (£83) per month or Rs60,000 (£1,000) per annum. In the 1999–2000 season over 50 players earned Rs500,000 (£8,300) per annum. The month for transfers in Indian football is April. The start of the new season varies in each state but it is generally in full swing from September to March. However, as Table 1, showing players' payments, reveals, the financial status of Indian football in the last two seasons is not encouraging.

TABLE 1
PLAYERS' EARNINGS (Rs LAKHS)

Player	1998–99	1999–2000	% change
Chima Okorie	27	14	–48
I.M. Vijayan	27	12	–56
Jo Paul Ancheri	20	9	–55
Basudev Mondal	12	8	–33
Dipendu Biswas	12	8	–33
Ranjan Dey	14	8	–43
Raman Vijayan	11	7	–36
Tushar Rakshit	14	5	–64

Note: figures are approximate; Rs10 lakhs is Rs1 million, although it has fluctuated, the conversion rate since 1998 has been about Rs60 to £1.

The loss of earnings for players is due to the declining income of the clubs. In the first years of the NFL, sponsors were eager to promote football. In the 1998–99 season, with the entry of Vijay Mallya's United Breweries Group into the management of Mohun Bagan and East Bengal and the success of two competitions for the Philips National League, financial investment in Indian football reached a peak. Mohun Bagan and East Bengal received Rs2.50 crores per season (1 crore is 100 lakhs). Chima Okorie and I.M. Vijayan were both paid Rs27 lakhs and Jo Paul Ancheri received Rs20 lakhs from Mohun Bagan for that season. Baichung Bhutia negotiated Rs24 lakhs from East Bengal.

This corporate interest lasted for just a year. Philips withdrew from the National League and the Kalyani Black Label Group stopped sponsoring the Federation Cup. Prices fell for the 1999–2000 season. The AIFF has received much of the blame for this. In an article in the *Durand Journal* of 1999 Jaydeep Basu, sports correspondent with New Delhi's leading newspaper the *Hindustan Times*, wrote that, 'Football officials in India are yet to learn the tricks of sustaining the flow of sponsors. The recent history shows that their callous attitude has resulted in many enthusiastic sponsors turning hostile.'[38]

Uncertainty now looms over Indian football in the new millennium. Declining sponsorship, dwindling team budgets and cash crises in newly formed professional teams such as FC Kochin and Bengal Mumbai Football Club (BMFC) are discernible after the interstate transfers concluded in early May 2000. With the AIFF unable to organize a domestic calendar for the season and the officials getting embroiled in factional politics and monetary disputes, the outlook for the 2000–01 season is bleak. Players' prices have slumped even further. Vijay Mallya has slashed the annual budgets of both Mohun Bagan and East Bengal from Rs2.50 crores to Rs1 crores[35] and only reluctantly increased these to Rs1.50 crores after the clubs protested. Both Salgaocar and Churchill Brothers have cut their annual football budget by about 30 per cent. FC Kochin, despite floating shares, is struggling to survive. Several of the club's key players have sought interstate transfers and only I.M. Vijayan and Ancheri remain as senior players.[39]

The only club to buck this trend has been Mahindras from Mumbai. The club has now renamed itself Mahindra United to gain an identity as a professional body instead of a company team. Their international striker Mohamed Najeeb is the highest paid player in Indian football this season as he receives Rs1 lakh per month. Striker Raman Vijayan from East Bengal is being paid Rs75,000 per month. The club has also bought the midfielders S. Venkatesh and the Nigerian Habib Adekunle from Salgaocar, as well as wingback Anthony Pereira from Churchill Brothers. In addition to this they have managed to retain their previous season's team and have engaged a new coach, the astute Shabbir Ali, who guided Salgaocar to the National League title in 1998–99.[40]

For a few seasons the money in Indian football was generous. But even now, since the game is not very physical and payment is reasonable, many foreign players are attracted to play in India. In the inaugural year of the National League there were about 20 foreign players. In the next two seasons this number increased to over 30 and by 1999–2000 the league contained about 35 foreigners. Except for corporate teams such as State Bank of Travancore (SBT), Border Security Force (BSF) and JCT, which have consciously adopted policies of the non-recruitment of foreigners, all of the other nine teams had their quota of four by 2000. The majority of the players were Africans, mainly Nigerians but with others coming from Kenya, Ghana and Zimbabwe. In addition to this, players came from Brazil, Jordan, Ukraine and Uzbekistan. The trend of Brazilian players coming to Indian football started in the 1997–98 season. During that season Dempo Sports Club of Goa recruited three Brazilian players from Sao Paulo and had a Brazilian coach. These players quickly ranked themselves among the highest earners so that, for example, in 2000–01 Mohun Bagan retained Jose Ramirez Baretto for the whole season by paying him an estimated Rs20 lakhs.

The professional club has also become a feature of Indian football. In the 1997–98 season FC Kochin, a newly formed club in Kerala, became the first real professional club in India. All of their squad were insured and the players were registered as professionals. In other leading clubs many players are paid to play, but they also retain jobs in banks or public sector firms. In their first season FC Kochin used a Scottish coach George Blues, who had considerable experience of coaching in Africa and western Asia. FC Kochin was formed by a trio of non-resident Keralites who had profited from business interests in the Gulf and were keen to develop football in their home state by setting up a professional club. In its first season the club was sponsored by the whisky makers KBL and later by Coca-Cola.[41]

Similarly a group of non-resident Indian jewellers formed a professional club in Mumbai. In the 1998–99 season they started BMFC by recruiting many prominent Indian players along with some Nigerian and Iranian stars.[42] Their success in the Mumbai league ensured them an entry into the second division of the National League. However, in the absence of regular and sustained TV coverage BMFC have not been able to attract many sponsors. Within two years of their formation the club are struggling to pay their playing staff and have dismissed all foreign players.

Traditional clubs such as Mohun Bagan and East Bengal have also realized that money secured from members, from prize money or from donations is insufficient to develop a top class team for the season. Hence both clubs organized lucrative corporate sponsorships with the names of the sponsors being displayed on the club shirts and track suits. They have also become public limited companies in order to cash in on their image and popularity.[43] The Goa FA is also trying to ensure that some of its best clubs become fully professional. The top six clubs of Goa compete in a semi-professional local league on a double leg basis in September and October each year. Birla and AT&T are sponsoring the venture. Churchill Brothers of Goa have obtained a club sponsor this season, Zee TV, and have adopted the name Zee-Churchill Brothers. By thoughtful promotion of the game Goa has now emerged as a major centre in Indian football to rival Calcutta.

INDIAN CLUBS INTO THE NEW MILLENNIUM

After a century of football and coming at the end of ten years of turbulence and change, Indian football is made up of a range of clubs and institutions. Some of these have long histories but others are little more than a couple of years old. This section will briefly introduce the key clubs as the sport enters the new millennium.

1. *Mohun Bagan* (Calcutta; maroon, green and white; founded in 1889)
Currently sponsored by the United Breweries group and previously sponsored by Tata Tea. India's most historic and successful club, it has won the National League twice in four years in 1997–98 and 1999–2000. It became the first Indian club to be chosen as Asian Club of the Month in January 1998, an honour it achieved for its remarkable unbeaten sequence of 11 matches in the Philips League. The club plays in a 4–3–3 formation with a flat back four or with a 1–3–4–2 formation.

2. *East Bengal* (Calcutta; red, yellow and white; founded in 1924)
Also sponsored by United Breweries. It has the best record against foreign teams in home matches. It had in its ranks Baichung Bhutia, who was the first Indian footballer to be sponsored by multinationals such as Reebok and Coca-Cola. He is also the only Indian player looked after by the International Management Group (IMG). East Bengal play in either the 4–3–3 or the 4–4–2 formation, with a flat back four.

3. *Salgaocar Sports Club* (Goa; green; founded in 1956)
This is the football team of a major corporate house in Goa that has interests in shipping, mining and iron ore. Its president Shivanand Salgaocar is committed to football and has consistently invested money to make his team one of the best in India. The players are hired on an annual or biennial contract basis. Salgaocar is noted for its strong defence and employs India's goalkeeper Juje Siddi who started his career as a boxer. Previously coached by the former international skipper Shabbir Ali the club plays in a 3–5–2 formation and often uses a sweeper back. It was the first team from Goa to win the National League in the 1998–99 season.

4. *FC Kochin* (Kerala; red and black; founded in 1997)
FC Kochin is the first fully professional club in Indian football. In just one year from its foundation it has achieved remarkable success and now receives massive support from Keralites living all over India and in the Gulf region. The team was trained by the Scottish coach George Blues and has recruited players from Ghana and Nigeria, including the goalkeeper Abubacker who played for the former in the Junior World Cup in 1997. For the 1998–99 season it recruited the entire group of trainees from the Tata Football Academy (TFA). Lively in attack but vulnerable in defence the club plays in a 4–4–2 or a 4–3–3 formation.

5. *Air India* (Mumbai; red and black; founded in 1952)
The only team that has never used a single foreign player because of company policy. Players either have jobs with Air India, the premier international airline of the country, or are on a contract basis. The team is traditionally a defensive, hard tackling unit that relies on the counterattack and a strong team spirit. The Wimbledon of Indian football, the club achieves success with a low budget and strong motivation. Its wily coach Bimal Ghosh has a reputation as a great motivator and was chosen as best coach of the 1997–98 Philips League.

6. *Dempo Sports Club* (Goa; white; founded in 1961)
Another team supported by a family that has shipping and mining interests in Goa. It was the first to bring in a Brazilian coach, Gonsalves, and three Brazilian players for the 1997–98 season. The team uses a slow, passing game and has maintained a tradition of trying to play skilful football with one touch, short passing build-ups. The club has also imported talented players from Nigeria and Sudan. The team usually plays in a 5–4–1 system or a conventional 4–4–2 formation.

7. *JCT Phagwara* (formerly known as *JCT Mills*; Punjab; red; founded in 1971)
JCT is a leading industrial house dealing in fabrics and electronics. Its young managing director, Samir Thapar, takes part in national level motor rallies and supports bodybuilding. JCT has the best gymnasium in the country. Thapar is keen on football and so provides the money to develop a successful team, which is also an important marketing ploy to spread the image of the company. It is the only major team from the northern regions of India where football is not so popular. As this is the case the club has not been able to develop much talent from the Punjab region and has relied on Nigerian players to survive in the National League. The team is coached by the former internationals Sukhwinder Singh and Parminder Singh and plays in either the 4–4–2 or the 4–3–3 formation.

8. *Indian Bank* (Chennai; blue and white; founded in 1958)
A company team financed by the largest bank of southern India. The club is unable to pay large sums of money and so is able to attract foreign players only from nearby Maldives and Sri Lanka. The bank employs many of the players. Its coach Albert Fernando, who is also a priest, excels at developing young talent. At home the team is always difficult to beat because of its spirit and well-organized midfield and defence. The team plays in the 1–3–4–2 or the 1–3–3–3 system.

9. *Churchill Brothers* (Goa; white and purple; founded in 1988)
A new club formed just over a decade ago and entirely funded by the football loving Alemao brothers who have made their fortune through restaurants, agriculture and shipping. Two of the brothers, Churchill and Joaquim, have been successful in politics. Churchill Alemao was twice elected as Member of the

Lower House of the Indian Parliament (Lok Sabha). Joaquim Alemao was a member of the Goa Legislative Council. The club was the first to get players from outside Goa to play in the state. The brothers increased payments to players in the early 1990s, thereby breaking the cartel-like monopoly in Goa of Dempo and Salgaocar. The club has imported talent from Zimbabwe, Nigeria, Sudan and Iraq. The departure of the Scottish coach Danny McLennan just before the Philips League 1997–98 season and of an Indian coach after two matches put the team in disarray. Runners-up in the inaugural Philips League, the club was relegated in the next season in March 1998 but is now back in the top division. The team plays in either the 4–3–3 or the 4–4–2 system, and has employed Grigory Schietsen, an Uzbeki coach, for the 2000–01 season.

10. *Mahindra United* (Mumbai; red; founded in 1962)
Another company team from Mumbai. The firm Mahindras manufactures jeeps and machinery. The club relied on young talent and a few imports from Nigeria and Nepal but finished last in both Philips League competitions. In consequence it frequently changes its coaches and there have been four in three seasons. Mahindras play in the 4–4–2 formation; however, the current coach Shabbir Ali has also experimented with the 3–5–2 system.

11. *Tollygunge Agragami* (Calcutta; orange and white; founded in 1943)
This club was established as the Russa Agragami Samity on Moore Avenue in Calcutta in August 1943. It remained an ordinary one till the late 1950s when the dynamic Bhairabb Ganguly took over as president. The name of the club was changed to suit the changing atmosphere. In 1961 the club entered the Calcutta League and had progressed from the fourth to the first division by 1970. In the late 1990s it replaced Mohammedan Sporting as the third force in Calcutta football. It qualified for the National League in 1999 by winning the 1998 second division national league. Based in south Calcutta, the club has local support and has attracted sponsorship as a result of its success. Its football budget has expanded to Rs15 million and it has recruited some Nigerians and Indian junior internationals from Tatas Football Academy. The former India junior coach Shanker Maitra started as team coach for the 2000–01 season but was replaced by the veteran Amal Dutta midway through the season. Both coaches have opted for a flexible 4–4–2 or 4–3–3 system.

12. *Indian Telephone Industries (ITI)* (Bangalore; blue and white; founded in 1956)
This is the football team of a public sector undertaking. Since the 1970s ITI has dominated football in Bangalore. Its greatest triumph was winning the inaugural Federation Cup in 1977 when the team beat the favourites Mohun Bagan 1–0 in the final. For many years it recruited players by offering them jobs and through this method produced several international stars, including India's finest winger of the 1970s, N. Ulaganathan. Now it has begun hiring players on contract and

has set a budget for football. It has recruited players from Nigeria, Kyrgyzstan and Kazakhstan. The club qualified for the National League in 1999 by finishing second in the second division. ITI just managed to avoid relegation in the 1999–2000 season. For the 2000–01 season it has hired the dynamic Mohammed Habib, a former Tata Football Academy and India junior player as coach. Habib is using either a 4–5–1 or a 4–4–2 system.

13. *Vasco Sporting Club* (Goa; white and black stripes; founded in 1956). Vasco was the first club from Goa to participate in India-wide tournaments, playing in Delhi in the Durand Cup in 1963. For the 2000/01 season, Vasco was sponsored by the Chowgule Group, and was coached by former international Derek Pereira for the second season. The squad was strengthened for this season by the arrival of three Brazilian and two experienced Uzbeki players. Vasco vary their playing systems and have recently used a sweeper system as well as the more traditional 4–4–2.

INDIAN FOOTBALL AND THE 2000 VISIT TO ENGLAND

The Indian national football team visited England in July 2000 for a three-match exhibition tour. This was the first such visit since 1948 and, although the official reason given for the tour was that it was a good opportunity to prepare the Indian team for the forthcoming World Cup qualifiers, the tour had a range of other objectives.

First among these was the introduction of Indian players to examples of good practice in the professional game. The national coach Sukhwinder Singh said that the tour was a learning experience for his players and commented that, 'The exposure helped the players to understand the need for better physical conditioning, the ability to play under pressure and that professionalism is commitment and not just money.'[44]

The second objective was to introduce the players to the standards of football played in Europe so as to encourage them to look at their own game. Singh claimed that the main conclusions reached by the squad after the tour were that players had to be faster on the ball and that Indian teams required more physical presence in midfield. However, the record of one win, one draw and one defeat was felt to be encouraging. India scored a solitary goal, Jo Paul Ancheri's match winner against Bangladesh at Leicester, but conceded just two in three matches. Both the goals were scored by the former German World Cup striker, 34-year-old Karl Heinz Riedle for Fulham FC in the opening match of the tour (which India lost 2–0). The 0–0 draw with West Bromwich Albion was seen as India's best performance and the win against Bangladesh was a positive result, despite some disappointment with the quality of the performance.

Analysing the results, Singh and the technical director P.K. Banerjee praised India's back four of Prabhjot Singh, Roberto Fernandez, Mahesh Gawli and Daljit Singh for their consistency and determination as they kept clean sheets in two successive matches. Considering the overall performances of the players, Banerjee felt that the defensive midfielder Ancheri was India's best player in the three matches. The injury to his left knee in the closing stages of the game against Bangladesh was a cause for concern. Ancheri hopes it is not a reoccurrence of the injury that plagued him earlier in his career.[45] The captain Baichung Bhutia was happy with the results of the tour but felt that India could have played much better. He concluded that 'We lost the ball too often by erratic passing'[46] and felt that, despite the win against Bangladesh, the fluency and rhythm in the team was missing in that game.

The final objective of the tour, however, was to establish links between football in India and among the south Asian communities of the United Kingdom. The tour was seen as successful in this respect as well. The largest attendance was in the second match at the Hawthorns, where a crowd of over 12,000 witnessed India play West Bromwich Albion.

Harpal Singh, a British Asian who is in the reserve team of the Premier League club Leeds United attended one of India's training sessions and greatly impressed P.K. Banerjee. This meeting led Banerjee to advocate the inclusion of non-resident Indians in the national team and he made it clear that he felt that 'the AIFF should tap these unknown sources of talent as it may hasten the development of Indian football.'[47] The Indian players also felt that the tour had been a success. Renedy Singh said that, 'I have never been made to feel so important and heroic before in my football career.'[48] The young players Prabhjot Singh and Hardip Saini were popular with the predominantly Punjabi section among the Indian spectators and both said, 'We are more popular in England than in Punjab.'[49]

THE SEASON OF REVOLT

The formation of the nine-team Indian Premier Football Association (IPFA) on 18 November 2000 led to an initial boycott of the National League and the delay of the start of the tournament. The members of the IPFA modelled themselves on the pattern of the G-15 (the top clubs of Europe) and acted as a pressure group. Years of frustration at inept marketing, inadequate resource mobilization and lack of a proper calendar of events had led to an internal revolt against the AIFF. The leading clubs of India were also exasperated with the constant politicking and bickering within the AIFF which had again erupted when Ranjit Gupta of the IFA (the controlling body of football in Bengal) filed a case against the AIFF president for embezzlement of funds.

The clubs that formed the IPFA were Mohun Bagan, East Bengal and Mohammedan Sporting (all supported by companies owned by Vijay Mallya's United Breweries group); Mumbai league champions Mahindra United; two clubs from Goa, Salgaocar and Zee Churchill Brothers; Tollygunge Agragami; JCT Phagwara; and FC Kochin. This move was seen as an important phase in the corporatization of Indian football as the business magnates challenged the politician–bureaucrat nexus that had controlled the game for decades.

The president of the IPFA Vijay Mallya said that, 'Our plans are simple: to popularize the NFL and raise the standard of Indian football at the international level. The IPFA want a player-friendly, spectator-friendly and sponsor-friendly National Football League.'[50] At present the NFL, which involves 12 teams playing on a home and away basis, is held in a period of just four months with teams travelling across the country and often playing twice in a week. The IPFA wanted the NFL to be spaced out over a period of from five to six months, with matches only on weekends to ensure proper TV coverage which would, in turn, attract sponsors. There is also a demand for repeat telecasts and a concerted effort to market the NFL. Mallya is adamant that the old formats of Indian sports need to be changed and that proper marketing is vital. At present the NFL is televised by Doordarshan, which has the rights for five years starting from 1998. The IPFA has promised a Rs6.5 crores deal with either Zee TV or Sony Max, both of which are confident of getting uplinking facilities on a shared basis with Doordarshan.

The IPFA's main aim was portrayed as an attempt to arrest the dangerous stagnation in Indian football. This may can be measured in the tournaments organized across the country. In the 1980s there were about a hundred domestic tournaments held annually and, indeed, in the 1960s and the 1970s there had been up to 125 such events. In Kerala alone nine major All India tournaments were held each year. In the new millennium there are barely two dozen tournaments held annually. The AIFF is just not able to attract sponsors. Thus the Federation Cup, billed as the knock-out Cup of India, has not been held since 1998. The Nehru Cup, started with much publicity in 1982 to provide international exposure for Indian players, has not been held since 1997.

The AIFF is seen as at best badly organized and at worst inscrutable and unaccountable. Prize money for the clubs in the National League is paid in instalments, months after the conclusion of the events. Mohun Bagan won the fourth NFL in March 2000 but got Rs3 million of the promised prize money of Rs4 million only in mid November. In fact none of the other clubs have been paid their full amount so far. The AIFF has been unable to attract a sponsor for the fifth NFL competition. Previous sponsors Philips (1996–98) and Coca-Cola (1998–2000) have backed out due to inadequate exposure and poor organization by the AIFF. Indeed, the AIFF was not the only target of the IPFA's criticism and the organization made it clear that it felt that only seven of the 31 state associations in the AIFF conduct a state league and organize football properly.

The revolt lasted 25 days and after protracted negotiations a truce was reached. The IPFA forced a compromise in the composition of the NFL committee and in the sharing of revenue. Representatives of the first six clubs in the annual NFL will serve on the League committee for the next season. The representative of the champion club will henceforth be vice-chairman of the committee. Shivanand Salgaocar of Salgaocar FC was included in the AIFF finance committee with cheque-signing authority. After deducting expenses for organization and conduct of the NFL, the premier clubs will get 80 per cent and the AIFF 20 per cent of the revenue. It was also decided to improve TV coverage and hold as many matches as possible in floodlight. It was decided to arrange corporate sponsorship worth Rs15 crores, but so far there has been no progress in this direction.

This truce helped Priya Ranjan Das Munshi's re-election as AIFF president for a fourth term. In the elections held at Delhi on 16 December 2000 he defeated Samir Thapar, managing director of JCT, in a straight contest. Alberto Colaco of Goa became the new AIFF secretary, beating the incumbent Kedarnath Mour in a close contest by 17 votes to 14. Mohammed Khaleel was retained as treasurer. A new post of executive president was created to accommodate P.P. Lakshmanan of Kerala. The industrialist Vijay Mallya, representing Pondicherry, was inducted into the AIFF as vice-president. The AIFF promised to set up a permanent office in Delhi by February 2001. It has appointed the former international referee Melwyn D'Souza as assistant secretary for coaching and refereeing. Three other appointments including two assistant secretaries, to look after 'administration' and 'finance and sponsorship', were to be announced. The outcome seems therefore to be an uneasy compromise. Some of the main movers behind the IPFA and behind the corporate interest in Indian football such as Vijay Mallya now hold posts in the AIFF. Administrators such as Alberto Colaco, with excellent reputations for organization, have been incorporated into the national structure. But representatives of the old order such as Priya Ranjan Das Munshi continue to hold power. The season of revolt may have only just begun.

NOTES

1. S. Banerjee, *Cluber Naam Mohun Bagan* (Calcutta: Aparna Book Distribution Centre, 1998).
2. Ibid.
3. Ibid.
4. Ibid.
5. Ibid.
6. See P. Dimeo in this volume for a more detailed analysis of these events.
7. Banerjee, *Cluber Naam Mohun Bagan*, p.41.
8. N. Kapadia 'India in International Soccer – Olympics', *Durand Journal* [Delhi] (1999), 102–6.
9. N. Ganesan, 'Rahim and After', *Sport and Pastime Magazine*, 16 July 1964.
10. Ibid.
11. Ibid., 'Captain for a Decade', *Sport and Pastime Magazine*, 12 Sept. 1964.
12. Ibid., 'Skilful Laiq', ibid., 3 July 1965.
13. N. Kapadia, 'Decline of Hyderabad Football', *DCM Football Tournament Journal* [Delhi] (1986), 35–9.
14. Ibid.
15. Ibid.
16. Ibid., 'Prelude', *DCM Football Tournament Journal*, 1.
17. M. Ghoshal, *Kolkatta Football* (Calcutta: Jaya Ghoshal, 1988).
18. N. Kapadia, 'Witness to an Era; a Profile of Harnam Singh', *The Telegraph*, 11 Feb. 1983.
19. R. Saha, *Ekadashe Surya* (Calcutta: Deepprakashan Publications, 1990).
20. H. Chattopadhya, 'East Bengal at Home against Foreign Teams', *The Telegraph*, 8 Aug, 1993.
21. S.L. Ghosh (ed.), *Indian Football* (New Delhi: Shaheed Prakashan Press, 1975), p.46.
22. Ibid., p.50.
23. Ibid., pp.54–6.

24. Ibid., p.56.
25. Ibid., pp.60–2.
26. M. Ghaus and N. Kapadia, 'Jarnail Who?', *Sportsworld Magazine*, 25 Aug.–7 Sept. 1993, 60–3.
27. Ibid.
28. J. Basu, 'The Glory Days of Indian Football', *Hindustan Times*, 7 Aug. 1997, 21.
29. See M. Rodrigues in this volume for a more detailed analysis of these events.
30. Indya.com, April 2000.
31. B. Sujit, 'Baichung Stars in East Bengal's Win', *The Telegraph*, 14 July 1997, 16.
32. N. Kapadia, 'It's Got to Be JCT', *Sportsworld Magazine*, 21 June–4 July 1995, 52–7.
33. Ibid., 56.
34. V. Ghosh (ed.), *Limca Book of Records 2000* (New Delhi: VG Communications, 2000), p.410.
35. Ibid., *Limca Book of Records 1999* (New Delhi: VG Communications, 1999), p.268.
36. 'Soccer Star Vijyan Makes Film Debut', *Hindustan Times*, 12 Oct. 2000.
37. R. Saha, 'Baichung! The Road to Bury', *Asian Age*, 26 Sept.1999.
38. J. Basu, 'Football Sponsorship', in N. Kapadia (ed.), *Durand Annual*, 1999, pp.8–9.
39. N. Kapadia, 'Turbulent Times for Indian Soccer', www.indya.com, Aug. 2000.
40. Ibid.
41. R. Upadhaya, 'Southern Light', *The Telegraph*, 4 May 1997.
42. S. Dutta, 'On the Ball', *The Telegraph*, 4 May 1997.
43. R. Saha, 'Just for Kicks', *The Telegraph*, 23 Feb. 1997.
44. N. Kapadia, 'P.K. Banerjee, Sukhwinder All Praise for the Back Four', *The Telegraph*, 31 July 2000.
45. Ibid.
46. Ibid.
47. Ibid.
48. Ibid.
49. Ibid.
50. Ibid., 'Nine Clubs in a Breakaway Mood', *The Telegraph*, 19 Nov. 2000.

2

Soccer as Moral Training: Missionary Intentions and Imperial Legacies

J.A. MANGAN

The nineteenth century was pre-eminently the European century in world history, the period in which Europe was able to impose its will and its ideas on the whole of the inhabited world. With the European conquerors of Africa and Asia went the religion of Europe – Christianity.[1]

Following on from previous work on the subject by the author, this essay will argue that the introduction of football into northern India was closely integrated with the colonial projects of the British and with the evangelical objectives of English Christian groups in the later part of the nineteenth century. The game was considered by the colonizers to carry with it a series of moral lessons, regarding hard work and perseverance, about team loyalty and obedience to authority and, indeed, involving concepts of correct physical development and 'manliness'. As such, it was used as a key weapon in the battle to win over local populations and to begin transforming them from their 'uncivilized' and 'heathen' state to one where they might be considered 'civilized' and 'Christian'.

The place of missionaries in the European colonialism of the nineteenth century was the consequence of European religious revivalism that was born in the second half of the eighteenth century and came to maturity in the late nineteenth. In Britain it resulted in the creation of numerous missionary societies committed to the conversion of those that such groups considered heathen. A number of these societies were Anglican and offered an image of evangelization as one with,

> churches built in the suburban Gothic style, with romantic missionaries expounding the authorized version of the Bible in the light of the Thirty-nine Articles to congregations differing from ourselves only in the colour of their skins and the absence of their clothes, while clean little black choir-boys in clean little white surplices sing their various versions of *Hymns Ancient and Modern*, or, it may be, the *Hymnal Companion*.[2]

A number of these missionary societies made a virtue of recruiting public schoolboys. This fact gave rise to a particular kind of missionary endeavour which reflected the style and purpose of English education of the Victorian and Edwardian eras. The endeavours of these societies were therefore imbued with the values of 'missionary muscularity'.[3] Two excellent examples of evangelists who came from within these traditions are Theodore Leighton Pennell and Cecil Earle Tyndale-Biscoe who were active in the North-West Frontier Provinces and in Kashmir respectively.

THEODORE LEIGHTON PENNELL AND THE NORTH-WEST FRONTIER

Theodore Leighton Pennell died from septicaemia at Bannu on the North-West Frontier in March 1912. He had been born at Clifton in 1867 and educated at Eastbourne College and London University. He was first and foremost a medical missionary but he was much more. It was at the urging of his mother that in boyhood he had determined to be a medical missionary, 'the work of a missionary was set before him from boyhood as the highest career which he could undertake, and the lives of great missionaries and explorers deepened the missionary enthusiasm implanted by his mother's training.'[4]

She was the supreme influence in his life. Pennell dedicated his autobiography *Among the Wild Tribes of the Afghan Frontier* to her with the following words, 'To My Mother to the inspiration of whose life and teaching I owe more than I can realize or record.'[5] To her he certainly owed the unshakeable conviction that India needed, and should be given, Christianity.

After qualifying as a doctor, having had conspicuous success as a student when he won several scholarships and medals, he was posted in 1892 by the Church Missionary Society (CMS) to the North-West Frontier of India. In 1893, on the instructions of the CMS, he established a medical mission at Bannu, a small military station in 'the wildest section of the border'. It had been decided by the British that healing their bodies was the surest way to win the trust of the Pathans and so a chain of medical missions was established along the Afghan frontier. Pennell himself subscribed to this strategy. He wrote in his autobiography, '... in no part of the country are medical missionaries more obviously indicated, not only for Christianizing the people, but equally so for pacifying them and familiarizing them with the more peaceful aspects of British rule'.[6] There were missionary medical posts at Srinigar, Marran, Peshawar, Korak, Teak, Tauk, Dera, Ismail Khan, Deva Ghazi Khan, Quelta and Bannu. 'Bannu was one of the last ... to be established, and it was to Pennell that the task was confided.'[7] There his commitment to missionary work and his dedication to preaching the Gospel became legendary.

Pennell travelled among the villages of the Waziri, dressed as one of them, speaking their language, displaying familiarity with their customs and 'with utter fearlessness [he] preached the Gospel in places where its message had never been heard before'.[8] His fearlessness was frequently tested to the limit, 'when Pennell began to preach in the Bannu bazaar [he was] hustled, kicked and buffeted in no gentle manner'.[9] Whatever the response to his preaching, his hospital work appears to have gradually won him the affection of the tribesmen and the esteem of the authorities.

However, he was not simply a missionary doctor and religious diplomat. He was also a teacher. Virtually from his first moments in Bannu war 'the supervision of a large school devolved upon him'. While being a brilliant surgeon, Pennell also seemed to have an aptitude for teaching. A reserved man, 'it was among the schoolboys that he seemed completely to unbend and to show the full attractiveness of his personality'. Pennell was a product of his time, class and education, 'He was a strong believer in the value of athletics in the development of character, and the boys of the Bannu High School ... obtained a great reputation for athletic prowess.'[10] It was to these boys that he introduced the game of association football.

Pennell made some interesting observations on the impact of modern sport (including soccer) on the North-West Frontier that have far wider resonance in the chapter in his autobiography entitled 'An Afghan Football Team'.[11] After a description of 'a flat open piece of ground covered by the hard alluvial earth known in the Punjab as *pat*', the place for the traditional sports of Afghanistan 'for centuries past',[12] he continued,

> this time we are in a large grassy sward between Bannu city and the cantonments. There is a crowd, as before, of some thousands of spectators, but the football goal-posts and flags show that the game is something different. It is the day of the provincial tournament of all the schools of the province, and teams of the various frontier schools from Peshawur, Kohat, Dera, Ismail Khan, as well as those of Bannu, have collected here to pit their skill and prowess against one another in games and athletics. The referee, an English officer from the garrison, has blown his whistle and the youthful champions come out, amid the cheers of their supporters, from the opposite sides of the ground.[13]

And then Pennell noted of this new activity,

> The old order changes and gives place to the new. Tent-pegging will always retain its charm, with its brave show and splendid opportunities for the display of manly courage and dextrous horsemanship, so dear to a militant nation like the Afghans, and will always remain their favourite pastime. But the simpler native games are gradually giving place to the superior attractions of cricket and football, and the tournaments which of recent years have been organized between the various native regiments and between the different tribes inhabiting each district and between the schools of the provinces are doing much to create a spirit of friendly rivalry, and to develop among these frontier people a fascination for those sports which have done so much to make England what she is.[14]

On his death one obituarist recorded the teacher's strenuous efforts to introduce soccer in Bannu and farther afield, 'on one occasion Pennell took the school football team for a tour in North India, playing matches with the various mission schools and colleges which they visited'. The memorial continued with a statement at once typical of the values of the time and of the convictions shared equally by the obituarist and by Pennell,

> this is a side of missionary work which is not often known, but it is worthy of note that some of the most successful educationalists in connexion [*sic*] with missions have recognized the fact that, especially among the Indian races, the proper use of athletics has served to strengthen moral backbone, which is often conspicuously weak, and has been an important auxiliary to Christian teaching.[15]

Pennell himself wrote of the purposes of the tour as follows:

> with the idea of developing the *esprit de corps* of the school, and gratifying their love of travel, while conferring on them the benefits of a well-planned educational tour of the chief cities of India, I arranged in the summer of 1906 to take the football team of the Mission High School at Bannu on a tour through a great part of Northern India.[16]

He was keen to point out that the team represented 'all classes, Moslims, Hindu, Christians and Sikhs'. Clearly he felt it important that soccer had a wide appeal among his pupils. The team travelled extensively and gained a wide experience so that 'we found ... that the football season differs in various places. While Calcutta plays football in July and August, Karachi plays from December to March, and Bombay in the spring'.[17]

On the field the tour was a great success. The Bannu boys rarely lost, 'in no place did we find greater enthusiasm among the colleges and schools for football ... than in Hyderabad ... and here our team experienced their first defeat.'[18] Off the field, however, the tour was a near tragedy. In Calcutta a mob mistook some of the team for a band of child-snatchers and attacked them, leaving them for dead. Fortunately the victims recovered in hospital but the series came to a premature end. Nevertheless, Pennell was able to look back positively on the trip, 'tours such as this undoubtedly tend to promote that feeling of friendship and union between the races of various parts of India which has hitherto been so little in evidence.'[19] He noted with pleasure that on their return to Bannu,

> we were honoured by a civic reception which went far to make up to the members of the teams for the discomforts they had undergone. The Civil Officer of the district, the Municipal Commissioners and a great number of the citizens met us with a band some miles before reaching Bannu and we were escorted in amid great rejoicing.[20]

What 'Pennell's Football Tour' reveals quite specifically is that the missionary played his part in the spread of association football throughout several parts of India. It also reveals how widespread, enthusiastic and organized soccer was in the secondary schools by the turn of the century.

Pennell, in fact, had a long experience of combining teaching, medicine and sport in the promotion of Christianity. While a medical student in London he 'took charge of the students' Christian Association [and] had an eye on the working lads in the Euston Road district, and with the aid of a few others, started and worked at a boys' club and gymnasium'.[21] By the time of his arrival in Bannu the use of sport as a means of making successful contact with the young was therefore a tried and tested strategy. As it was later recorded of his approach in Bannu, 'while the old ... came to be treated in his hospital, and they were very good friends with him ... they were not much influenced by his teaching ... the boys were different.'[22]

A brief glimpse of Pennell's school at Bannu in his early days is offered by Brigadier-General Scott-Moncrieff, the missionary moralist who visited it at the turn of the century,

> His school at first was a very small affair, but by the time I came into touch with him it had flourished so far that it was just being established on the public school boarding system, and a block of dormitories and classrooms had then been completed. Close to this building was a fine swimming-tank, over which there was a big tree, on which were erected diving platforms at various heights. Every morning, even in the sharp cold winter, the boys all had to swim, the doctor himself often leading them; and if any lad shirked it, he was thrown in, clothes and all. The elder boys had quite imbibed the spirit, good form and honour. They all adored the doctor, and his greatest pleasure in life was in his association with them, playing football and cricket with the utmost keenness.[23]

CECIL EARLE TYNDALE-BISCOE AND KASHMIR

At virtually the same time as Pennell was teaching soccer to his mainly Waziri pupils, Cecil Earle Tyndale-Biscoe was teaching soccer to his mostly Hindu boys. In 1891 Tyndale-Biscoe, who was educated at Bradfield and Cambridge, took a soccer ball and a wife to his Church Missionary Society School in Srinagar, Kashmir. His wife excited interest while the ball stimulated irritation.

Tyndale-Biscoe later recorded its hostile reception. The whole school was assembled. The ball was presented to them,

T-B: This is a football.
Boys: What is the use of it?
T-B: For playing a game.
Boys: Shall we receive any money if we play that game?
T-B: No!
Boys: Then we shall not play that game.
Boys: What is it made of?

T-B: Leather.
Boys: Take it away! Take it away!
T-B: Why should I take it away?
Boys: Because it is *jutha* (unholy) we may not touch it, it is leather.
T-B: I do not wish you to handle it. I want you to kick it ... and today you are
         going to learn how to kick it, boys.
Boys: We will not play that *jutha* game.[24]

Tyndale-Biscoe was not to be dissuaded. He was used to getting his own way. A year earlier he had observed a fire close to the school from his classroom window. He had ordered his pupils to provide help to put it out. As high-caste members of society they had preferred to continue their lessons rather than indulge in demeaning manual activity. It was a point of view that failed to win his sympathy. In his own words,

> I then took action and drove them out of the classroom ... at the double I herded them with my stick to the fire. Arrived there, we found that scores of citizens had already taken their seats at every available place in order to enjoy themselves at an entertainment for which they would have nothing to pay. As the flames spread from one house to another they seemed highly delighted, shouting out 'Hurrah!'

Tyndale-Biscoe was appalled. He commandeered pots from reluctant boatmen, armed the larger boys with sticks to prevent the police from stealing valuables from the burning houses and organized the rest of his pupils as a fire-fighting force. The school fire service, which later fought many fires in Srinagar, had been created.[25]

Shortly afterwards, when his pupils refused to take up swimming as it was also felt to be beneath their dignity, he employed Machiavellian cunning,

> Boys were persuaded to swim by the age of thirteen by the simple expedient of increasing the school fees by one-quarter every twelve months for non-swimmers beyond that age. Eventually swims across the local Dal and Wular lakes (four miles and five miles, respectively) became a regular annual event for the stronger school swimmers, and one of the proudest achievements of his years in Kashmir was to establish a life-saving corps which over the years rescued more than 400 people from drowning.[26]

On yet another occasion Lord Lansdown, Viceroy of India, visited the school on a prize-giving expedition. With a nostalgia 'natural to a sporting English gentleman trained from his youth in an atmosphere of manliness and fair play'[27] he looked out of a school window at the smooth, dark waters of the Jhelum river and observed how pleasing it would be to have headship of the Jhelum to match the headship of the Thames. Tyndale-Biscoe, as an equally nostalgic, ex-rowing Cambridge Blue took up the challenge and decided that the boys would now learn rowing.

The obstacle to his plans was obvious. 'Oarsmen developed low-caste muscular arms and no Brahmin had so vulgar an appendage as muscle on the arm.'[28] Nevertheless, Tyndale-Biscoe built a boat. It proved impossible to get pupils or indeed any of his staff into it. However, he forcibly persuaded two young teachers to inspect the craft and in no time at all, with a firm push from behind, they were sprawled in it floating swiftly downstream. The incentive to row was self-evident. In Tyndale-Biscoe's jaunty words 'minus the moral article ... they bent their material backbones and ... made a beginning in making that low-caste stuff commonly called muscle'.[29] Rowing became part of school life as did boat outings for families, the sick and the elderly. 'The school emblem of crossed paddles with heart-shaped blades was a fitting symbol of this transformation – exemplifying the virtues of the products of the muscular Christian in Empire – strength, kindness and service.'[30] Enthusiasm for rowing spread throughout Srinagar schools and in 1909 the first interschool regatta was held. State, Hindu, Islamic and Christian schools took part. The Church Missionary Society School won by 30 lengths.

Thus the challenge presented by soccer held no terrors for Tyndale-Biscoe. He ignored the pupils' fears and proceeded to give them instructions about the pitch, positions and rules. Their sullen response was not encouraging. He wrote later,

> before the end of school I perceived that there would be trouble, so I called the teachers together and explained to them my plans for the afternoon. They were to arm themselves with single-sticks, picket the streets leading from the school to the playground, and prevent any of the boys escaping *en route*. Everything was ready, so at 3 o'clock the porter had orders to open the school gate. The boys poured forth, and I brought up the rear with a hunting-crop.

He added,

> then came the trouble, for once outside the school compound they thought they were going to escape, but they were mistaken. We shooed them down the streets like sheep on their way to the butchers ... All were clothed in the long nightgown sort of garment I have described before, each boy carrying a fire-pot under his garment and so next to his body. This heating apparatus has from time immemorial taken the place of healthy exercise. We dared not drive them too fast for fear of their tripping up (as several of them were wearing clogs) and falling with their fire-pots, which would have prevented their playing football for many days to come.[31]

Then followed an unforgotten moment in the modern history of Kashmir. The ground was reached, the sides were picked, the ball put in position, the whistle blown, and blown again. The boys were adamant. They had absolutely no intention of kicking 'an unholy ball'. Tyndale-Biscoe, for his part, had every intention that they should. The masters were lined up with their sticks raised menacingly along each goal line and the boys were given five minutes to reflect on their decision. Five minutes passed. The masters charged, sticks and voices raised. The game began,

> all was confusion ... as [pupils] tried to kick the ball but generally missed it, their clogs flew in the air and their *pugaris* were knocked off while their nightgowns flapped in one another's faces; a real grand mix-up of clothes and humanity ... suddenly there were squeals of agony and horror and the game came to a halt. One unfortunate had stopped the ball with his face. He was polluted. His horror-stricken friends took him sobbing to Tyndale-Biscoe. A wash in the canal was brusquely prescribed. The game, or rather the rough and tumble, proceeded until time was called. The first game of football in Kashmir played by Brahmins was over.[32]

Another description of the 'game' was, if anything, even more picturesque,

> As soon as the pandits saw the sticks there was one concerted rush by the whole lot to see who could get nearest the ball and so avoid the stick-bearers. Not only did they kick the unholy leather, but with hands and claws they fought each other to get near it. *Pugarees* flew out like pennants, clogs and shoes shot into the air. Football had started in Kashmir ...[33]

There were immediate repercussions. One bearded player (a number of 'boys' were often young men in their twenties hoping to learn English at the school) was expelled from his home for having touched the polluting leather. He went to live with relatives. Some enterprising pupils then carried pins hidden in their sleeves and over 50 balls were punctured before Tyndale-Biscoe hit on the idea of fining those responsible for the burst bladder and the practice ceased.

Despite the unpromising start, soccer prospered at Srinagar High School and the Christian gentleman's code of behaviour was partially, if not wholly, assimilated. At the time he wrote *Kashmir in Sunlight and Shade*, which was published in 1922, Tyndale-Biscoe could observe that he had recently watched 'an inter-class match, most keenly contested, the referee being not a teacher, but a schoolboy. His decision was not once disputed, nor was there any altercation between any of the players, it was a truly sporting game.'[34]

Tyndale-Biscoe's son Eric, in his biography of his father, *Fifty Years Against the Stream*, wrote later, 'Now, not only is football played by the school boys, but the general public have taken to it with enthusiasm. They have a football league of various teams ...'[35]

As with so many others in the length and breadth of the Empire, Tyndale-Biscoe had practical objectives in mind in his determination to take soccer to Kashmir. The game would introduce the local youth to a new code of ethics,

> It was his profound desire as a Christian to introduce his pupils to HIM who taught all men to love one another and show it by practice ... talking

would not accomplish this ... bundles could not do this, therefore bundles must be turned into boys by athletic exercises and athletic boys turned into manly citizens by continued acts of kindness.[36]

The game would also transform the bodies of the local boys as they needed to be strengthened to make them suited for roles that the British wanted Indians to play. His football-playing schoolboys became the agents of a range of social programmes that he imposed on the local community. During cholera epidemics staff and pupils would fill up cesspools and clean streets and compounds of filth; in summer hospital patients of all denominations were treated to outings on the local lake; in winter the pupils provided fuel for the poor; all year they saved lives from fire and water and they even rescued animals that they felt had been mistreated.

While football in Kashmir has its origins in the force of a colonial zealot and his determination to transform the ethics and the bodies of the young Indians that he encountered, the legacy of the game in the region hints at a more complex story once the game has been adapted and adopted by Indian groups. The school continues to develop excellent young footballers and in a recent All-India school soccer tournament in Delhi the school won the tournament handsomely with an average of five goals per match. Soccer continues to be a widely played game in Kashmir and its early moments in the colonial past are still directly and explicitly acknowledged. At the school, recently renamed the Tyndale-Biscoe School, pupils act out a bizarre play for visiting dignitaries. They recreate the chaos of the first game of football at Srinagar described above and take on the roles of frightened schoolboys and truculent masters. In a remarkable post-colonial performance and with great enjoyment and hilarity, modern Kashmiris acknowledge the origins of the game in which they now excel in the reluctance of their ancestors and the bloody-mindedness of the British headmaster.

THE BOARDING SCHOOLS OF THE RAJ

Elsewhere in India British missionaries made their contribution to the spread of soccer through the boarding schools of the *Raj*. British hill-stations were originally created as sanatoria for the military in the first half of the nineteenth century. By mid-century they were populated by soldiers, civil servants and *box-wallahs* and their wives luxuriating in the 'Englishness' of their climate. It was sensible in this unrelenting climate to create such schools for their offspring. Among the most famous of the hill-stations were Simla, Mussoone, Darjeeling and Ootacamund.

The first of the hill-station schools was Mussoone School established by the Revd Robert North Maddock in 1849 as 'a public school for boys *of the upper grade*'.[37] This set the tone for the future, as in time it became 'a very *pukkah* establishment'. In the 1860s it became a Diocesan school with a new headmaster, the Revd A.O. Hardy. In a report on the European Hill Schools by A.J. Lawrence in 1872, reference was made to the nascent interest in 'manly games', including association football. The seed had been sown. The Lawrence Schools, created on the initiative of Henry Lawrence (later Sir Henry), an Army officer, also played their part over the next half century in spreading English games across India. By 1860 there were four schools – Sanewar, Mount Abu Lovedale, Ootacamund and Ghora Gali, Murnee.

Perhaps the clearest link between the English public school games ethos and India is George Edward Lynch Cotton, who became Metropolitan Bishop of Calcutta in 1858. Cotton had earlier been headmaster of Marlborough College where he did so much to establish public school games.[38] On his arrival in India he became 'concerned that the Government of India had not played its part in providing education for its poorer European and Eurasian subjects'.[39] He proposed a string of schools in the hills and on the plains. One of the eventual outcomes was the creation of Simla Public School in 1863. After Cotton's death by drowning in 1866, it was renamed Bishop Cotton School in his memory. As might be expected, games, including soccer, were a central feature of the school. The soccer 'seed' was now being spread more and more widely among the children of India. The school experienced various vicissitudes, mostly associated with finance, but it survived into the twentieth century and in 1923 the speech of the headmaster, the Revd W.S. O'Neill, on its Diamond Jubilee, included this self-confident, institutional self-appraisal,

> ...we are fully confident that no boy who passes through this School and takes full advantage of the corporate life, *the games*, and the course of studies provided will be at any disadvantage in the great game of life ... I have no hesitation in saying that this School compares most favourably with any of the lesser English public schools.[40]

It should be noted that Cottonians over the years were prominent in many walks of life. Today the school is flourishing, as 'strong in its Christian ideals as it ever was'.[41] It has a chapel, houses and many sports, including cricket, basketball, hockey, boxing, athletics, tennis and, of course, soccer 'all contributing to the retention of the public school ethos'.[42]

Even before Cotton's death Cotton Schools for boys were set up in Nagpur, Bangalore and Darjeeling. They too were characterized by the same public school, games-playing ethos. Nowhere was this more in evidence than at St. Paul's School for Boys, Darjeeling, established in 1864 under the headship of the Revd J.C. Nesfield, who was recruited from England. Life at the school in the late nineteenth century is described in *My Thirty Years in India*, written by Edmund Cox (later Sir Edmund) who joined the school in 1877 as classics master. His credentials were impeccable as he had studied at Marlborough and Trinity College, Cambridge. Like Tyndale-Biscoe a little later in Srinagar, he was unimpressed by his pupils '... a nice prospect for me, fresh from an English public school and university, to have to look after such a rabble.'[43]

Displaying a confident Anglo-Saxon belief in himself[44] and 'with the assistance of another Master, the redoubtable Edmund Cox threw himself heart and soul into teaching and organising cricket, football, riding and swimming; and order emerged out of chaos.'[45] Many of the boys at St. Paul's were the sons of tea-planters. Indeed, 'St. Paul's maintained a connection with the tea-planting fraternity until the *Raj* had packed up its tents and gone'.[46] The tea-planting fraternity was a mix of the local and 'Home' educated, 'but the one thing they all had in common was their obsession with games'.[47] There was invariably a Planters XI of cricketers and footballers in Darjeeling, mostly old boys, who would go back to the school to take part in matches against the boys and other visiting teams.[48] The schoolmasters had one view of games, the boys may well have had another. Helen Craig Innes has remarked that no doubt 'it was his prowess at sport which tipped the scales in a St. Paul's boys favour when he went for interviews with the managers of the many tea gardens of the Darjeeling District.'[49]

At St. Paul's 12 headmasters attempted to make their mark to a lesser or greater degree between 1864 and 1870, Richard Cartiman (King Edward's School, Birmingham and The Queen's College, Oxford), was the first lay headmaster (1878–98) and by 1934 Leslie James Goddard (Trinity College, Cambridge), with a Blue in association football and cricket and experience in both English and Indian public schools, was in charge. He is crucial to the story of the success of the school. When he arrived in 1936 there were 102 pupils. Some two years before he left in 1964 there were 300, mostly Indian. Today there are more than four times that number. Goddard was important in another way. He ensured the popularity of soccer at the school as he created new pitches and played in the school eleven. He did the same for cricket. The games tradition that he made secure lives on to this day in the Anglo-Indian St. Paul's. In the school's *Commemorative Volume, 1823–1973*, it is recorded of 'The Goddard Era' that he was responsible 'for transforming a crumbling monument to inefficiency and woolly-mindedness into one of the finest educational institutions in Asia. Renowned for its academic and athletic achievements, for its highly-disciplined, well-mannered boys and its healthy cosmopolitanism.'[50]

It must not be overlooked that well into the twentieth century soccer and other games in the hands of English schoolmasters had a serious moral purpose. L.C. Taylor, a young master at St. Paul's during the Second World War, put it as well as anyone,

> The Rector and his staff had a clear sense of mission, which was to train an elite in India, and to instil what we would call the Victorian 'noblesse oblige', high ideals and so on, into the young men of India's rising middle class.[51]

He noted two things about his exercise in responsibility: its timelessness and its 'strangely abstract values to a race concerned more with putting families first'.[52] As mentioned earlier, inculcating an English sense of 'fair play' was integral to this responsibility and the games field was integral to this.

There is a sizeable roll-call of schools like St. Paul's, too many to mention in this chapter, but it may be interesting to single out one or two in order to further underline the role that educationalists played in the assimilation of soccer (and much else) in India. One was Sherwood College for Boys in Naini Tal, founded in 1839 as the Naini Tal Diocesan School (it became Sherwood School only in 1937). Arguably its most famous headmaster was Alwyn E. Binns (1932–47) 'the legendary man who made Sherwood what it was, an Anglican school which produced muscular Christians ... with corporate life centring on chapel worship, academic excellence and *compulsory games*.'[53]

Roman Catholic schools as well as Church of England schools had their games fields on which soccer was played. James Richard Staines was sent to the Patrician Brothers' St. George's College, Missoorie in 1917 and recalled hockey and soccer matches against the Jesuit orphanage St. Fidelis School. The Jesuits, of course, also had their schools and games in several major cities in India, including Bombay, Madras and Calcutta. Staines, incidentally, draws attention to the interest in hockey in the hill-station schools,

> no mention of the hill schools in India would be complete without some reference to their prowess in hockey. In the 20s and 30s practically the entire Olympic teams representing India were composed of young men from hill schools, St. George's, Oakgrove, Bishop Cotton's, etc.[54]

Staines provides a practical reason,

> because it was difficult to grow grass, possibly on account of the altitude, our playing fields in the hills consisted of *bujree*, a kind of flinty surface, and although we played football on it, as well as cricket using a mat, it was most suitable for hockey, and that became our main game and the one we were best at.[55]

Not only the Irish St. George's, but other European schools such as the Belgian Jesuits St. Joseph's North point, Darjeeling, established in the 1880s, were created in the English public school image, 'it was a very English public school. The Belgians spoke perfect English.'[56] As in the case of Tyndale-Biscoe's school in Srinagar, soccer was a means to a moral end. On one occasion, overnight floods washed away a nearby village,

> The football team went up next morning ... village people stood nearby. No spades could be found, so schoolboys rushed to get *kooktees* from bystanders ... [one] woman, who had been totally buried, was near death. She looked pitifully at her two little dead babies in her arms. A member of the football team gave her his shirt to wear: she had been deprived of almost all her clothing. A *charpoy* was found and the sick woman placed on that, the boys carrying her through waist-deep mud. None of the bystanders would touch the load.[57]

In the late nineteenth and the early twentieth century the public school games ethic was embraced in the middle-class, English-initiated schools of India as fully as it was in the middle-class schools of 'Home'. In the famous hill-stations of India, the schools 'were as besotted with games as were their counterparts at "Home". "*Mens sana in corpore sano*" and "Play up! Play up! and play the game" vied with each other in importance, particularly in boys' schools.'[58] This state of affairs was true of India as a whole,

> sports and games-mad were those 'Anglo-Indian' public schools in India, and this obsession can be said to have sprung from the Christian gentlemen who left England to promote ... a healthy mind in a healthy body in Queen Victoria's fast-expanding empire.[59]

CONCLUSION

> In certain important ways, *culture* was what colonialism was all about. Cultural forms in newly classified 'traditional' societies were reconstructed and transformed by and through colonial technologies of conquest and rule.[60]

This study has begun to explore the origins of football in south Asia in the educational programmes of the British during the colonial period. Two main conclusions have been made. First, the origins of modern sports in parts of modern-day India and Pakistan are in the exporting from Britain of its own experiences of developing modern sports in the eighteenth and the nineteenth century. It is certainly possible to use south Asian examples to agree with C.L.R. James's observation in the Caribbean that 'the organisational drive for sport had come from Britain. It was from Britain that cricket, and soccer more than cricket, had spread as nothing international had ever spread for centuries before.'[61]

The second conclusion is that sport in general, and football in particular, were important 'colonial technologies of conquest and rule', to borrow the phrase from Nicholas Dirks. The examples explored above show that the missionaries and teachers involved in integrating the game with the educational programmes of the schools opened for Indians by the British were very conscious of its power to transform bodies and minds. The game carried within it a moral order based on the ethics of commitment and dedication, of team spirit and the subjection of the individual to the demands of the group and of valour and personal bravery. Colonized peoples were often portrayed as lacking just such attributes and thus football was seen as one method of introducing them to such desirable characteristics. Football was certainly one of those sports that was believed to be a 'stylized epitome of a moral order and the metaphoric essence of a cultured civilisation'.[62]

But the game also had the practical impact of transforming Indian bodies into the shapes and to develop the capabilities considered desirable by the British who required local servants to put in place their wider visions of imperial reform. Many of the Indians that the British took charge of in their schools had bodies that demonstrated their own belief in the degrading nature of physical exertion. Masters such as Tyndale-Biscoe entirely ignored the claims of such a culture and forcibly imposed their belief in the virtues of physical action on the muscles and physiques of the local youth. He did this as he had a moral commitment to the ideal of the 'muscular Christian' but also because he had a broad vision of 'improving' local society through a series of interventions. These interventions were aimed at imposing his order on the local town through such initiatives as a fire brigade and a life-guard and this required a cadre of loyal agents with the physical capacity to carry out such duties. Football and the other sports that he introduced had the practical result of creating just such an order of brave and strong young men to implement his projects of social reform.

One final point should also be made, however. A study such as this outlines the intentions and the programmes of the colonizers. An assessment of the impacts of these intentions and programmes is a different matter altogether. As the story of the Tyndale-Biscoe School and its re-enactment of the first ever game of football in Kashmir shows, it is no easy matter to begin untangling the responses of Indian communities to the introduction of football. The first game is a stark example of colonial coercion and local resistance as the masters used sticks to make the young Indians pollute themselves. Yet the transformation of this traumatic event into a play in which post-colonial schoolboys gleefully act out all the roles for the amusement of visitors hints at all manner of responses after the initial rejection. As this author has observed elsewhere, interpreting these events is no simple matter but they certainly offer the opportunity 'to place the grand ... discourses of colonial knowledge and control in the context of their often partial and ironic realizations'.[63] How far soccer actually taught 'fair play' and for how long the lessons of men such as Tyndale-Biscoe have continued to be learnt are important issues for future research.

NOTES

1. J.A. Mangan, *The Games Ethic and Imperialism: Aspects of the Diffusion of an Ideal* (London and Portland, OR: Frank Cass, 2000 [reprint of 1986 edn]), p.168.
2. Ibid., p.169.
3. Ibid., p.171.
4. Obituary, *British Medical Journal*, 1 (1912), 761.
5. T.L. Pennell, *Among the Wild Tribes of the Afghan Frontier* (London: Seeley, 1909), Dedication.
6. Ibid., p.53.
7. Brig-Gen G.K. Scott-Moncrieff, 'Dr. Pennell of Bannu', *Blackwood's Magazine*, 192, 1211 (July 1912), 5.
8. Obituary, *Lancet*, 6 April, 1912, 961.
9. Scott-Moncrieff, 'Dr. Pennell', 7.
10. Obituary, *British Medical Journal*, 761.
11. See Pennell, *Among the Wild Tribes*, pp.153–67.
12. Ibid., p.155.

13. Ibid.
14. Ibid., p.157.
15. Obituary, *British Medical Journal*, 761.
16. Pennell, *Among the Wild Tribes*, p.157.
17. Ibid., p.159.
18. Ibid.
19. Ibid., p.160.
20. Ibid., p.167.
21. Reminiscence of Devereaux Marshall, one-time fellow student, in *British Medical Journal*, 767.
22. Scott-Moncrieff, 'Dr. Pennell', 7.
23. Ibid.
24. Mangan, *Games Ethic and Imperialism*, p.184.
25. Ibid., p.181.
26. Ibid., p.182.
27. Ibid.
28. Ibid.
29. Ibid., p.183.
30. Ibid.
31. Ibid., p.185.
32. Ibid.
33. E.D. Tyndale-Biscoe, *Fifty Years against the Stream* (Mysore: Wesleyan Missionary Press, 1930), p.20.
34. Cecil Earle Tyndale-Biscoe, *Kashmir in Sunlight and Shade* (London: Seeley Service, 1922), p.277.
35. Tyndale-Biscoe, *Fifty Years*, p.20.
36. Mangan, *Games Ethic and Imperialism*, p.187.
37. See *Under the Old School Topee*, by Hazel Craig Innes, privately printed, 1996, p.xi. This labour of love, and rightly unashamed exercise in nostalgia, will prove to be a record of considerable value to future social historians who reflect on the cultural influences of the English public school system on modern Indian culture and society.
38. See J.A. Mangan, *Athleticism in the Victorian and Edwardian Public School: The Emergence and Consolidation of an Educational Ideology* (Cambridge: Cambridge University Press, 1981).
39. Innes, *Under the Old School Topee*, p.60.
40. Ibid., p.68. Emphasis added.
41. Ibid.
42. Ibid.
43. Sir Edmund L. Cox, *My Thirty Years in India* (London: Mills & Boon, 1909), p.26. Cox has a nice line in bland sarcasm and his descriptions of his time at St. Paul's School, Darjeeling are often vehemently hilarious.
44. This characterized his devastating criticism of headmaster, pupils and servants.
45. Cox, *My Thirty Years in India*, p.28.
46. Innes, *Under the Old School Topee*, p.76.
47. Ibid., p.77.
48. Ibid.
49. Ibid, p.96.
50. Ibid.
51. Ibid., p.112.
52. Ibid.
53. Ibid., p.119.
54. James Richard Staines, *Country Born: One Man's Life in India 1909–1947* (London: Croscomb Press, 1986), p.56.
55. Ibid.
56. Gloria Jean Moore, *The Anglo-Indian Vision* (Melbourne: AE Press, 1986), p.149.
57. Ibid.
58. Innes, *Under the Old School Topee*, p.197.
59. Ibid., p.202.
60. Nicholas B. Dirks (ed.), Introduction, *Colonialism and Culture* (Ann Arbor, MI: Michigan University Press, 1992), pp.3–7. Emphasis added.

61. C.L.R. James, *Beyond a Boundary* (Harmondsworth: Penguin, 1964).
62. Ibid., pp.157–8.
63. See J.A. Mangan, 'The Early Evolution of Modern Sport in Latin America: A Mainly English Middle Class Inspiration', in J.A. Mangan and Lamartine DaCosta, *Sport and Society in Latin America: Past and Present* (London and Portland, OR: Frank Cass, forthcoming).

3

Football and Politics in Bengal: Colonialism, Nationalism, Communalism

PAUL DIMEO

By his legs you shall know the Bengali. The leg of a free man is straight or a little bandy, so that he can stand on it solidly ... The Bengali's leg is either skin and bones; the same size all the way down, with knocking knobs for knees, or else it is very fat and globular, also turning in at the knees, with round thighs like a woman's. The Bengali's leg is the leg of a slave.

G.W. Steevens (journalist, 1899)[1]

Above all, do not think that speech is ever a substitute for action.

Lord Curzon (Viceroy of India, 1902)[2]

The Calcutta FC was the last European civil side to reach the Shield final [in 1936]. The sun had set on the British soccer empire. A jubilant Calcutta greeted the victory of Mohammedan Sporting with bands, processions and fireworks.

S. Mookerjee (historian of Calcutta football, 1989)[3]

INTRODUCTION

In championing the virtues of action in his role as the British leader of imperial India, Lord Curzon concluded his speech on education with a reference to the importance attached by the colonial government to sport. Yet his remarks also captured the spirit of the age in Bengal,[4] which was certainly a centre of action and energy at the end of the nineteenth and at the beginning of the twentieth century. Calcutta, as the administrative capital, mercantile entrepôt and industrial heart of the British Empire in India, was a centre of imperial enterprise and endeavour. Europeans there made fortunes from Asia but also planned societies in their role as imperial governors and shaped cultures in acting as colonizers.

The city was also the base for a vibrant Indian population, the English-educated elite which dominated local society, while the middle classes competed for posts in the local service sector the working classes and rural migrants found jobs in industry and on the *ghats*. Differentiated by class, caste and religion, the Indian communities of Bengal in general and of Calcutta in particular vigorously pursued a range of economic, political and cultural agendas so that by the early twentieth century nationalism, communalism and anti-colonialism had developed as powerful forces. The people of Bengal and Calcutta, be they of Indian or British origin, certainly believed in action.

The broader currents of history and society in Bengal and Calcutta are important in understanding the emergence and development of the game in what has traditionally been the powerhouse of Indian football. Bengal has the oldest, richest and most successful clubs in the Indian game, it hosts some of the longest-running competitions in the world and the popularity of the game there is such that local derbies have commanded attendances of over 130,000. The region has this status in Indian football precisely because the game and its institutions became powerful vehicles for the energies that emerged during the history of the period. As such, tracing the changing nature of football in Bengal is in many ways an exercise in tracing the history of the region itself. Football has been at the heart of the action that has defined modern Calcutta and West Bengal.

THE BRITISH AND FOOTBALL IN INDIA

Football was quickly to become important to Indians and in many ways to become dominated by Indians, but it was in the first place a British introduction. The game had been played by Europeans since the 1870s in Bengal. Football was an important part of Army life and it was the large garrison stationed at Fort William in the centre of Calcutta that played a major role in the early introduction of football to the city. For officers educated in the games ethic, sports were a useful way of developing specific characteristics among soldiers. Indeed, while presenting the Durand Cup in Simla to the King's Own Scottish Borderers in October 1892 Lord Roberts articulated the perceived link between sports and martial efficiency, 'the same qualities, discipline and combination, were equally necessary in good soldiers and football players.'[5] As Mason has argued, team sports encouraged *esprit de corps*, fitness and relief from boredom.[6] For these reasons regimental teams quickly became a dominant force in Indian football during this period. An Army team won the Calcutta Football League on all but nine occasions between its foundation in 1898 and 1933.

Football was not solely the preserve of the Army in Bengal, however, and European civilians from groups of merchants, civil servants and missionaries began to form clubs in the 1870s. The Calcutta Football Club (CFC) was established to play rugby in 1872 but found that there was little interest in the game among the British of Bengal. By 1894 the club had forsaken rugby in favour of football and had donated its silver to fashion the Calcutta Cup for the annual Scotland–England rugby union fixture back home. Little is known of the early days of this club but the fact that it was in a position to donate a trophy for the most important rugby match of the British calendar indicates that its members were well connected in metropolitain sporting circles. The club represented the colonial elite of Calcutta and was filled with 'the *burra sahibs* of the city's commercial establishments'.[7]

Whatever the exact origins of the club, CFC quickly established itself as a football institution and won the Calcutta League in its second year in 1899.

Indeed, CFC continued to be a presence in Indian football as it won seven of the nine league titles taken by a non-Army team before 1933 (1899, 1907, 1916, 1918, 1920, 1922 and 1923). It was the most successful British civilian team and symbolized the colonial elite that Indians so wanted to beat.[8]

In 1878 the Dalhousie Club was established by members of the Indian Civil Service, which was mostly filled with former public school boys and mercantile groups associated with the Trades Association of India. Dalhousie would take the other two non-Army League successes in 1928 and 1929. Elsewhere, the Trades Club drew its members from the British employees of the jute mills.[9] Other civilian clubs were established, such as the Naval Volunteers (which became the Calcutta Rangers), Police, Customs and the Armenian Club.[10] In other words, the establishment of football clubs to participate in regular competitions was a rapid development from the 1870s onwards in Bengal. The apparently close identification of clubs with specific groups, whether regiments, employment associations, ethnic groups or geographical affiliations, was an integral feature of early Bengal football and mirrored the early organization of football elsewhere.[11] It reflected the social structures of European society in Bengal, which was far from a homogeneous unit, fissured as it was by class, profession and geography.

While a variety of European clubs were being formed, a number of competitions was being organized for these teams to compete in. The oldest cup tournament, the Durand Cup, was established in 1886 just 15 years after the FA Cup competition began in England, and in 1889 the Trades Cup was established. In June 1893 the disparate clubs and competitions that were leading the way in Indian football prompted the establishment of a ruling body to oversee these initiatives and to formalize the sport's rapid development. The colonial press in India immediately saw the value in such a move,

> We are glad to welcome the formation of an Indian Football Association, a copy of the Rules and Regulations of which we have the pleasure to acknowledge. The Association is modelled on the lines of the International Football Association at home.[12]

> The objects of the Association at present are to form a governing body that will be able to finally decide any disputes on the field ... Of far greater interest than this to the many, however, is the proposal to start in connection with the Association a Challenge Cup to be competed for by every Football Club in India.[13]

A modest sounding group of British men formed the working committee: Capt G.A. Williams, W. Bushby, the Revd J.L. Peach, E. Jackson, J. Kidston, B.C. Lindsay, H.S. Ashton and A.R. Brown. The first accusation that they had to fend off was the claim of Calcutta bias within the organization's set-up, they were all 'Calcutta men', the meetings were to be held in Calcutta and the design of the

Challenge Cup assumed the superiority of Calcutta teams. The IFA Shield became the most prestigious competition, taking precedence over the Trades Cup for the European teams and did much to establish Bengal as the centre of Indian football.

The philosophy behind the IFA was typical of the British in the nineteenth century. Its regulations were derived from the rules of the game drawn up by the public-schools-dominated English FA in 1863. The model of the English FA (before FIFA was formed in 1904 there was no challenge to its 'International' status) was used and was assumed to be appropriate for the organization of football in any country. In other words, from the crucible of English public schools and Oxbridge colleges came the method employed by the British in Calcutta to organize sport across the entire subcontinent. The small band of amateur enthusiasts, including an Army captain and a Church minister, was considered capable of organizing football in India, using established and authoritative English models.

The most obvious points to make about the early organization of football in India are that it was dominated by Europeans and that it excluded Indians to the extent that 'the Anglo-Indian clubs were chary of including a footballer who was not fair-skinned'.[14] In this, football largely reflected the broader currents of colonial society in India, as the British by the end of the century had self-consciously isolated themselves from local communities as a result of the repositioning of the *Raj*'s authority after the 1857 Mutiny. Control had passed from the East India Company to the British government that, in turn, exercised its power through the exclusively British and heavily bureaucratic Indian Civil Service. India was no longer the place for adventure and cultural exchange of the nineteenth century and attitudes hardened as the British dug in to preserve their economic asset. The emphasis shifted, as outlined by Judith Brown, towards privilege and imperial prestige,

> In the later nineteenth century a distinctive imperial life-style developed among the British in India. The new rulers exported and recreated, even in the most isolated parts of India, a culture and life-style fashioned in upper middle-class Britain. It was a life free of manual exertion, dependent on Indian servants for its smooth functioning. It was meticulous in its codes of dress and manners, of elaborate social courtesy, and of appropriate behaviour in relations between dominant and subordinate, male and female. It surrounded itself as far as possible with all the domestic trappings of British life, even to the extent of dressing for dinner in the jungle. From this domestic and social world Indians were largely excluded.[15]

This was the context for the establishment of the football clubs and of the IFA: a closeted world of business, family life, leisure and manners. Hunting, horse racing, polo, cricket and football went alongside tea parties and cocktails on the lawn. The IFA was specifically a British institution, created from the sporting amateurism of middle-class England, brought to India to recreate the playing fields of Harrow and Eton on the Calcutta Maidan. Indeed, as Moorhouse has argued, the deliberate separation of British and Indian was most obvious in the social realm and anti-Indian prejudice among the British in India was 'always most powerfully exercised in the composition of their clubs'.[16]

INDIANS, EDUCATION AND THE CULTURE OF FOOTBALL

The urge to exclude Indians from British society extended to sports and to football in particular. However, the complexities of colonial agendas are also reflected in football since among the British in India other objectives actually resulted in the colonizers' encouraging Indians to learn the game and to organize teams and clubs. In other words, while many British organized football in India so as to exclude Indians, many others took the game to the locals.

The reasons for the desire of many British to have Bengalis play the game lies in a range of discourses about 'race' and 'orientalism' that coloured British thinking about India after the uprising of 1857. By the nineteenth century the British had become fascinated by 'race' and tried to classify and categorize Indians on the basis of perceived 'racial' qualities. A healthy 'race', it was claimed, was characterized by 'manly' vigour and strength, capable of defending itself through warfare but also capable of self-sacrifice for weaker allies. As such the strong and independent nation had 'male' qualities while a colonized people was largely portrayed as weak and effeminate and in need of the benevolent protection of a 'male' civilization.[17]

Bengalis were represented by the British as an example of just such a weak and effeminate people and they were dismissed by the colonizers as possessing 'the intellect of a Greek and the grit of a rabbit'.[18] The image of the effeminate *babu* became a dominant feature of colonial life and a general slur upon all Bengalis. *Babu* was a term of derision specifically relating to the English-educated, Bengali, middle-class male who was employed in the service of the empire as an administrative or professional worker. The *babu* was widely reviled as physically weak and morally suspect for collaborating with British interests.[19]

The origins of this 'colonially-constructed image of the weak Bengali' are instructive, since they point to the wider cultural and social changes within which football emerged and which made it politically significant.[20] The 1857 mutiny of Indian soldiers serving the British originated among Bengali officers and thereafter soldiers from the region were viewed as unreliable. Indeed, recruitment policy after 1857 deliberately excluded Bengalis and chose to focus on soldiers from parts of India that had remained loyal to the British. The association of men from these regions with military service and of Bengalis with treachery and exclusion from the Army led to a series of images being constructed of the martial and the non-martial races of India. 'Manly' races such as the Punjabis and the Gurkhas were constructed as essentially 'different' from the effeminate, enervated race of Bengalis.[21] As Stanley Wolpert explains,

> The British soon [after the Mutiny] developed their spurious theories about 'martial races' and 'nonmartial races', based for the most part upon their experience with 'loyal' and 'disloyal' troops during the mutiny. Not only were there 'martial races', but also – and here Hinduism supported British prejudice – 'martial castes', least of which was the Bengali or Maharashtrian brahman, whose rebel leaders had fought so bitterly [in the Mutiny].[22]

These constructions had a profound effect on social relations in Bengal where the British became convinced of the Bengalis' physical inferiority because of their lack of service in the post-1857 armies. Sir George Campbell, Lieutenant-Governor of Bengal in the 1870s, believed 'that if the educated Bengalees, instead of giving way to intellectual vanity, set themselves to rival Europeans in qualities depending on physical and moral tone, they are capable of very great things.'[23] Consequently the following stipulations were made for those Bengalis who applied for posts in the Native Civil Service,

> By every candidate a certificate of character must be produced, as also a medical certificate of fitness for employ in any portion of Bengal. Candidates for appointments of over Rs100 a month must show that they can ride at least 12 miles at a rapid pace; candidates for inferior posts must have similar qualification or be able to walk 12 miles within 3 1/2 hours without difficulty or prostration. Good character, health, and physical energy [are] thus secured.[24]

Through such statements and mechanisms the British transmitted to the Bengali elites the idea that they were considered physically inferior. However, in sports the British offered Indians a means of developing their bodies. Indeed, many among the British saw it as part of their imperial duty to help Indians to 'improve' themselves and deliberately set about encouraging Bengalis, men in particular, to engage in games. Many Indians quickly realized that physical prowess was necessary for success in the colonial order. The lesson learnt was that an ability to demonstrate to the British that Bengalis did possess physical vigour was necessary both to get ahead in colonial India and to gain the respect of the imperial power. While there were British officials and civilians encouraging Indians to play football there were also many Bengalis who realized the value and importance of taking advantage of these opportunities to play the colonizers' games. The most obvious place where British 'improvement' met with ambitious young Indians was in the Anglo-Indian schools and colleges.

Middle-class Bengalis were educated in British-run, Anglo-Indian colleges modelled on the British public schools of the nineteenth century. That such models were adopted for these institutions should come as no surprise since the colonial administration was dominated by graduates of the public school system in Britain. There were large numbers of former public school boys in powerful positions in India at this time and three Governors-General and four Viceroys were schooled at Harrow alone.[25] Lord Curzon himself was educated at Eton and Balliol College, Oxford.

The education of Indians within these colleges was designed to produce 'Oriental Englishmen'[26] and to train them for colonial service. These institutions adopted the games ethic of the public schools back in the England where there was a faith in the 'desirability of games, especially team games ... for the development of ethical behaviour and the formation of sound social attitudes'.[27] The implication of this in India was that sports would be introduced for Indians, as it seemed self-evident to the British that 'team games were ... valuable for teaching conformity and solidarity and football, cricket, hockey and rugby were rapidly established as central parts of the curriculum in schools all over the empire from the 1880s.'[28] Sir George Campbell, for example, emphasized the importance of sport in the curriculum of the College of Engineering in Calcutta,

> I spared nothing to make that college complete, but the Bengalis seemed infinitely to prefer literature, law, and politics to anything that required some physical as well as mental exertion. At the same time I am bound to say that when I introduced gymnastics, riding, and physical training in the colleges, they heartily accepted these things, and seemed quite ready to emulate Europeans in that respect.[29]

Campbell was clear in his intentions. Sport was as valuable for education, for the making of able men, as was scholarly activity. His implication that Bengalis embraced these benefits indicates his belief in both the superiority of British ways and his strategy for Bengali improvement. It was one that the students apparently accepted wholeheartedly. Although Campbell makes no mention of football *per se*, another Briton resident in Calcutta in 1885 realized its place in the larger picture of British sports and Indian inferiority,

> Many educated Natives, in Bengal specially, have for years past felt the reproach which attaches to their want of courage and corporeal activity and have earnestly set themselves to remedy these defects: hence on all sides we find efforts to follow the example of Europeans among native students. Football and cricket are becoming popular, and gymnasia introduced.[30]

Another example of similar colonial attitudes towards sports comes from the Lieutenant-Governor of Bengal in 1891, Sir Charles Elliot, who proposed measures to assist in the improvement of the Bengali 'race' through physical culture,

> For some years past the physical training of schoolboys had been encouraged by the formation of clubs for athletics, by drill and gymnastic exercises, in Collegiate competitions and annual sports. In 1891–92 it was particularly noticed on every hand that there was a great increase of the zeal

with which the national English games, especially football, were played. On tour Sir C. Elliot constantly watched the performances of the boys with great interest ... He looked forward to great improvement in the physique of Bengalis in the course of one or two generations from this source ... Sir C. Elliot expressed a hope that some generous and public-spirited individuals would come forward and provide means for the physical improvement of their race: and with the aid of Government and private subscriptions Marcus Square in the centre of the town was cleared and made available for recreation.[31]

Sports were considered a source of improvement necessary for the Bengali 'race'. Such was the success of sports within Anglo-Indian colleges that their ethical virtues continued to be extolled as the twentieth century progressed. In August 1915 the First World War was a year old and the President of Presidency College, H.R. James, beseeched his young Indian charges to offer the ultimate sacrifice. He did this by portraying death in battle as profoundly honourable, to pass 'in one brief moment of exalted action to an immortality of youth and renown'.[32] His speech, however, softened the prospect of death in the British Army with sporting metaphors,

> we have acquired a fighting temper peculiarly our own. Nursed in a succession of heroic struggles for ideas more than for material power, and called upon to uphold interests wider than national by force of arms in every quarter of the globe, we have learnt to wage war in a chivalrous spirit and have wedded humanity to courage in fight. We know how to win without insulting the vanquished and to suffer defeat without rancour. For in the course of ages of warfare all the world over, and in the development of the games by which, even in peace time, we train our youth to manliness, we have acquired a love of fair play, which has become a national character. Alike in peace and war we seek 'to play the game'.[33]

James was unwavering and solid in his belief in empire, illustrating to the boys that it stood for justice, liberty, Christian tolerance and civilization. For these ideals Indians were asked to lay down their lives, and many did, of course, accept the call to arms.[34] The preparation for these battles lay, for James, in the lessons of the playing fields,

> Throughout this fierce ordeal it was seen how the British regiments were so many bands of athletes, disciplined and practised equally to stand shoulder to shoulder, to scatter without losing cohesion, to fight singly or in groups, or in their unyielding khaki lines: not athletes only but men of heroic temper, sublime in endurance, in unflinching constancy, in gaiety.[35]

James's commitment to the lessons of the sports field is obvious. He was militaristic and uncompromising in his conclusion that sports prepared men for battle and for death. The link was yet again established between sport, physical culture, honour and manliness and was made central to elite education in Bengal. Games remained important even after the devastations of the Great War. Presidency College made sport compulsory. Also, the College expressed a desire for applicants who had physical prowess,

> Participation in games or regular physical exercise will be compulsory for those admitted into the 1st year classes. Other things being equal, preference will be shown in making admissions to those who have previously played in their School or College teams.[36]

The diffusion of this ideal through Anglo-Indian colleges had a powerful effect. Its legacy was the commitment of graduates to team sports. Mason has speculated that members of the educated classes filled the Bengali football clubs that emerged in the 1880s and the 1890s,

> We do not know much about the social origins of the players, but it seems likely that they came from the educated lower-middle and middle classes, an expanding group without whose existence and positive support such a structure as the British Empire in India could not have been sustained.[37]

Evidence exists to support Mason's speculation on this direct link between the middle-class, English-educated students and the formation of league clubs, and points to the influence of British pedagogues. One important player was Nagendraprasad Sarbadhikari, a graduate of Hare School, who helped to establish the Wellington Club in 1884 and the Shovabazar Club in 1885.[38] The story of 'the first encounter of a Bengali with a soccer ball',[39] has taken on a mythical status but it does contain all of the elements discussed above,

> One morning in 1879, ten-year-old Nagendraprasad Sarbadhikari of Hare School was accompanying his mother on her morning trip to bathe in the Ganga. As their carriage crossed the Maidan, they saw some English soldiers kicking a round object about. The curious boy got down to watch. The ball landed near his feet. He picked it up: it was surprisingly light. A soldier called out, 'Kick it to me'. Nagendraprasad complied.[40]

From this encounter Nagendraprasad and his friends purchased a football (though their first ball was a rugby ball) and were helped by Professor G.A. Stack of Presidency College and his colleague J.H. Gilliland to learn the rules and techniques of football. Their passion for the sport quickly developed and they helped to develop the structure of Indian football clubs.

The colleges soon produced teams, beginning with Presidency College in 1884, followed by Sibpur Engineering College, Bishops College, Medical College, St. Xavier's College and La Martiniere College. Graduates from these were instrumental in forming other teams, including some of the most prominent clubs in the history of Indian football, 'it was these students, after they left college, who founded the first of today's open clubs in the 1880s and 1890s to enable them to go on playing the game. Chief among their number were Nagendraprasad himself, Kalicharan Mitra, Manmatha Ganguli and Haridas Sheel.'[41] The umbilical connection between British educationalists, the Anglicization project, the public school games ethic and the development of Indian football clubs was central to the sport's development.[42]

However, the educational experience of sport was certainly not uniform. It seems that where Indian and mixed race ('Anglo-Indian') students attended the same schools, those that had some European ancestry were privileged. Bengali students were often excluded from competing on the same level as mixed-race students and they were,

> debarred from these college teams. They could only watch and learn [as] the Europeans and the Anglo-Indians were not prepared to concede that Indians would be able, in the course of years, to combat them on equal terms. This attitude only added fuel to the fire of new-born nationalism.[43]

As stated earlier then, there was a tension within the British colonial community in India since there were those who wished to encourage Indians to play British games and others who were eager to maintain the maximum possible distance between the colonizers and the colonized. Thus the origins of many football clubs run by Indians may have been the English educational institutions designed to turn out 'Oriental Englishmen', but this did not mean that these clubs were allowed to compete with teams of European origin. Indeed, the exclusion of Indian clubs from the major competitions was a feature of football in south Asia until the 1930s.

The organization of the leagues had been discriminatory from the beginning and prohibited Indian teams from freely entering the competitions. In 1893, when the IFA Shield tournament began, only one Indian team was allowed entry. Mohun Bagan was not allowed into the IFA Shield until 1909 by which time it had won the Trades Cup three times. The Calcutta Football League of two divisions was formed in 1898 and was viewed as a European competition. The first Indian team to play in the League was Mohun Bagan in 1914, which was allowed entry to the second division. Between 1914 and 1925 only two Indian teams were permitted to play in the first division.[44] In 1925 Mohun Bagan and Aryans occupied the allocated places in the top division when East Bengal qualified for promotion. They pursued their claim for promotion even though the exclusionary rules prohibited this. Their eventual success proved the catalyst for the ending of what was popularly referred to by Indians as the 'colour bar' in football. It was not until 1930 that equal representation between Indians and Europeans on the Council of the IFA was obtained and this only after the threats of secession by Indian clubs that necessitated the creation of a reconciliation commission.[45]

This apparent contradiction in colonial policy, between using sport as a means of establishing Indian 'separateness' or inferiority and of offering British-style strategies for improvement on the one hand and dismissing equal competition in the leagues on the other, is important in understanding the ways in which football became more than simply a game for Indians. The tension between these themes against the background of racial discord and emerging nationalist dissent gave a deeper social meaning to football clubs in Bengal in the first decade of the twentieth century.

NATIONALISM, COMMUNALISM AND THE RISE OF INDIAN CLUBS

In response to growing Bengali demands for political power Lord Curzon announced a Machiavellian strategy designed to undermine the coherence of Indian nationalism. The Presidency of Bengal was partitioned in 1905 and separated the largely Hindu West Bengal from the more Muslim districts of East Bengal and Assam. However, the Bengalis were far too suspicious of colonial intentions to accept the lame excuse offered that the pressures inherent in administering such a large region were too great. The partition was perceived as a policy of divide and rule, and across Bengal opposition was expressed through violent attacks on prominent officials, mass protest, media criticism and ultimately through the *swadeshi* campaigns.

Indian football clubs came to symbolize the wider protests and attracted as much nationalist attention as the rallies held by political agitators. The Shovazabar Club was the first to beat a British team in 1892, and Mohun Bagan won the Trades Cup three years in a row, from 1906 to 1908. The club first entered the IFA Shield in 1909, the only Indian club to be allowed such a privilege, only to lose to the Gordon Highlanders. Representatives of other Indian clubs who watched the match 'smirked in envious glee' at this defeat, claiming that Mohun Bagan's place in the IFA Shield was like 'a dwarf ... reaching for the moon'.[46] Mohun Bagan's run to the final of the Shield just two years later had a rather more unifying impact on local communities.

After seeing off St. Xavier's (3–0), Rangers (1–0), the Rifle Brigade (1–0), and the 1st Middlesex Regiment (1–1, 3–0), the Indian club was recognized as having a serious chance of winning the 1911 tournament. Described as having 'simply walked over the military defence' in the semi-final, the scene was set for an exciting final against the 'crack' East Yorkshire Regiment.[47] The final brought a crowd estimated at between 60,000 and 100,000[48] that travelled to the ground from as far afield as Patna, Assam and the outlying regions of Bengal. They travelled by specially arranged trains, steamers and trams to see the game. A temporary telephone was installed at the nearby CFC ground to transmit reports throughout Bengal. Mookerjee sums up the feelings of the day thus, 'Soccer fever had engulfed Calcutta. The IFA Shield final pushed everything else to the background. Hope, once kindled, whatever the odds against be, refuses to be snuffed.'[49] In an exciting match, the Indians came from a goal down to score twice in the last five minutes, 'wild excitement burst out amongst the Indian spectators

... When the referee blew the long whistle, shirts, hats, handkerchieves, sticks and umbrellas started flying in the air.'[50]

This was a moment to be savoured, a victory that unified Bengalis of different religions against their colonial rulers.[51] One local newspaper, the *Basumati*, emphasized the cohesive nature of this sporting success by claiming that Mohun Bagan had 'held up before the Bengali an ideal of striving in concert. The Bengali must ever remain indebted to those who have, in the dark days of disunion, found the secret of union.'[52]

However, some other responses point to the complexities of the relationship between sport, colonialism and nationalism in Bengal at this time. A month before the final another local newspaper, the *Nayak*, had restated the sense of inferiority and dependency felt by middle-class Bengalis,

> We English-educated *Babus* are like dolls dancing on the palms of Englishmen. The education which makes *Babus* of us, and gives us our food whether we are in service or in some profession, is established by the English. Our ... political efforts and aspirations are all kinds of gifts of the English people ... English education and the superficial imitation of English habits and manners have made us perfectly worthless, a miserable mixture of Anglicism and *swadeshism*.[53]

In the wake of Mohun Bagan's success, the newspaper's tone altered dramatically,

> Indians can hold their own against Englishmen in every walk of art and science, in every learned profession, and in the higher grades of the public service ... It only remained for Indians to beat Englishmen in that peculiarly English sport, the football. It fills every Indian with joy to learn of the victory of the Mohun Bagan team over English soldiers in the Challenge Shield competition. It fills every Indian with joy and pride to know that rice-eating, malaria-ridden, barefooted[54] Bengalis have got the better of beef-eating, Herculean, booted John Bull in the peculiarly English sport. Never before was there witnessed such universal demonstration of joy, men and women alike sharing it and demonstrating it by showering of flowers, embraces, shouts, whoops, screams and even dances.[55]

This exemplifies the type of reaction that gave a sporting moment deeper meaning in Bengali society. It is a victory that continues to be celebrated as a profound moment in the Independence struggle,

> Barefoot Bengali *babus* had battled with their British 'bosses' on equal terms, and had got the better of them. A subject race, humiliated by hauteur, ridiculed by so-called racial superiors and derided by a discriminating ruling class, had, at last, delivered a fitting reply. In a moment, Mohun Bagan Athletic Club was transformed from a Calcutta

football team into a symbol of nationalist aspirations. The Bengalis had found their voice on a football field, and the voice echoed and re-echoed all over India.[56]

The relationship between sporting triumph, nationalism and colonialism therefore seems centred on a paradox that Indians were fully conscious of even at the time of the game. The 1911 victory was a moment of nationalist resistance when the ideological underpinnings of colonialism, the belief in innate British superiority and in Indian physical frailty, were dramatically and publicly undone. Yet in celebrating the undoing of these stereotypes there was the acceptance of the British moral system introduced through the Anglo-Indian colleges in which only success in sport and the demonstration of physical prowess could signal strength and self-reliance.

Despite this paradox, however, it certainly seems to be the case that by 1911 football had been embraced by Indians as an activity with far broader social and cultural meanings than that of simply a pastime activity. Historians have even suggested that the attachment of these meanings meant that football became overtly politicized and that what happened on the park had much wider implications,

> Oddly enough, it was in the same year, 1911, that the British shifted the capital of the *raj* from Calcutta to Delhi. Recent memorialists of Mohun Bagan's victory have, alas, failed to notice this coincidence. *If* it is a coincidence, for it is highly likely that one was the cause of the other and that to pre-empt further humiliation the British adroitly and deliberately moved the seat of power from Bengal, away from its skilful footballers and its bomb-wielding nationalists. The link between sporting prowess and militant anti-imperialism was thus undermined, to be finally rent asunder by Gandhi and the Bombay capitalists.[57]

This relationship between football and politics continued throughout the period of British rule. The year 1925 saw East Bengal's promotion, which came at a time of sustained nationalist dissent that included industrial strike action in Calcutta and a visit from Mahatma Gandhi. This year also saw the Bengali newspaper *Amrita Bazar Patrika* publish a series of articles on the need for the physical improvement of Bengalis if nationhood were to be established and successful. Physical prowess, sporting achievement and anti-colonial agitation all combined in a political and cultural storm.

By the 1930s, when Mohammedan Sporting became the first Indian team to win the Calcutta League, still the most important football tournament in India, the values of the games ethic were consistently being expressed by Indians. In a celebratory speech the Mayor of Calcutta, Nalini Ranjan Sarkar, expressed views that would have been met with the approval of Curzon, Campbell or James,

> Sports and games are fine things. They develop some of the best qualities

in the individual ... apart from the qualities of concentration and single-mindedness of efforts, in a game like football, where team work is an important thing, a successful team must develop an *esprit de corps* to a high pitch of excellence. The Duke of Wellington after seeing a cricket match observed that Waterloo was won on that field. The same indeed may be said of football, only with greater emphasis. And those who succeed in cultivating the qualities which collectively go by the name of sportsmanship are, I think, well-equipped generally for almost every walk of life.[58]

Sarkar went on to bestow additional virtues on to football: that of bonding disparate groups, and of providing a fine example which should be matched in political life, if the fragmented nationalist movement were ever to succeed. The irony was that the unity against the British was being undermined by the communal divisions that would eventually lead to the partition of India and the murderous events of 1947 and which were fuelled by the successes of Mohammedan Sporting.

The club went on to a series of famous triumphs in the 1930s. It won the Calcutta League five years in succession from 1934 to 1938 and it won the Shield and League 'double' in 1936 and carried off the Durand Cup in 1940. By this time, Indian teams were dominating football and the question was not whether they could take on the British but which Indian club would emerge triumphant. As a club founded for Muslim players, Mohammedan Sporting's achievements proved a focus for that community's identities and the club's triumphs were followed by Muslims from all over India.[59] The 1930s were, of course, a period when divisions between Muslims and Hindus were hardening into the communal identities that would eventually lead to violence. Indeed, it was at the end of the 1930s that Mohammed Ali Jinnah first articulated the confidence and identity of south Asian Muslims in expressing a desire for a separate state.[60] The successes of Mohammedan Sporting in the 1930s had acted as one vehicle for the emergence of the confidence and identity of Indian Muslims that would eventually lead to violence and Mookerjee concludes that 'with each victory, a communal wedge was driven deeper into Calcutta football if not into Calcutta society'.[61]

CONCLUSION

The early history of football in Calcutta is probably even more complex than has been identified here. The composition of the teams that came from such organizations as trades clubs or from visiting ships is uncertain and may reflect teams of mixed racial origins in the 1880s and the 1890s. The fact that Indian teams were able to compete in greater numbers for the Trades Cup at a much earlier stage than they were allowed to enter the IFA Shield similarly hints at other histories to be written to fill out the picture of football in Calcutta in the nineteenth century.

This study has, however, attempted to begin tracing the outlines of this picture and to uncover the complexities in this history. Previous such studies have been useful in identifying key themes. J.A. Mangan's studies of Kashmir have shown how football was used as a tool of empire for transmitting moral codes considered desirable by the British. Mason's account of the 1911 Mohun Bagan victory demonstrated how football had become the site for the contestation of colonial power and for Indian resistance to the ideologies of empire by which Indians were represented as physical, and therefore moral, inferiors to the British.

It has been shown that these two themes are inextricably linked and that they highlight the complexities of sport in a colonial setting. Football may well have been used by many members of the British community as a tool of empire in Bengal and this was nowhere more obvious than in the Anglo-Indian colleges. But not all of the British saw the sport in this way and many within the ranks of the colonial presence deliberately attempted to organize the game so as to exclude Indians and to emphasize their 'otherness'.

Similarly, football may well have become a site of resistance and each victory for an Indian team and each successful attempt to gain entry to football competitions broke down the ideological structures of colonialism that were based on exclusion and the superiority/inferiority opposition. However, while Indians were busy beating the British at their own games in order to demonstrate the bankruptcy of the idea that Indians were physical and moral inferiors, they were still implicitly recognizing the legitimacy of the ethical order underlying success in games. This ethical order had its origins in the public schools of Britain and so a determination to defeat the colonizers in football was on the one hand resistance but on the other a submission to the cultural imperialism of the British.

As was stated earlier, however, Bengal is the traditional powerhouse of Indian football precisely because the game and its institutions became a powerful vehicle for the energies that emerged during the history of the period. Once these energies turned towards organizing communities to compete for the spoils in the event of British decolonization football took on communal significance, and by the 1930s it seems that a consideration of the place of football in Indian society and politics required no focus on the British at all. The game had become dominated by Indians on the field, while off it supporters celebrated victories less for their demonstration of superiority over the British and more for their meaning in terms of Muslim and Hindu rivalry and the creation of a Muslim identity.

Looking beyond the immediate scope of this study, it seems that football in the post-colonial period in Calcutta has continued to be shaped by, and to articulate, the wider tensions and energies of society in Bengal. After 1947 a 'new intoxicating political current seized Calcutta football as soon as the old nationalistic one had died away'.[62] This was the intense rivalry between the indigenous West Bengalis and the immigrants from what became Bangladesh, with the former adopting Mohun Bagan and the latter supporting the East Bengal Club. The flow of new arrivals continued steadily throughout the 1950s and the 1960s, but peaked again after the fight for Independence in 1971 that resulted in the separation of Bangladesh from the rest of Pakistan. In all, over four million people arrived in West Bengal, mostly into Calcutta.[63] The East Bengal–Mohun Bagan rivalry has dominated Indian football ever since and only recently has the clubs' supremacy been challenged by teams from Goa. The consistent attendances of over 100,000 at the Calcutta derby overshadows crowd sizes between any other matches.[64] The fanaticism of the clubs' supporters led to the suicide of one Mohun Bagan fan in the 1970s and to 16 deaths in August 1980 at the Eden Gardens stadium.

In other words, while football was at first important for understanding and demonstrating the divisions and energies within the European communities in Bengal, it quickly became a means of identifying those within the Indian communities of the region. Nandy has claimed that 'Calcutta loves football with a blind love'[65] and, while this is certainly the case, it is also true that love of the sport has always co-existed with a love of what the game represents. As such, football may be used to trace the history of Bengal itself, as the game may be used to identify those who had power and those who sought power at any one time in Calcutta.

NOTES

1. Cited by I. Chowdury-Sengupta, 'The Effeminate and the Masculine: Nationalism and the Concept of Race in Colonial Bengal', in P. Robb (ed.), *The Concept of Race in South Asia* (Oxford: Oxford University Press, 1995), p.298.
2. Cited in S. Nurullah and J.P. Naik, *A History of Education in India (During the British Period)*, (Bombay: Macmillan, 2nd edn, 1951), p.447. The quotation comes from Curzon's Convocation Address to staff and students of the University of Calcutta, 1902.
3. S. Mookerjee, 'Early Decades of Calcutta Football', *Economic Times: Calcutta 300* (Sept. 1989), 157.
4. The name Bengal refers to the Presidency in the north-east of British India. It was partitioned first and unsuccessfully between 1905 and 1911. However, in the partition of India after independence and the creation of Pakistan, it was divided again. The East Bengal region became East Pakistan, until independence was won from West Pakistan in 1971 with the creation of Bangladesh.
5. *Englishman*, 5 Oct. 1892.
6. T. Mason, 'Football on the Maidan: Cultural Imperialism in Calcutta', *International Journal of the History of Sport*, 12 (1990), 85.
7. Mookerjee, 'Early Decades', 146.
8. Ibid.
9. Ibid. The Calcutta Football Club merged with the Calcutta Cricket Club in 1964 to form the Calcutta Cricket and Football Club. To this day, the club continues to organize sporting events such as golf, cricket, football, rugby and hockey competitions in Calcutta. Having been taken over by Indians after the British departed, the club continues to hold a prominent place in the city's sporting life, owning grand facilities and hosting important competitions. The legacy of their British past and the elitism of their predecessors are still evident, 'Today the CC&FC stands as a brilliant sentinel to youth and active sportsmanship in every sense of the term. In a city where open space is a precious rarity the green swards of the Club are a matter of considerable pride and envy'. See www.ccfc.org for more details.
10. A large community of Armenians have resided in Calcutta since the city's beginnings in the late seventeenth century.
11. For a more detailed discussion of the sociological features of football's development see R. Giulianotti, *Football: A Sociology of the Global Game* (Oxford: Polity Press, 1999).
12. *The Indian Planters' Gazette and Sporting News*, 10 June 1893. This weekly newspaper was aimed at residents, British colonialists and, as the title implies, covered issues of news, trade and sport.
13. Ibid., 24 June 1893.

14. Mookerjee, 'Early Decades', p.147.
15. J.M. Brown, *Modern India: The Origins of an Asian Democracy* (Oxford: Oxford University Press, 2nd edn, 1994), p.98.
16. G. Moorhouse, *India Britannica*, (London: Harvill Press, 1983), p.176.
17. S.B. Cook, *Colonial Encounters in the Age of High Imperialism* (New York, NY: HarperCollins, 1996); M. Harrison, *Climates and Constitutions Health, Race, Environment and British Imperialism in India, 1600–1850* (Delhi and Oxford: Oxford University Press, 1999).
18. J. Rosselli, 'The Self-Image of Effeteness: Physical Education and Nationalism in Nineteenth Century Bengal', *Past and Present*, 86, 1980, p.123.
19. M. Sinha, *Colonial Masculinity: The 'Manly Englishman' and the 'Effeminate Bengali' in the Nineteenth Century* (Manchester: Manchester University Press, 1995).
20. Chowdury-Sengupta, 'The Effeminate and the Masculine', p.282.
21. See Sir G. MacMunn, *The Martial Races of India* (London: Sampson, Low, Marston, 1933); R. Fox, *Lions of the Punjab: Culture in the Making* (London and Berkeley, CA: University of California Press, 1985); P. Dimeo, 'Race, Colonialism and the Emergence Of Football in India', in M. Allison, J. Horne and L. Jackson (eds), *Scottish Centre Research Papers in Sport, Leisure and Society, III* (Edinburgh: University of Edinburgh Press, 1999).
22. S. Wolpert, *A New History of India* (Oxford and New York, NY: Oxford University Press, 5th edn, 1997), pp.241–2.
23. Sir G. Campbell, *Memoirs of My Indian Career*, ed. Sir C.E. Bernard, (London: Macmillan, 1893), p.267.
24. Ibid., p.266.
25. B. Gardiner, *The Public Schools: An Historical Survey* (London : Hamish Hamilton, 1973), pp.108–9.
26. J.A. Mangan, *The Games Ethic and Imperialism: Aspects of the Diffusion of an Ideal* (Harmondsworth: Viking, 1986).
27. Ibid., p.43.
28. Mason, 'Football on the Maidan', p.85.
29. Campbell, *Memoirs*, pp.273–4.
30. 'Trust and Fear Not', *Ought Natives to be Welcomed as Volunteers?* (Calcutta: Thacker, Spink, 1885), p.18. This paper was written anonymously; however, Sinha (*Colonial Masculinity*, p.82) suggests that the author was Henry Harrison, Chairman of the Corporation of Calcutta.
31. C.E. Buckland, *Bengal under the Lieutenant-Governors: Being a Narrative of the Principal Events and Public Measures during Their Periods of Office, from 1854 to 1898*, 2, (New Delhi: Deep Publications, 2nd edn, 1976), pp.117–8.
32. H.R. James, *The Empire's Immortal Dead August 1914–August 1915: An Address to the Staff and Students of Presidency College, Calcutta* (London: Longman, Green, 1995), p.28.
33. Ibid., pp.10–11.
34. D. Omissi, *The Sepoy and the Raj: The Indian Army, 1860–1940* (Basingstoke: Macmillan, 1994); D. Omissi, *Indian Voices of the Great War: Soldiers' Letters, 1914–18* (Basingstoke: Macmillan, 1999). Recruitment policies changed to suit the needs of the day. By the First World War Bengalis were accepted more readily into the Army.
35. James, *The Empire's Immortal Dead*, p.21.
36. Advertisement in *Amrita Bazar Patrika*, 'Admission Requirements for Presidency College', 23 April 1925.
37. Mason, 'Football on the Maidan'.
38. M. Nandy, 'Calcutta Soccer', in S. Chaudhuri (ed.), *Calcutta: The Living City, 2: The Present and Future* (Calcutta: Oxford University Press, 1990).
39. Ibid., p.315.
40. Ibid., p.316.
41. Ibid., p.317.
42. See Kapadia in this volume, for a discussion of the pedagogical attitudes the organizers of Mohun Bagan had towards their players. Their attempt to produce morally healthy young men through sport echoes the games ethic of the British colonialists. As such, the club simultaneously up held the values of the games ethic while seeking victory over the very people who introduced both football and its concomitant social virtues.
43. Mookerjee, 'Early Decades', pp. 146–7.
44. Ibid., p.153.

45. Mason, 'Football on the Maidan', 94–5.
46. Mookerjee, 'Early Decades', 149.
47. Ibid., 150.
48. It should be noted that Calcutta had a population of around 1,200,000. A crowd of the size suggested means that the proportion of the total population who attended this match was similar to that at a popular match in a British city around this time.
49. Mookerjee, 'Early Decades', 150.
50. Ibid., 151.
51. Nandy, 'Calcutta Soccer', p.318.
52. 5 August 1911.
53. 14 June 1911.
54. The Bengalis did not wear boots during this period, while the British did, and so boots became symbolic of British culture.
55. 30 July 1911.
56. Mookerjee, 'Early Decades', 151.
57. *Calcutta Telegraph*, 20 June 1998. Guha's claims are interesting and suggest that football had a wider political impact. However, at present only evidence of association is available, rather than proof of any direct relationship of sport and politics.
58. *Amrita Bazar Patrika*, 1 Aug. 1934.
59. See Kapadia in this volume.
60. Brown, *Modern India*.
61. Nandy, 'Calcutta Soccer', p.318.
62. Ibid., p.319.
63. P.Dimeo '"Team Loyalty Splits the City into Two": Football, Ethnicity and Rivalry in Calcutta', in G. Armstrong and R. Giulianotti (eds), *Fear and Loathing in World Football* (Oxford: Berg, 2001).
64. See Kapadia in this volume.
65. Nandy, 'Calcutta Soccer', p.320.

4

Football in Goa: Sport, Politics and the Portuguese in India

JAMES MILLS

What above all needs to be noted in Portuguese India is the mentality, the outlook on life, the spiritual atmosphere. No qualified traveller passing into Goa from the Indian Union can fail to gain the impression that he is entering an entirely different land.[1]

Football in Goa is different. It has unique origins in the activities of an indigenized Catholic Church, in a history of emigration, in a forced industrialization, in the processes of decolonization and in a search for a means of protecting the difference described above of a Goa that found itself immersed in the Indian Union after 1961. The opening quotation emphasizes this difference, not just of Goan football, but of the region itself. It also hints at the origins of this difference as the writer is Oliveira Salazar, the Portuguese dictator and the last European ruler of Goa.

To write the history of Goan football is to write the story of one of India's two most powerful soccer regions. Along with West Bengal, Goa dominates Indian football. At the inception of the National League in 1996 Goa and West Bengal were the only football federations invited to enter two teams. Salgaocar, Goa's most successful club, won the National Football League (NFL) in 1999 and the Rovers Cup in 2000. With the promotion of Vasco Sports Club to the NFL in 2000, Goa now has three teams in the top flight. Goan players are also heavily represented in the national team and such players as Francis Silveira of Churchill Brothers and Robero Fernandes of Salgaocar toured England with the Indian team in July 2000.

This study then will look at the key moments and events which have shaped this footballing power in relation to the five factors mentioned above: the Church, emigration, industrialization, decolonization and the struggles for Goan independence in post-colonial India. This will show how the game there has developed in ways that are unique to the region and that are directly related to the political, economic and cultural history of Goa.

EARLY ORIGINS AND THE CHURCH

The Catholic Church came with the Portuguese invaders of Goa when Vasco da

Gama's expedition arrived in 1498 and throughout the sixteenth century the Church took the projects of the Counter-Reformation and the Inquisition into Asia. Closely allied with the colonial state in the Portuguese territories of Goa, Daman and Diu, the evangelical clerics spread Christianity and attacked Hinduism, banning the practice of the latter in Portuguese domains and employing programmes of forced conversion among the local Indian population where persuasion and preaching failed to get results. Of course, this alliance between church and state was not peculiar to Portuguese India, as both Iberian powers had closely integrated religious objectives with the commercial interests that had driven them to take on empires in Africa and the Americas as well as in Asia.

Although these initial religious campaigns were strident and often violent, the energy which marked the early years of Catholicism in Goa was not sustained. The evidence suggests that the Church had lost much of its momentum by the second century of the Portuguese presence, and Pearson suggests that 'a slackening of zeal even in the Inquisition seems to be discernible in the seventeenth century, while the Jesuits also by then had lost their earlier élan and enthusiasm and seem to have concentrated on trade.'[2] Rather than continuing as an aggressive vector of an alien cultural imperialism, the Church established local roots and quickly became embedded in Indian society. By the middle of the nineteenth century, when figures may be taken as broadly reliable, about two-thirds of the population of Goa were Christian.[3] Moreover, by 1834 about 280 of Portuguese India's 300 or so regular clergy were of local extraction and in 1833 the laws against the practice of Hindu rites within Portuguese territories had been rescinded. In other words, by the nineteenth century the Catholic Church was in the hands of local Goan society and was no longer at pains to set itself at odds with other beliefs within that society.

The reasons for this were that the Catholic Church was felt by many Goans by the nineteenth century to be their Church rather than a colonial institution. A process of adoption of and adaptation to Christian ways had occurred since the arrival of the Portuguese in 1498 and a recent study emphasizes that 'the religion that the converters brought over four centuries ago has been "familiarized", accepted and configured in terms of the local matrix.'[4] Indeed, Robinson goes on to conclude that 'one may wish to say that the faith itself, European in origin, seems to have been indigenized, incorporated into and adapted to the existing socio-ritual order and pattern of hierarchy and privilege.'[5]

An understanding of the nature of the Catholic Church in Goa in this period is important as it was to play a central part in the early spread of football in Portuguese India in the later nineteenth century. It was a visiting British priest who first brought football to Goa in 1883. Fr William Robert Lyons arrived in Siolim from Udipi, to recover at the coast from a bout of illness that he had experienced inland. Soon enmeshed in the activities of the local church, he founded St. Joseph's School at Siolim, which was later moved to Arpora. Like so many of his fellow missionaries in British India,[6] he saw sports as integral to a

Christian education since it was believed by such men that 'Christianity is a life that has to be lived. Christ Jesus was a perfect man as well as God, and to be a Christian one has to strive after perfect manliness, strength of body, strength of intellect, strength of soul.'[7] Sport was certainly a means of strengthening the body, and, by teaching the rules of fair play, submission to authority and team work, it was also seen as the means of creating the obedience and compliance that the Church considered to be signs of a strong intellect and a strong soul.

Other headmasters soon became convinced of the attractions of integrating football into their educational programmes and by 1893 the private English language school at Assolna was also playing the game under the leadership of its senior master Antonio Francisco de Souza. Although working in south Goa, de Souza was from Siolim, where football had first been introduced. The Rachol Seminary, which was the chief centre for the training of local priests in Goa, was also soon fielding teams. In later years these were banned by edict by the Bishop of the East Indies from participating in football tournaments since he considered the spectacle of 11 cassocked, future priests kicking about a ball to be one that undermined the dignity of their calling. The significance of the players at the seminary was that they took the game with them when they went to serve in the villages and so football quickly found its way into rural areas away from its original introduction to the urban-educated elites. In many ways the village set-up in Goa, known as the *gaunkar* system, was ideal for the introduction of football,

> The *gaunkars* were the male members of the dominant caste, either *brahmin* or *kshatriya*, in a village: in theory they were descended from the original settlers of the village. They could be either Hindu or Christian. They ran village associations which controlled most of the affairs of the village: roads, drainage, irrigation, public security, religion (they supported the local church or temple depending on whether the village was Christian or Hindu), education and health.[8]

In other words, the villages had pre-existing organizations with experience in mobilizing the local population for community matters. Moreover, they concerned themselves with education and health and were closely allied with the local priests. Quite simply, the structure of village society in nineteenth-century Goa (and it is worth remembering that 85 per cent of Goans lived in villages in 1910)[9] was well suited to the formation of local football teams by enthusiastic clergy.

By the beginning of the twentieth century the competitions held were between teams that had either Catholic school[10] names or village associations. St. Mary's College at Saligao, St. Mary's School at Assolna and St. Xavier's High School at Margao competed with such village teams as the Boys Social Club of Colva and Calangute. The latter were the winners of Goa's first recorded organized tournament, the Grande Torneio de Futebol do Gremio Literio e Recreativo de Mapuca. The final was played in 1925 in front of a crowd of 4,000.

Although introduced by a British missionary, the Church's involvement with football in Goa is more directly comparable with the experience of Catholic teams in Scotland than with mission sport in British India. The latter was a direct exercise in colonial hegemony, where 'sport was a significant part of imperial culture and an important instrument of imperial cultural association and subsequent cultural change.'[11] Games were self-consciously adopted as a means of imposing an alien moral order on a reluctant local population in British India, 'sport was a means of transmitting a set of British beliefs and standards about fairness, honesty and straightforwardness in a context of respect for traditional authority'.[12] Indeed, they were often violently imposed by such men as Cecil Earle Tyndale-Biscoe, head of the Church Missionary School, Kashmir. He threw staff into boats, herded boys on to football fields and publicly harangued failed cricketers in order to force the local population into abandoning their own cultural beliefs about physical exercise and hierarchy and into accepting his own concept of the 'muscular Christian in Empire'.[13]

In Goa, however, the indigenized state of the Church by the end of the nineteenth century meant that the historian needs to look elsewhere for an understanding of the role of religious institutions in promulgating football. The game was similarly adopted by priests within the Irish Catholic community in Scotland in the later nineteenth century. Famous Scottish clubs such as Hibernian and its west coast imitator Glasgow Celtic were initially closely bound up with the Church and with individual priests such as Canon Hannan, who energetically helped to form Hibernian from his parish in Edinburgh's Cowgate.[14] Their aims in founding these clubs had less to do with the imposition of an alien moral order on a colonized population and more to do with the consolidation and improvement of an existing religious constituency. In focusing on Hibernian, Celtic and Dundee Harp in the nineteenth century, Weir concludes that,

> it is certain that the original intention of those Roman Catholic clergy involved in football clubs was a patristic, rather than a managerial one. Results on the park were not of importance, rather the immersion of young Catholics in the ways of the Catholic Church, providing relief for the catholic poor, and keeping Catholics away from the influence of non-Catholics were the goals.[15]

The Catholic Church was, and indeed still is, important in promoting football in Goa as it provided an institutional means of introducing young men to the game in both the cities and the villages and among both the schooled elites and the church-going peasantry. A look at comparisons from other contexts where priests involved themselves heavily in promoting sport among their congregations suggests that in sport and sporting organizations the clergy saw a means of perpetuating religious and community ties and in promoting 'virtuous' pursuits.

It would have been in the English language schools mentioned earlier rather than in the Catholic establishments that Hindu Goans first experienced football.

English schools were popular since the language was the means of gaining opportunities in nearby British Bombay and a range of teams from such institutions flourished under names like Colegio Ingles de Assagao and English High School Margao. This was especially so after 1910 when all anti-Hindu laws were rescinded. The new-found equality of Hindus in Portuguese India, who made up about 49 per cent of the population in that year, meant a new enthusiasm for access to opportunities that they had previously been denied. As such, as Pearson points out, 'they flooded to schools, joined actively in public life and founded libraries and journals'.[16] From playing football in the English language institutions, Hindus went on to form their own clubs, which seem to have specifically used their religion as a means of creating a football identity and, conversely, to have used football to celebrate their religious identity. Before 1910 Hindu Boys Club was able to field two teams to play an exhibition match at Margao on Diwali,[17] and Goa Hindu Club appears in the records after this period. Neither did these Hindu clubs quickly disappear nor become peripheral to football activity in Portuguese India. The first all-Goa football tournament to include entrants from North and South Goa was, for example, hosted in 1930 by the Hindu Sporting Club of Mapuca.

The Catholic Church in Goa seems to have been the means by which football was first introduced into Goa and by which it quickly spread in the towns and in the villages, among the educated elites and into rural society. However, to focus exclusively on the role of priests is to ignore the range of groups and processes which quickly took on football and promoted its spread. This is evident in the discussion of Hindu clubs which, in turn, focuses attention on the second of the four factors outlined as important in understanding the history of Goan football. This is emigration.

MIGRATION, BOMBAY AND FOOTBALL

The Goan economy under Portuguese rule stagnated for much of the nineteenth and early twentieth century and historians tend to point to 'the backwardness of Goa's agricultural sector' and to observe that 'the commercial sector remained feeble [and] there was no industrial development at all'.[18] For many, the expanding Asian economy of the period and the growth of nearby Bombay, British India's west coast commercial centre, provided important opportunities for success not available in the tightly controlled, village hierarchies mentioned earlier or in the moribund commerce of Portuguese possessions.

By 1921 then it was estimated that 469,000 Goans lived in Goa, Daman and Diu while up to 200,000 lived away from home, in British India, East Africa or Mesopotamia. About a quarter of the expatriate community lived in Bombay alone. Most of those in Bombay worked in low status employment servicing the vibrant economy of the ports, although up to a fifth were part of that floating group just out of a job, in town looking for a job or recently out of a job, 'Of those in Bombay, the main occupations were seamen (37 per cent), cooks and waiters (18 per cent), clerks, tailors and ayahs (each eight per cent) and musicians (two per cent) but another 18 per cent were unemployed.'[19]

With such a sizeable community in the city and with such difficulties to negotiate as unemployment, homesickness and cultural alienation, Goans in Bombay quickly organized themselves into clubs and institutions based on the familiar loyalties from back home. Pearson emphasizes this, concluding that,

> a notable feature of this migration was the way in which village and family ties were maintained ... the famous Goan clubs in Bombay, to which the majority of the community belonged, were village-based. A Goan in Bombay joined people from his home village in a club, and his social life, and many aspects of his social welfare, were focussed on these clubs.[20]

The implications of this for football were both cultural and practical. On a practical level, expatriate communities used their emerging economic clout[21] to expand the institutional base of Goan football by founding and funding clubs for migrants to Bombay. They began to send these clubs back to Portuguese India from an early period, St. Mary's College of Bombay competing against Panjim Boys in 1905, for example. This shows that expatriate football was also important for the cultural emergence of football in the Goan psyche. The sport was being used as a means of confirming ties with the homeland by migrant communities through the sending back of football teams to compete there. It also shows how football had quickly become established as a means of Goan self-identification when abroad.

Indeed, football remained an important part of expatriate relations with Goa throughout the twentieth century. By the 1940s the best of the Bombay migrant teams, Young Goans, were touring Portuguese India and well-connected individuals such as Augusto de Noroha e Tavora were arranging exhibition matches in Goa for major teams such as the Tata squad from British India. As recently as January 2000 there was a Goan World Cup organized by Goan communities from around the world in which each migrant group arranged to send a team back home to compete for a trophy.

By the time that the British left India in 1947 the number of Goans living outside the Portuguese-controlled states far outnumbered those who actually remained at home and it has been pointed out that,

> it is estimated that by 1954 there were 1,800,000 Goans outside of Goa and in India and East Africa, three times as many as remained in the colony. As many as a million Goans were residing in India, 100,000 in the Bombay area alone.[22]

Such a large and economically healthy[23] community gave a momentum to the development of football by ensuring that the organizations existed for its encouragement among Goan communities outside as well as inside the home states.

Importantly, however, the migrant experience of Goans meant that football was from an early date tied in with Goan identity, as the playing of the sport became central to Goan association when abroad and to the establishment and maintenance of relations between expatriates and the society that they had left behind.

THE END OF PORTUGUESE RULE AND INDUSTRIALIZATION

The 1950s were a curious decade in the history of Goa since it was the last one in which the Portuguese dominated and it was the first in the twentieth century when Portugal seemed to wake up to the possibilities of Goa. Under increasing pressure to cede Goa to the Republic of India, Portugal embarked on an ultimately doomed policy of drawing the territories closer to it. It did this through two main strains of policy: industrial development and cultural bonding, both of which had important implications for football in the colony.

Portugal's cultural policies in the 1950s grew from an attempt to assert that Goa was in no way Indian and was an essentially European society that had grown out of four centuries of Portuguese rule. As such, it was argued, the Indian Republic had no legitimate claim to the territories, which were portrayed not as colonies but as integral provinces of the state of Portugal with full and equal representation in the metropolitan Parliament,

> The Portuguese have always revealed the tendency to create a morally united motherland with territories and peoples which in time would become incorporated in the nation; at no time was an impediment to this seen in racial or religious differences or in the dispersal of lands ... the truth is that the peoples in question have demonstrated throughout history the same living solidarity with Portugal as the branches of a tree have with its trunk and roots.[24]

Writing this in 1956, the Portuguese dictator Oliveira Salazar was adamant that 'he who is born and lives in Goa or in Brazil or in Angola is as Portuguese as he who lives and is born in Lisbon.'[25] The problem with this attempted justification for the continuation of Portuguese rule was that most of it was self-evidently untrue. By the 1950s only 3 per cent of Goans in Goa could speak Portuguese and during this period even the Catholic Church was becoming careful to dissociate itself from the colonial government, 'Cardinal Gracias, himself of Goan background, laid down from Bombay that "as far as the Catholics of Goa are concerned their culture is not Portuguese but Goan".'[26]

Thus the Portuguese attempted some last-ditch attempts to create in Goans an awareness of the benefits of European rule and of their ties to the Iberian state. Football proved to be an important means of attempting to promote this and of highlighting the effectiveness of Portuguese administration. In 1951 the Conselho de Desportos da India Portuguesa was established and for the first time an all-Goa league was set up with a first and a second division. This replaced the

Associacao de Futebol da India Portuguesa which had become defunct within a decade of its foundation in 1939 and which had failed either to organize a league or to gain recognition from the Portuguese Football Association.

The objective of the Conselho de Desportos was to rejuventate Goan football and to demonstrate through a popular medium the efficiency of Portuguese rule. Infrastructure was improved in the period with such innovations as floodlit games being introduced in 1958. Improvements were also made in the administration of the game as players were for the first time expected to register with a single club and the Conselho introduced and administered an identity card system. Goan football was now divided into four zones: Bardez, Panjim, Margao and Mormugao, and each had an administrator appointed to oversee it. The first league was won by Clube Desportivo Chinchinim which beat off FC Siolim to take the title. Clube de Desportos de Vasco da Gama won the title three times; Associacao Desportiva de Velha Goa won it twice; and Sporting Clube de Goa, Grupo Desportivo da Policia, Clube Independente de Margao and Clube Desportivo Salgaocar each won it once under Portuguese rule, which ended in 1961.

In an attempt to have Goans become aware of their place in the Portuguese world, tours of major teams from around the Portuguese Empire were arranged in the territories. In 1955 Ferroviarios de Lourenco Marques travelled from Mozambique to play a state representative team. In front of crowds of 20,000 they forced a 2–2 draw in the first leg before going on to thrash the Indian team 5–1 the next day. The political agenda behind the selection of touring teams was obvious in the invitation extended to one of Pakistan's leading clubs in 1959. Port Trust Club of Karachi played in front of crowds of 7,000 and 15,000, winning the first game and losing the second and, of course, symbolizing the solidarity of two anti-India footballing nations. Perhaps most famously of all, the Benfica team visited Goa in 1959. They played the Military and won 2–1 and then played Goa twice. The Portuguese government of the state was careful to associate itself with this prestige visit and the final game was played in front of the Governor-General of Portuguese India, General Vassalo de Silva. Goa lost the first game 4–0 and the final one 1–0.

The momentum generated by the visit of one of the greatest teams in the world to Goa was carried forward into the separation of football from the other sporting concerns of the Conselho de Desportos da India Portuguesa, which, as its name suggests was a general sports council. On 22 December 1959 the Associacao Futebol de Goa was founded, a body which under the name of the Goa Football Association continues to administer the sport.

The second part of the Portuguese attempt to create an enthusiasm for its rule in Goa was economic,

> Portugal in the 1950s also made belated efforts to develop Goa with a view to making its people clearly better off than those in neighbouring India. In 1952 a Development Plan was decreed. This boosted Goa's fledgling iron

ore exports. Revenue from this, and from migrant remittances, meant than per capita income in Goa was some one-third higher than in India.[27]

Alongside the exploitation of the territories' iron ore reserves, which were chiefly exported to Japan, the Portuguese also developed manganese exports to the United States. The result of this was that, while the ordinary mine workers were exploited, a small clique of well-placed Goans profited enormously from this sudden expansion in the industrial sector.

Football clubs that grew out of industrial organizations had been a minor if consistent feature of Goan football since its earliest days, as the Western India Portuguese Railway school had regularly organized a team from among its students. However, the 1950s saw the beginning of substantial investment being made by private industrial corporations in clubs that came to carry their names and to act as both advertising and self-aggrandizement for the companies concerned.

The most successful of these clubs has been Salgaocar Sports Club. Founded as Vimson FC in 1955 by the House of Salgaocar company, a major miner and exporter of iron ore to Japan and South Korea, the club benefited from enormous financial support and won the second division in 1957 with an unbeaten record. It then won the First Division League Championship in the last year of Portuguese rule in 1961. In an interesting reflection of the continuity in both industry and football between Portuguese rule and membership of the Indian Union, Salgaocar then went on to win the first two seasons of the Goan league after liberation. In total they won the league four times in the 1960s, twice in the 1970s, five times in the 1980s and four times in the 1990s. They were the first Goan team to represent the state in a major all-Indian competition, the Durand Cup in 1962 in Delhi, where the Prime Minister Jawarharlal Nehru was careful to have himself photographed with them on the lawns of his residence. At a time when the Indian Union still had occupying troops in Goa and Goans were appealing to the United Nations for independence, this was an important image of incorporation and reconciliation designed for the newspapers. Salgaocar is the only Goan team to have won the Durand Cup, in 1999, the season when they became the first team from the state to win the National Football League started in 1996. They also won the Rovers Cup and the Super Cup in that season. While the team has been a playing power in India football since liberation, it is also worth pointing out that the House of Salgaocar has always been careful to maintain a close relationship with administrative power in the state football structure. In 1959 a Salgaocar was vice-president of the General Body of the Goa Football Association and 40 years later the president of the club was also the president of the Goa FA's executive committee.

Other major industrial players similarly adopted or founded clubs. Dempo Sports Club grew out of the adoption of Bicholim Football Club by the House of Dempo in the 1960s and went on to be the first Goan club to win the Rovers Cup, the oldest competition in Bombay. Sesa Goa Sports Club was founded and the football team established in 1965 by the Sesa Goa company, a subsidiary of the

Italian iron ore company Ilva. The team quickly flourished and won the Goan League in 1968 and in 1973. However, the parent company moved from Italian to Japanese hands and, with this, the commitment to a football team waned. Moreover, by the 1990s the wage demands of players had spiralled and, reflecting on its original foundation as a means of giving back to the community through sports, the management decided that the budget was better spent on a football academy for youngsters than on paying the wages of players. In 1998 the team was formally disbanded and the Sesa Goa Football Academy was established with the aim of providing both formal education and football training for 25 boys in the 14 to 18 age bracket.

In short, the final decade of Portuguese rule was an important one for understanding the evolution of Goan football since it was in this decade that the great industrial companies of the region were established. These companies would go on to provide extensive funding for Goan football and to finance and provide the administration for its most successful clubs. If this appears to be the chief legacy of the period then it must also be remembered that the Goa Football Association also grew out of this decade. This was because the Portuguese attempted to use football administration as a means of demonstrating the efficacy of their rule on a popular level in the years when they were trying to justify their presence in the face of growing pressure from India to decolonize.

INDEPENDENCE AND IDENTITY

Football had become a language by which the Portuguese attempted to communicate the benefits of their rule to the Goan population. After liberation, the game continued to develop because it was similarly used by Indian politicians as a way of driving home messages to the public.

The key issue after the Indian Army ended Portuguese rule in 1961 was of the way in which Goa would be integrated into the rest of India. This was an issue not simply of power but of identity, as different claims were made by a range of political parties as to where Goa belonged in the Indian Union on account of its history and its languages. The Maharashtrawadi Gomantak Party (MGP), formed in 1963, insisted that 'the language of Goans is Marathi'[28] and therefore the state should be swallowed up by its giant northern neighbour Maharashtra, with its capital in Bombay. In reaction to this, 'the primarily Konkani speaking Christian minority which had dominated the colony under the Portuguese, founded the United Goans Party (UGP) in September 1963 to prevent the dilution of their community's distinct culture and language.'[29] Meanwhile, the Indian state to the south, Mysore, was also bidding to incorporate Goa into its jurisdiction.

This was a period of division in Goan politics. The MGP appealed to low-class and low-caste Hindu voters. Wealthy and high-caste Hindus voted for the Congress in a show of loyalty to the Indian Union since it was the Indian National

Congress that had led India to independence and that dominated Indian politics until the 1970s. The Christian population voted for the UGP in order to articulate its desire to protect its distinct culture and to promote Goa as a unique unit.

The most significant politician of the period was also the most skilful manipulator of the football medium,

> The individual who led the campaign for merger was Dayand Bandodkar, who simultaneously served as chief minister and president of the Maharashtrawadi Gomantak Party ... a merchant who had become wealthy because of mining ventures, Bandodkar acquired a reputation among the masses as a sportsman and a philanthropist.[30]

Bandodkar was careful to associate himself with football in Goa from the start of his campaign for merger. He became vice-president of the Goa FA in 1962, the first year after the departure of the Portuguese. He set up the All India Bandodkar Trophy tournament. With Rs60,000 paid for the gold cup, this was a showcase for Goa on the Indian national football stage as the state for the first time offered and hosted a trophy for teams from across India. The first winners were Leaders Club from Jalandhar, but Vasco were the first Goan club to win it in the following year, playing with the famous four strikers known as the 'ABCD' of football: Andrew, Bernard, Catao and Dominic.

Perhaps most tellingly of all, Bandodkar adopted the relatively obscure Panvel Sports Club which was founded in 1965. Under the Bandodkar family the club briefly became a symbol of a bright Goan future as it nurtured future internationals such as Brahmanand Shankwalkar and Francis D'Souza. However, the degree of his influence over the club and the extent to which it was taken on as a personal vehicle is demonstrated by the fact that it won its only major cup, the Bandodkar Trophy, in the season in which he died, after which it abruptly went into terminal decline and was wound up after relegation just three years later in 1977.

Bandodkar was committed to integration with Maharashtra and his governments in Goa adopted heavy handed and often unpopular tactics to attempt to make this a reality,

> The Bandodkar administration promoted Marathi as the language of government and education, while denigrating Konkani ... and enacted tenancy legislation which gave property to those who worked the land at the expense of those Goans – mainly Christians – who lived abroad or worked in Bombay but maintained land in the territory. Perhaps most offensive of all, the government inundated the bureaucracy at all levels with 1,100 deputized civil servants from Maharashtra at a time when qualified Goans were available to fill the positions.[31]

By financing Goa's premier tournament, by promoting a new team in Goan football and by publicly encouraging the development of a new generation of Goan players (Henry Britto, who was to captain and manage Salgaocar, recalls

Bandodkar's personally prescribing and paying for Ovamaltine to encourage the physical development of the young Britto), Bandodkar was demonstrating a commitment to Goa's development and Goa's future. By doing this in football, a subject of constant popular interest, he was carefully manipulating the Goan love of the game in order to ensure that people came to believe that he had this commitment. He gambled that a public commitment to Goan football would result in a public conviction that Bandodkar had a knowledge of Goa's best interests and therefore his political stance on integration ought to be supported.

It did not have such a result. In 1967 there was a referendum on the issue of integration with Maharashtra which was 'the most unprecedented and intense political activity in Goa's history'.[32] Merger was rejected, as elite Hindus, fearing the power of the low classes and low castes mobilized by Bandodkar, joined Christians in denying him a vote for integration. The result of this was the closing of the divisions that had been exploited for the sake of the merger campaign, 'whereas the 1963 election campaign had highlighted sectarian differences among Goans, the 1967 Opinion Poll served to solidify Goan identity ... it once again became permissible for Hindu Goans to emphasize their local identity.'[33]

Football was at the heart of this re-emphasis of Goan identity. B.M. Parkkot had taken over Goa's oldest club, Vasco Sports Club, in the 1964–65 season, having successfully established Salgaocar in Goan football between 1955 and 1964. His impact was immediate as Vasco won the Goan league that season and in total three times out of the next five seasons. They also became the first Goan team to experience success in important all-India tournaments, reaching the Rovers Cup Final in 1966 and winning the Kerala Trophy in 1968.

Parkkot's influence, however, went far beyond the successes of the clubs that he ran. He was deeply committed to an independent Goa FA. As a mirror to wider political events, both the Maharashtra and the Mysore FA had proposed swallowing the Goan organization after liberation in 1961. The issue awaited the outcome of wider political events since it made little sense for the Goan FA to become incorporated into an organization that did not reflect the political affiliation of the state. Upon the rejection of merger in 1967, Parkkot had himself elected as president of the Goa FA in 1968 and held the post until 1972. He successfully lobbied the All India Football Federation, and the Goa FA was finally declared to be a full constituent member under his leadership. To celebrate this and to emphasize in footballing terms Goa's new-found independence, the FA hosted the all-India Santosh trophy in 1972. This is the tournament contested by state representative teams and Goa was knocked out in the semi-finals by Bengal.

Indeed, football was again used as a symbolic medium when Goa finally secured its status as a fully-fledged state within the Indian Union. This was granted in 1987 and by 30 May 1988 the foundation stone was laid for the new Fatorda stadium in Margao to be the showpiece of football in Goa. This was not simply the result of energetic work by the Football Association, since the newly independent Goan government paid for the work and through the supervision of

Monte Cruz, the sports minister, the project was completed in time for its inauguration in January 1989.

Since the liberation from Portugal, football has been used as a medium for the transmission of a range of political messages. Dayand Bandodkar attempted to establish himself as a champion of Goan interests by adopting positions in the region's football which plainly communicated his commitment to Goan success. He did this in order to harness popular support to his campaign for the merger of Goa with Maharashtra. Football has similarly been used at crucial moments since the failure of Bandodkar's campaign, with the independence of the Goa Football Association following closely on the rejection of the merger plan and with the birth of a modern stadium to celebrate the rise of Goa to full status as a state in the Indian Union in 1987. It can only be concluded, somewhat in contradiction to traditional concerns about a close relationship between sport and politics, that this integration of football and political agendas has been a good one for Goan soccer. Its independent status, its prestige cup competitions and its showpiece stadium were all achieved in specific political contexts.

CONCLUSION

With a healthy, village-level tournament system continuing to flourish underneath the club leagues, football in Goa remains a mass sport at the beginning of the new millennium. It is played in the towns and in the rural areas of the state and stars of Goan football continue to emerge from within the population. Sukhdev Arwade, the Golden Boot winner of the Goan League in the 1998–99 season, is an indicative example. He learnt football simply playing with friends as a child, 'my friends [in Curtorim] always provoked and insulted me because of my technique and said I would never rise to become a good player ... then I had a reason to play and practice football hard.'

As well as a sport of mass participation, it is a game of popular emotional involvement. Finals played out at the Fatorda Stadium still draw crowds in excess of 10,000, and the attendance at the Rovers Cup games in Bombay tends to be dominated by those of Goan extraction. The celebrations of successes involving teams from the state show the emotional meaning that football has for Goans. The captain Brahmanand Shankwalkar recalls that, at the first victory of the Goan State team in the Santosh Cup in 1984, 'we had tears of joy rolling down our cheeks. Goa had won the nationals for the first time ever ... we had written history.'

The game is now embedded in Goan culture precisely because it has been so closely related to Goan history. The key processes and institutions that have shaped society in the region are an indigenized Catholic Church, economic migration, a forced industrialization, decolonization and the search for a means of protecting the difference of a Goa which found itself immersed in the Indian Union after 1961. This study has demonstrated how closely football has been related to each of these institutions and processes and the changes that they have wrought in Goa throughout the last 120 years.

NOTES

This essay relies heavily on the collection of documents and articles assembled by Noel da Lima Leitao and Francis Ribeiro. Most of the historical information comes from this source and the author expresses his thanks for access to this collection. See N. da Lima Leitao and F. Ribeiro, *The Grass is Green in Goa* (Panaji Goa FA, 2000)

1. O. Salazar, 'Goa and the Indian Union: the Portuguese View', *Foreign Affairs*, April 1956, 3.
2. Ibid., 148.
3. M.N. Pearson, *The New Cambridge History of India I: The Portuguese in India* (Cambridge: Cambridge University Press, 1987), p.150.
4. R. Robinson, *Conversion, Continuity and Change: Lived Christianity in Southern Goa* (London: Sage, 1998), p.214.
5. Ibid.
6. For a full discussion of British missionary attitudes on the role of sport in Empire see J.A. Mangan, *The Games Ethic and Imperialism: Aspects of the Diffusion of an Ideal* (Harmondsworth: Viking, 1986), pp.168–92.
7. Ibid., p.178.
8. Pearson, *New Cambridge History of India*, p.154.
9. Ibid., p.152.
10. Both Catholic schools and non-religious English language schools (see discussion later in text) formed the basis for some of the earliest Goan teams. This is directly comparable with the origins of football in other contexts. See, for example, T. Mason, *Association Football and English Society, 1863–1915* (Sussex: Harvester Press, 1980), pp.22–4.
11. J.A. Mangan, 'Britain's Chief Spiritual Export: Imperial Sport as Moral Metaphor, Political Symbol and Cultural Bond', in J.A. Mangan (ed.), *The Cultural Bond: Sport, Empire, Society* (London : Frank Cass, 1992), p.4.
12. T. Mason, 'Football on the Maidan: Cultural Imperialism in Calcutta', in J.A. Mangan, *The Cultural Bond*, p.142.
13. Mangan, *The Games Ethic and Imperialism*, p.183.
14. J. Weir (ed.), *Drink, Religion and Scottish Football 1873–1900* (Renfrew: Stewart Davidson, 1992), p.43.
15. Ibid., p.44.
16. Pearson, *New Cambridge History of India*, p.152.
17. A Hindu religious festival held in November.
18. Pearson, *New Cambridge History of India*, p.154.
19. Ibid., p.156.
20. Ibid.
21. By 1951 it was estimated that Goa's net gain from remittances from migrant communities was Rs 22 million. See A. Rubinoff, *The Construction of a Political Identity: Integration and Identity in Goa* (London: Sage, 1998), p.39.
22. Ibid., p.38.
23. By 1951 total payments from people in India to those in Goa totalled Rs68 million; ibid., p.39.
24. Salazar, 'Goa and the Indian Union', 9.
25. Ibid., 4.
26. Pearson, *New Cambridge History of India*, p.159.
27. Ibid.
28. Rubinoff, *Construction of a Political Identity*, p. 87.
29. Ibid.
30. Ibid., p.91.
31. Ibid.
32. Ibid., p.92.
33. Ibid., p.94.

1. Captain of the Indian national team, Baichung Bhutia

2. National football coach, Syed Nayeemuddin

3. Friends and rivals. I.M. Vijayan (left) of FC Kochin and the Nigerian Chima Okorie (right) of Mohun Bagan

4. I.M. Vijayan in action for FC Kochin against Mohun Bagan in the 1997 Durand Cup semi-final

5. Tension and stone-throwing after a disputed decision during the 2000 Durand Cup final between Mohun Bagan and Mahindra United

6. Syed Nayeemuddin gives instructions to his East Bengal team

7. Mohun Bagan players celebrate their 2–1 triumph over Mahindra United in the 2000 Durand Cup final

8. Priya Ranjan Das Munshi (left, in blazer) with FC Kochin players after winning the Durand Cup in 1997

9. Mohun Bagan players and supporters celebrate winning the 2000 Durand Cup at Ambedkar Stadium, Delhi

10. The East Bengal team, 1995

11. The Mahindra United team, 1998

12. The Salgaocar team (Goa), 2000

5

'Kicking the Buddha's Head': India, Tibet and Footballing Colonialism

ALEX McKAY

INTRODUCTION

While the other contributions in this volume examine the place of India during the colonial period as a receptor of football and footballing cultures, this essay will demonstrate that it also came to act as a centre from which the game was transmitted to other parts of Asia. Using Tibet as a case study, it will look at the way in which British officers and Indian soldiers who were sent from British India to maintain a presence in regions that bordered the Asian empire took football with them. The game was used to keep themselves entertained but also to transmit certain messages about the British in Asia and also as a strategy for reshaping local societies and cultures. This study will not simply look at colonial designs in taking football in particular and sport in general to Tibet, it will also consider the reactions of those societies and cultures to the imperial game.

In focusing on sport in Tibet and the arrival of 'modern' games from India, the study begins to explore a neglected area in Tibetan studies. Tibet in the popular imagination is the home of monks, mystics and magicians, and is seen as a land of gilded aristocrats, free-spirited nomads and simple, honest peasants. The reality is, of course, different and scholars in the field of Tibetan studies today are gradually dispelling such images and uncovering the prosaic realities underlying that Shangri-La construction.[1] But while new understandings of the Tibetans are slowly emerging, one image has not changed. Westerners simply do not imagine the Tibetans as a sporting people. It is easy to associate Brazilians with association football, New Zealanders with rugby union and West Indians with cricket, but it has been difficult to imagine a monk in midfield.

The perception of a people as sporting, or in this case non-sporting, is of course a construction, although like most such it is not without foundation. But even within the academic field of Tibetan studies sport is not an issue that has attracted attention. Far more is known about the burial practices of Tibetan kings in the seventh century than is known about the place of sport in contemporary Tibetan society. Indeed, most Tibetan scholars, in their concern with Buddhist dialectics, monastic structures and political dynasties, have simply avoided all mention of sport. Even the writings of anthropologists and sociologists working among Tibetan communities rarely contain any reference to the subject.

Contemporary Tibetan society and culture, both as they exist within what is now the Chinese-administered province of the Tibetan Autonomous Republic (TAR) and within the Tibetan exile community,[2] have been the subject of many studies by Western academics during the last four or five decades. But only two or three of these are even peripherally related to sport.[3] To these works it is possible to add a handful of studies by Chinese scholars whose work has appeared in English.[4]

There are many aspects of Tibetan society and culture that have been neglected by scholarship due to their failure to fit into the usual categories by which academics analyse, or construct, Tibet. Some issues have been ignored because Tibetan scholars (who are, in the main, sympathetic to Tibetan aspirations to self-determination) have feared that they might cast Tibet in a negative light and thus provide ammunition to support the Chinese position in Tibet. So issues such as crime, punishment, violence, corruption and class inequalities have tended to be ignored in favour of studies of matters that reflect more positively on Tibet and the Tibetans.

Yet sport is one issue that may be considered without immediate implications within the Sino-Tibetan problem. It is possible then to speculate that this failure to consider the issue of sport within Tibetan society has much to do with the academic preoccupation with the study of 'high' culture commonly associated with Tibetan Buddhism. Sport is popular culture and secular culture and is consequently ignored. But the Tibetans had considerable leisure time and the role of leisure-time pursuits must be considered if a balanced and realistic picture of Tibetan society is to be obtained.

SPORT IN TIBET BEFORE THE BRITISH

Certain physical activities undertaken by monks as part of their monastic training might be classified by Loseries-Leick's term, 'Psychic Sports'.[5] These were physical exercises that were part of a programme aimed at spiritual enlightenment. While many of these practices were restricted in circulation, it does appear that the majority revolved around exercises of the yogic type which were not competitive. As they were not a leisure-time pursuit it is open to debate as to whether they can be termed sporting.

This does, however, raise the issue of the extent to which the primarily Buddhist orientation of Tibetan elite society affected Tibetans' own perception of sporting endeavours. Ideas of beauty and of the desirable body are cultural variables and it seems that the body of the ascetic represented a cultural ideal among significant sectors of Tibetan society, rather than the body of the sportsman or the labourer. Thus artistic representations of cultural 'heroes', such as the archetypal renunciant Milarepa, depicted figures whose achievements were in the spiritual realm and did not generally focus on the detailed physique other than to portray extreme mortification. The great physical endeavours that these 'heroes' were credited with in myth and text were attributed to their spiritual power rather than to their inherent, or developed, bodily strength.

The one commentator to devote any real attention to Tibetan leisure activities was Sir Charles Bell. For most of the period 1908–21 Bell served as the British Political Officer for Sikkim, Bhutan and Tibet. This position effectively meant that he was British India's ambassador to Tibet and he soon became a friend and confidant of the thirteenth Dalai Lama (1873–1933). In *The People of Tibet*[6] Bell described a variety of sporting activities of both indigenous and imported origins in which the local population engaged.

It is possible to categorize these activities in three areas. The first involved those physical activities that were undertaken for pure enjoyment. These included long jumping competitions in which a running jump was taken from a springboard and 'round stone' (*do-kor*), a cross between weight lifting and shot putting.[7] Also in this category was skipping (*tak-chom*) which Bell described as the 'national pastime' and which seems to have been particularly favoured by women and monks. The type of skipping preferred was that in which two persons hold a rope while another skips over it in as many ways as possible, such as springing up and down from a lying down position. One variety that Bell noted was for two persons to be skipping while fighting each other.[8]

Another activity of this type was the 'big toe kick' (*te-pe*) which could be played individually or competitively by a group. The game involved keeping a shuttlecock in the air by kicking it with the instep. Bell described this game as particularly popular among women.[9] It is still a very popular contemporary pastime among Tibetans both in the TAR and in the exile community, although it now seems to be a predominantly male activity. Finally in this category there was kite flying. Mainly an urban sport, kite flying had its competitive edge. Some Tibetan enthusiasts made 'killer kites' by gluing powdered glass to the string. These were used to bring down other kites by means of sawing through their string.[10] It is notable that none of these activities involved a ball. The wheel was not used in Tibet until the arrival of Europeans and their troops in the early part of the twentieth century and similarly the use of a ball for any recreational purposes was apparently also unknown until that time.[11]

The second group of activities that Bell recorded comprised the various dice and board games that might be classified as recreational rather than sporting since they were not physical activities. These included one game that was consistent with the popular image of Tibet. *Sa-lam Nam-sha* is a board game played with dice and similar to snakes and ladders, but in the Tibetan variety the players attempted to ascend the board to heaven while avoiding the descent into hell.[12]

More commonly, however, the atmosphere surrounding these activities was purely secular. They were generally accompanied by gambling. There were professional gamblers in Tibet and many aristocrats employed their own gambler for whose wins and losses they were responsible. The most common of these pursuits were those involving dice. Wang Yao describes how dice games (*sho-bshad*) were accompanied by verbal sexual innuendoes and were thus restricted to male participation. The lasting popularity of dice playing within Tibet is attested to by textual and archaeological sources that demonstrate that Tibetans played dice at least as far back as the eighth to the ninth century AD.[13] It has also been suggested that in certain parts of the country dice could have a spiritual rather than a sporting function because Tibetans used them for divination rather than gambling.[14]

The third group of Tibetan leisure activities consisted of those sports derived from martial pursuits. These ranged from childrens' games of throwing stones at a target or to the greatest distance, to adult activities such as wrestling, archery and horseracing. From the seventh to the ninth century AD Tibet was a great Central Asian military power and was strong enough to sack the Chinese capital of Chang'an (Xian) in 763. Tibetan forces ranged as far west as Samarkand and their troops were famed for skilled horsemanship. Tibet subsequently declined as a military power and by the early years of the twentieth century had military forces numbering only around 5,000. But echoes of the skills acquired in the martial period survived. There were horse races between riderless horses that were spurred on by horses with riders chasing behind them. There were also riding skill competitions that involved a combination of riding at speed and firing either arrows or bullets at a fixed target.

Some regional variations appear to have existed in regard to the form of these competitions but there were certainly no written rulebooks. William Rockhill was an American diplomat and adventurer who travelled in north-eastern Tibet in the nineteenth century. He recorded that,

> horseracing is one of [the Tibetans'] favourite pastimes, but they do not understand this amusement as we do, confining themselves rather to showing off their horses, and themselves in their finest trappings, or else racing by twos and threes, but not for a purse or any reward.[15]

The martial sports had particular Tibetan characteristics. Wrestling appears to have been free-form, with the added element of the use of handfuls of roasted barley flour (*tsampa*, the Tibetan staple diet) that could be thrown into an opponent's eyes.[16] Archery was conducted with a longbow and Bell informs us that he was told by one competitor that 'beer must be drunk when shooting arrows. Otherwise the shoulder shakes and the arrow does not go hot to the target'.[17] Tibetan sporting contests usually took place during festival and feasting days, as part of the general entertainment, rather than as the focus of events and they were the subject of raucous attentions from the crowd.

What these types of activity have in common is that they involve skills essential to the warrior. This militaristic aspect to a sporting activity may explain one feature of the element of competition in traditional Tibetan sporting endeavours. Individual performance was more important than mere victory when an activity was militarily orientated and the overall standard was the issue. It was not enough to have one great warrior, rather all of a group's warriors must be proficient if they were to be victorious in battle. Thus the Tibetans were apparently as concerned with abusing the losers as applauding the winners. Bell notes that those who had done well in competition may have been rewarded, but also that 'those who have failed receive little or nothing; their food is doled out to them in markedly poor vessels and they are jeered at by their fellows'.[18]

The problem with exploring the history of sport in Tibet before the arrival of Europeans is that most written sources were compiled inside the monasteries. On the whole, life outside these institutions was accorded low priority in these records and physical activities were considered especially unimportant in a period when Tibet's military prowess was in decline. Martial traditions may have survived among the *Kham-pa* and other tribal groups in eastern Tibet, but by the nineteenth century the Tibetan social ideal was primarily a religious, rather than a military or a sporting one.

Within the monasteries themselves, however, there was a group that engaged in physical competition and which maintained a strong physical culture. This was the 'dop dops' (*ldab ldob*) who were monks singled out for their size and imposing appearance. Their function was to serve the monasteries internally as police and keepers of order and externally as soldiers who could fight to defend their particular institution from attack. Some came to act as a sort of mercenary and were hired out to serve as guards protecting caravans; monasteries even cashed in on the prowess of their 'dop dops' by using them as bounty hunters.[19] The role of the 'dop dop' may at first sight appear far from the monastic ideal. But while the popular image of monasteries may be of a spiritually focused community engaged in meditation and ritual performance, these institutions actually admitted large numbers of men unsuited to matters of the spirit. This was only to be expected in a monastic population that at any one time contained about a fifth of the male population. Those unsuited to the spiritual work of the monasteries were, however, more suited to many of the other roles of the institution such as that of cooks, cleaners or clerks. Those whose temperament and physique made them ideal for martial pursuits found a place within the order of the monastery as 'dop dops'.

The 'dop dops' had a reputation for unruliness and for vendettas and they engaged in pitched battles with their counterparts from other monasteries. They were, therefore, concerned with physical fitness and their strength and athleticism were part of their identity. 'Dop dops' practised and competed with one another in such activities as jumping and stone throwing and such was the skill that they developed in these pursuits that they were often hired by aristocrats to give displays.[20]

There was therefore a limited conception of sporting performance within Tibetan society. But, in general, popular entertainment was more commonly provided by and associated with storytellers, minstrels and strolling players or, in the more formal context, with their monastic equivalents. As performers in the Tibetan language and within Buddhist culture these popular and monastic performers acted as cultural agents. As such, they were responsible for the transmission of notions of a shared culture and identity that it is possible to discuss in the context of what Hobsbawm has called 'proto-nationalism'.[21] Sport before the arrival of the Europeans appears to have had no place in the formulation of this proto-nationalism. Indeed, most sporting activities seem to have had regional variations so that it is not even possible to identify a Tibetan game common to all ethnic groups or to all regions. In the early part of the twentieth century, however, the British arrived and brought with them association football. This was to be Tibet's first encounter with modern sport and its first experience of sportsmen as cultural agents.[22]

THE BRITISH, FOOTBALL, SPORT AND MODERNITY

A permanent British presence in Tibet dated from 1903–04 when a mission under the command of Col Francis Younghusband (1863–1943) fought its way to the Tibetan capital of Lhasa. The mission was dispatched by the Viceroy of India, George Curzon, with the primary aim of excluding Russian influence from Tibet and thereby securing British interests on the borders of the Empire. Throughout the nineteenth century the Tibetan government had sought to exclude Europeans in order to preserve the Buddhist religious and social system. The government had refused to accept communications from the Government of India and had succeeded in excluding all but a handful of Europeans from entering central Tibet.[23]

The Younghusband mission forced the Tibetans to enter into treaty relations with the Government of India and to accept the presence of British officials. These were placed at two 'Trade Agencies' situated at Yatung in the Chumbi Valley, just across the border from Sikkim and at Gyantse in central Tibet, around 130 miles south of Lhasa. The so-called 'Trade Agents' posted at Yatung and Gyantse were actually officers of the Indian Political Department which was, in effect, the diplomatic corps of the Government of India. Trade was of little concern to the Trade Agents whose primary duty was to cultivate the friendship and cooperation of the Tibetans and to obtain information about political and socio-economic conditions there. These officers were under the direct control of the Political Officer for Sikkim, Bhutan and Tibet, who was stationed at Gangtok, the capital of Sikkim. A British medical officer and one or two other British officers in command of the 50-man Indian Army escort accompanied the Gyantse Trade Agent. Three or four non-commissioned and civil officers were also stationed there to organize communications and clerical matters. Gyantse was thus home to from six to eight Europeans as well as 50 Indian soldiers, along with around a dozen Sikkimese or Indian servants.[24]

The officers who served in Tibet were products of the British public school system and of universities or military colleges. These institutions sought to produce a particular type of individual with what were regarded as the necessary attributes for service in the Empire. Sports, particularly team sports (and equestrian skills), were seen as an important part of the process that shaped men of suitable character for these roles. Team sports were considered necessary to foster the physical and moral virtues an officer would need, that is, fitness, endurance, self-control, team spirit and a sense of 'fair play'. This emphasis on sport could tend to produce a narrow anti-intellectualism, but among those who served in Tibet a reasonable balance seems to have been the result. The officers were strongly imbued with the required love of sports but were by no means anti-intellectual.[25]

During the early years of the British presence sports were played by the Trade Agency officers and the soldiers who accompanied them for a variety of reasons, such as enjoyment and exercise and, as the men were far from busy there, simply in order to pass the time. The records of the officers in Tibet show that they played several sports including polo and hockey but that football was by the far most popular. There is no record of when Tibetans first joined in but members of the local community were employed by the Agencies in various capacities and these employees were soon drawn into taking part in the games.

The Agencies also had sports days, based on the British public school model, to which the local people were invited. This was part of the process of establishing good relations with the Tibetans since food was provided and prizes were given to all comers. Athletics, polo, football and novelty events such as sack races were held. These soon became popular events so that, for example, the Armistice Day event in 1918 attracted a crowd of around 3,000 Tibetans although most were poorer citizens who came for the free food and drink that the British provided.

Tibet had gained de facto, if not de jure, independence from China after the 1911 Chinese revolution that led to the collapse of their position in Tibet. Under the rule of the thirteenth Dalai Lama, Tibet then embarked on a period of experimenting with modernization. This was a process supported by the British Indian officials responsible for Anglo-Tibetan relations. As part of this process four young Tibetans were sent to Rugby School in England in 1913. The traditional Tibetan education system was centred on the monasteries and sport was not a part of their curriculum. At Rugby, a traditional public school, it was a very different matter and one of the young men was reported to have quickly shone at cricket. This was a skill, however, that was to serve him little on his return since the lack of grass on the Tibetan plateau meant that cricket was not one of the games cultivated by the British who were based there.

Education as a force for modernization in Tibetan society was quickly developed and in October 1923 an English medium school was opened in Gyantse. It was unpopular with the conservative Tibetan aristocracy who proved reluctant to send their children to it. However, one aspect of the curriculum proved overwhelmingly successful with the pupils. This was football.[26] The headmaster of the Gyantse school was Frank Ludlow who was a Cambridge graduate and noted botanist employed by the Tibetan government. Having been a teacher with the Indian Education Department, Ludlow naturally followed the usual British imperial practice of emphasizing sports as a character-building activity. He took several footballs with him to Gyantse and soon had to send for more as his pupils proved so keen on the game that they wore them out. As the traditional robe-like Tibetan dress known as the *chuba* proved unsuitable for the game, Ludlow also sent for football kits. These he ordered in the 'Tibetan colours' of yellow and maroon. These colours were first worn by the schoolboys in a match against the Gyantse military escort team. A competitive league was then established in Gyantse with the school team and the British Trade Agency civil and military 'A' and 'B' teams. There was apparently a keen rivalry between them. Ludlow acted as referee in these games and recorded in his diary that he had to lecture his boys on 'keeping their temper when playing football and generally playing the game'. On one occasion he had to send off two of his own pupils for quarrelling on the field.[27]

The attempt to instil the Tibetan youths with the moral sporting codes and ethos of the British Empire is explicit here and is in common with other colonial attempts to introduce sport across Asia. However, in Ludlow's endeavours it is possible to glimpse another project underlying his introduction of football and its organization in Tibet. This project was the inculcation of a sense of nationalism among the local population. There were no 'Tibetan colours' as such that had traditionally been associated with the region. When Ludlow put his boys into 'Tibetan colours' he drew upon no apparent local precedent. Yellow was the colour of the hats worn by the monks of the dominant Tibetan sect, the *Gelugpa*, popularly termed the 'Yellow Hats'. Maroon was probably derived from the colour of the monks' robes. In other words, Ludlow was creating a set of national colours for the strips rather than relying on any well established precedent. In his choice of livery for the football kits Ludlow was entirely in line with other British attempts to create symbols upon which they hoped to encourage a sense of 'nation' among the Tibetans.[28]

Historically there was a distinct Tibetan identity based on such elements as shared language, religion, diet, dress and culture. It is not at all clear, however, that this constituted a Tibetan *national* identity. Tibet included large areas, such as the eastern regions of Kham, where the population acknowledged the religious authority of the Dalai Lama but denied Lhasa's secular authority. Lhasa also laid claim to the ethnically Tibetan region of Amdo, or Kokonor, in the north-east where the largely nomadic Tibetan Buddhist population had not actually been ruled by Lhasa since the eighteenth century. Even in the central provinces of U and Tsang a sense of unified Tibetan identity was far from well established. Shigatse, Tibet's second largest town, was the domain of the Panchen Lama, who was the second highest figure in Tibetan Buddhism. He maintained his own court and even conducted an independent foreign policy. Much of the local population considered the Panchen Lama to be their supreme leader and were hostile to attempts at centralization by the court at Lhasa. Tibetans therefore appear to have had a sense of cultural identity, of 'Tibetan-ness'. However, their political and social loyalties were to region, to sect, to family and to local leaders rather than to a 'nation'.[29]

The British were enthusiastic about trying to create this 'national' identity and about having Tibetans rally around the symbols of such an identity for very pragmatic reasons. The primary concern of the British in their relations with Tibet was that the area should provide a stable northern frontier for the British Indian Empire. The legal status of Tibet actually mattered little to them as long as it provided the required secure barrier against Russia, Britain's great rival in central Asia. China had proved incapable of controlling Tibet in the late nineteenth century and Chinese attempts to regain control there in the years before 1911 had only added to instability in Tibet. British officials therefore tended to support Tibetan self-government and to promote policies designed to strengthen and unify Tibet to the point where it would take its place among the world's nation-states and would be capable of resisting Chinese and Russian influence. While international agreements and a desire to avoid upsetting the Chinese government meant that the British government did not officially recognize Tibet as an independent state, their officials worked at encouraging processes that would lead the country in that direction.

In addition to providing Tibetan colours Ludlow also defined Tibetan character on the lines favoured by the Tibetan government as to the primarily religious identity of Tibet. For example, when the Political Officer offered a prize of Rs11 to the winning team in a school versus military match, Ludlow proposed that the school use the money to buy a photo of the Dalai Lama. The Dalai Lama, incidentally, was receiving regular reports on Ludlow's school, including its football matches and Ludlow recorded that at one point the Tibetan ruler was 'rather fed up' because he had been unable to contact the local Tibetan administrators on the newly installed telephones. The officials at the time were all away watching the football.[30]

British plans for the modernization of Tibet largely collapsed in the mid 1920s. Conservative opposition to the innovations brought by modernity proved too strong and the Dalai Lama changed direction. He reduced the growing power of the military and the Gyantse school was closed in October 1926. Sport was a casualty of this change and there is no mention of football in the British records for a decade, although it apparently continued to be played among the British and the Indians at the Trade Agencies. However, in 1936 a British mission under the command of the Sikkim Political Officer Basil Gould was dispatched to Lhasa. The thirteenth Dalai Lama had died in 1933 and a Chinese 'condolence mission' had arrived in 1934. When it became clear that the Chinese had no intention of leaving Lhasa and had, in effect, established an embassy there, the British responded by establishing their own mission in the town. The British Lhasa Mission remained there, theoretically on a temporary basis, until Indian independence in 1947 when the mission passed to the control of the new Indian government.

The Gould mission included seven British officers and more than 50 Indian, Sikkimese and Tibetan support staff. Gould was very much in the sporting mould and had good experience of Tibetan conditions, having already served there as a Trade Agent in Gyantse. In this role in 1912–13 he had put on an exhibition polo match during a visit to the town by the Dalai Lama in an apparently successful attempt to impress the Tibetan leader. The Gould mission deliberately and consciously initiated the reintroduction of football to Tibet as a political tool. Gould was quite clear about his motives. His reports specifically state that he felt that matches between the mission and the Tibetans were an important means by which to cultivate the friendship of the locals.[31]

Gould, playing in goal, led a team known as the 'Mission Marmots', after the animal that is indigenous to Tibet, and the team went unbeaten without conceding a goal in their first season. But they did have the advantage of playing in boots, which rather overawed their barefooted opponents. A team called Lhasa United was formed by Lhasa residents and included Tibetans, Ladakhis, Sikkimese, Nepalese and even a Chinese tailor. The three Tibetan officials in the side were somewhat handicapped because they wore the traditional charm boxes on their heads and thus were unable to head the ball. This detail is an important one for it is an indication of the way in which modernization had implicit requirements. In this instance, of course, the requirement was the need to dispense with traditional dress in order effectively to play the modern foreign game.[32]

As had been the case in Gyantse, a competitive league was formed in Lhasa, although in this case the games were seven-a-side. In addition to the Mission Marmots and Lhasa United, there were teams made up of players from the Nepalese community, the Lhasa Muslim community (mainly composed of Ladakhis) and an additional Tibetan side.[33] The second Tibetan team was composed of soldiers from the Dalai Lama's personal bodyguard, the Trapchi Regiment. They provided strong opposition and forced a draw with the Mission Marmots. The 1936 season came to an abrupt end, however, when someone stole the goalposts for firewood.[34]

Football seemed to be firmly established in Tibet and eventually there were 14 teams in the Lhasa competition. The British reported that Tibetan officials were practising the game twice a week, that football boots were for sale in the Lhasa market and that street urchins were playing the game with a ball made of paper and string. Even the Regent who ruled Tibet in the intervals between the thirteenth and the fourteenth Dalai Lama, a young man in somewhat poor health, took up playing the game. Significantly, it appears that this was on the advice of the British mission doctor.[35]

While the Tibetans were playing the game for enjoyment their activities were seen in another light by the British and the Chinese whose missions in Lhasa were in competition for influence over the locals. The Chinese were not without their own cultural sporting weapon of influence. When Hugh Richardson (who headed the Lhasa mission for much of the period from 1937 to 1950) returned in October

1938 after an absence of 15 months he reported that '*Mah Jong* has completely taken hold of Lhasa since I was last here'. To which report an amused official in Simla added the question of whether this represented 'sinister evidence of Chinese influence?'.[36]

Badminton is also reported as having found great favour around this time, but Richardson had a tennis court built at the British mission where he took on all-comers, including the Chinese representatives. Football remained the most popular foreign sport in Tibet until 1944 when it was suddenly banned by the Tibetan government. It was stated that kicking a football was 'as bad as kicking the head of the Lord Buddha'.[37] The overt cause of the ban was the occurrence during a football match of a hailstorm. This was considered to be a very bad omen by the Tibetans. However, the underlying cause of the ban was monastic opposition to the game. Too many monks were playing when they should have been engaged in religious activities and it was felt that too much money was being spent on uniforms and equipment. In the wider sense, the introduction of football to Tibet threatened to generate passions and rivalries outside the traditionally acceptable channels of Tibetan society. The monastic powers were hostile to any changes in their social system and structures and feared that football was the thin end of a wedge that would undermine the system and their privileges. Football was consciously introduced by the British coming from India as a tool of colonialism and modernization. It was as consciously banned because it was recognized by the monastic elite in Tibet as just such a tool. The British and their Indian and Sikkimese employees continued to play football among themselves, although the British players had always struggled to perform well due to the altitude which left them breathless after a short run. But their efforts to encourage football in Tibet as a means of inculcating a sense of national identity were a failure. The only consolation for the British was that *mah-jong* was soon banned as well.

The British encouragement of football must have hardened opposition to their presence in conservative Tibetan circles and particularly among the monastic institutions. But probably more significant in that regard was the British love of field sports, shooting or *shikar*, as it was known in British India. Shooting was a popular and perfectly proper recreation for the British officer class of the time and Tibet was something of a paradise for the hunter. The British officers bagged enormous amounts of game, including wolves, bears and snow leopards as well as countless birds. But to the devout Tibetan Buddhist population the unnecessary taking of life was morally unacceptable. Tibetans certainly did hunt wildlife but for skins or meat not for recreation. Indeed, the Tibetan government made several official complaints about British officials shooting in central Tibet. As the Nepalese and Chinese representatives were apparently equally keen on slaughtering the local wildlife (much of which was in fact semi-tame due to the Tibetan ban on killing), the Tibetans' anger must, in fact, have been directed at all foreigners rather than specifically against the British.

For the Tibetans, football's introduction and its failure may also have had broader implications. The only hope for Tibet of obtaining permanent independence was to establish a separate political status and identity in the world arena. Football has certainly played a part in the assertion of a visible, national identity on the international stage in other cases, and a Tibetan football team could have made a small contribution to presenting the world with a strong symbol of independent Tibetan identity, while also countering the predominant popular images of Tibetans as an entirely spiritually-orientated people whose political aspirations were therefore of no importance. The failure of Tibet to represent itself in these terms has played a large part in its recent history of domination by the Chinese state.

BRITISH DEPARTURE AND CHINESE INVASION

In October 1950 Tibet was invaded by Communist Chinese forces and the country's fragile independence was ended. Much of Tibet was absorbed into the neighbouring Chinese provinces and what remained is now designated the Tibetan Autonomous Republic. Ironically, the sense of nationalism that the British had tried to foster has received its greatest boost from the hostile Chinese presence in Tibet and Tibetan nationalism has developed as a strong force both among the exile and the TAR population in opposition to the invasion and occupation.

In the contemporary TAR Tibetans are largely excluded from participation in much of the government and administration by the nature of the Chinese system of education, in which higher education is only in the medium of Chinese. Such sporting activities as there are in Tibet are similarly dominated by the Chinese and the facilities that have been built in Lhasa and elsewhere are designed more for the benefit of the vast number of Han Chinese settlers on the Tibetan plateau than for the local population. Probably the most popular pastime for Tibetans in Lhasa today is pool which is often played in the open air on tables that the owners carry around on their backs. Tibetans, however, do organize some ethnically-based competitions which may include traditional Tibetan sporting events such as rock carrying and flying kites.

The influence of television and Chinese state sporting celebrations and culture has stimulated Tibetans' interest in sporting participation. They compete as individuals in Chinese national sporting competitions. Indeed, several ethnically Tibetan athletes have been included in Chinese teams competing in international events such as the Asian Games, and particularly in such sports as archery and shooting. As far as football is concerned, there are hints that the game continues to be played in Tibet and a Tibetan football team was recorded as winning the 'Second National Unity Cup' in 1984.[38] While football is played in the TAR, it is not particularly common. Tibetans in the TAR cleverly display a variety of manifestations of their indigenous culture as signs and symbols of national identity[39] but football is not indigenous and seems to have no political or nationalistic implications to encourage its playing. The Chinese clearly have no intention of establishing Tibetan sporting teams that would act as a focus for indigenous nationalism. Thus the Tibetan team competes against other 'National Minority Groups' rather than in international competition or in competition against Han Chinese teams. Much more research is needed within the TAR to examine the ethnic and social background of Tibetan sporting competitors and the extent to which they preserve indigenous sporting traditions or use sport as a vehicle for resistance to the dominant, Chinese, imperialist culture.

The situation among the Tibetan exile community is different. The 'Big Toe Kick' (*te-pe*) remains a popular pastime among the Tibetan refugee communities in India especially since it is a cheap game to play and an easy one to organize. Those traditional sports that derived from military activities such as horse racing do not appear to have survived in exile. This may be partly explained by the non-violent image of Tibet which the government in exile promotes as an ideological centrepiece. This does not accord with the militaristic sports of old Tibet so these have fallen into disuse. Within the TAR, however, these activities are still carried out, particularly among the eastern Tibetan tribes.

It is intriguing that mountaineering, which has become a defining element of Sherpa culture, has not become an activity with which the Tibetans are closely associated. The Sherpas are of Tibetan origin, while the names of a number of Chinese citizens known to have climbed Everest indicate that they are also Tibetans. At least one member of the first successful Chinese Everest expedition in 1960 was Tibetan. But for reasons that are difficult to explain, the Tibetans have failed to establish an identity as climbers.

The refugee community in south Asia is open to both Indianization and Westernization, and the Tibetans in India are increasingly at home in the world of globalized sport. Football and even cricket are played in Tibetan exile communities, along with hockey, volleyball and several other sports. Tibetan exile schools have athletic carnivals and sporting curricula which are designed on the British model. The idea that football was banned in pre-1950 Tibet is at best an amused memory and at worst an embarrassment. There is now even a film entitled *The Cup* that deals with young Tibetan monks sneaking out of their monastery in India to watch the World Cup on television. A gentle portrait of the clash between cultures and generations and of the potential of football to cross cultural borders, its young Tibetan heroes look to the footballers of Brazil and France rather than to the religious heroes of the Himalayas. Written and directed by an incarnate monk, Khyentse Norbu, and financed by Australians, it was well received at the 2000 Cannes Film Festival. It would seem that at the end of the twentieth century football in Tibetan culture was still seen as a symbol of and a metaphor for modernity.

CONCLUSIONS

The cultural structures of traditional pre-1950 Tibetan society did not include a significant sporting component. The monastic focus of society meant that sporting activities were not a means of gaining wealth or increased social status and games were played almost entirely for recreation. Many of these activities were derived from martial skills and the low status of the military in Tibetan society further acted to prevent their being a prominent cultural feature.

British efforts to encourage football in Tibet as a means of fostering a sense of Tibetan nationalism were largely a failure since the game was associated with the wider policy of modernization that aroused considerable opposition in elite and monastic circles. There, Western innovations were regarded as a threat to the existing social system and were successfully resisted by Tibet's elites. The failure to modernize was a key factor in Tibet's loss of independence (although it is unlikely that any changes would have enabled Tibet to resist the full-scale military invasion of 1950). A Tibetan football team at international level might have made a small contribution to the recognition of Tibet as a nation-state. Thus the ban on football may be seen as part of a lost opportunity for the Tibetans.

In the wider sense, the failure of the Tibetans to become a sporting nation raises issues of how a society defines itself and is viewed by the outside world. Sport is a cultural manifestation and, in a society with a primarily religious orientation, it is restricted at best to a role in 'popular' rather than 'elite' culture. Nevertheless, the popularity of various recreations among the Tibetan peoples both historically and in the contemporary world is an aspect of Tibetan culture that is ignored by the popular and academic media largely because of preconceived images of the Tibetans as non-sporting people.

NOTES

A version of this essay was presented at a joint History/Sports Studies Seminar at University College Northampton in May 2000. I am grateful to Paul Dimeo, Jim Mills and colleagues for their comments on that paper. I am also pleased to acknowledge the assistance of the International Association for Asian Studies, Leiden, The Netherlands.

1. Regarding these images, see for example, D. Lopez, *Prisoners of Shangri-La: Tibetan Buddhism and the West* (Chicago, IL: University Press, 1998); P. Bishop, *The Myth of Shangri-La: Tibet, Travel Writing and the Western Creation of Sacred Landscape* (London: Athlone Press, 1989); T. Shakya, 'Tibet and the Occident: The Myth of Shangri-la', *Tibetan Review*, 27 (1992), 13–16.
2. At least 100,000 Tibetans fled into exile in India during the 1950s in response to the Communist Chinese take-over of Tibet. The refugees included the Tibetan leader, the fourteenth Dalai Lama, who now resides in Dharamsala in the Indian Himalayan foothills.
3. I exclude my own work: see n.21. See M. Calkowski, 'Contesting Hierarchy: On Gambling as an Authoritative Resource in Tibetan Refugee Society', in C. Ramble and M. Brauen (eds), *Anthropology of Tibet and the Himalaya: Proceedings of the International Seminar at the Ethnographic Museum of the University of Zurich, Sep. 21–28 1990* (Zurich: Ethnographic Museum, 1993), pp.30–8. This article concerns gambling rather than sport *per se*, although given recent events in cricket this is perhaps quite relevant. Also see A. Loseries-Leick, 'Psychic Sports – A Living Tradition in Contemporary Tibet?', in E. Steinkellner (ed.), *Tibetan Studies: Proceedings of the 7th Seminar of the International Association*

for Tibetan Studies, Graz 1995 (Wien: Verlag der Österreichischen Akademie der Wissenschaften, 1997), 2, pp.583–93. I have not had access to Loseries-Leick's other work, cited there; 'Traditionssport in Tibet', in B. Günther, K. Günther and A. Loseries-Leick (eds), *Spectrum der Sportwissenschaften, Zeitschrift der österreichischen Sportwissenschaftsgesellschaft* (ÖGS), Heft 1 (1996).

4. The Chinese scholar Wang Yao has made two contributions to the field. He has argued rather unconvincingly that polo originated in Tibet, later spreading to Persia, usually considered the home of that game; see W. Yao, 'An Inquiry into Polo – Tibet's Contribution to Athletic Sports', in S. Ihara and Z. Yamaguchi (eds), *Tibetan Studies: Proceedings of the 5th Seminar of the International Association for Tibetan Studies* (Narita: Japan, 1989), pp.849–52. Also see W. Yao, 'On the Origin of *sho* (Dice) and *shag* (Domino): Exploration in the Amusement Culture of the Tibetan People', in E. Steinkellner (ed.), *Tibetan Studies: Proceedings of the 7th Seminar*, 2, pp.1055–67. Also see D. Linhui, 'Tibetan Sports: Thirty Years of Development', in *China's Tibet*, 6 (1995), 2–4.

5. Loseries-Leick, 'Psychic Sports'.

6. Sir C. Bell, *The People of Tibet* (Oxford: Oxford University Press, 1968) [first published 1928].

7. Ibid., pp.268–9.

8. Ibid., pp.214, 268–9.

9. Ibid., p.215.

10. T. Skorupski (ed.), *Adventures of a Tibetan Fighting Monk* (Bangkok: Tamarind Press, 1986), p.131.

11. The absence of a ball as a recreational device is difficult to account for. Tibet's mountainous terrain cannot be the explanation for it, given that most of the population actually live in the relatively flat river valleys.

12. Bell, *People of Tibet*, pp.265–9.

13. See Yao, 'On the Origin of *sho*'.

14. Ibid., p.248.

15. W. W. Rockhill, *The Land of the Lamas: Notes of a Journey Through China, Mongolia and Tibet* (New Delhi: Asian Educational Services Reprint, 1988), p.247 [first published 1891].

16. Bell, *People of Tibet*, pp.279–80.

17. Ibid., p.271.

18. Ibid., p.283.

19. On the *ldab ldob* see M. Goldstein, 'A Study of the *Ldab Ldob*', *Central Asiatic Journal*, 9, (1964), 125–41. Also see R. Ekvall, *Fields on the Hoof: Nexus of Nomadic Pastoralism* (London: Holt, Rinehart and Winston 1968), p.41.

20. D. Snellgrove and H. Richardson, *A Cultural History of Tibet* (London: Weidenfeld & Nicolson, 1968), p.242.

21. E. Hobsbawm, *Nations and Nationalism since 1780* (Cambridge: Cambridge University Press 1990), p.46.

22. See A. McKay, 'The Other "Great Game": Politics and Sport in Tibet, 1904–47', *International Journal of the History of Sport*, 11 (1994), pp.372–86. Where not otherwise noted that article is the source for the following section.

23. Just three Europeans reached Lhasa in the nineteenth century: an eccentric Englishman Charles Manning in 1812 and two Lazarist monks, Huc and Gabet, in 1846.

24. Regarding the British presence in Tibet see A. McKay, *Tibet and the British Raj: The Frontier Cadre 1904–47* (Richmond: Curzon Press, 1997). Regarding the wider diplomatic history of Tibet in this period see A. Lamb, *Tibet, China, and India 1914–1950* (Hertingfordbury: Roxford Books, 1989); M. Goldstein, *A History of Modern Tibet, 1913–1950: The Demise of the Lamaist State* (Berkeley, CA: University of California Press, 1989).

25. See McKay, *Tibet and the British Raj*, pp.77–86, 183–94. Also see J.A. Mangan, *The Games Ethic and Imperialism: Aspects of the Diffusion of an Ideal* (London and Portland, OR: Frank Cass, 2000 [reprint of the 1985 edn]); Clive Dewey, '"Socratic Teachers": Pt 1 – The Opposition to the Cult of Athletics at Eton, 1870–1914', *International Journal of the History of Sport*, 12 (1995).

26. The main primary source in regard to sporting activities at Gyantse school is the diary of Frank Ludlow; see Oriental and India Office Collection, [hereafter OIOC], MSS Eur D 979; the Ludlow Collection, Gyantse diary of Frank Ludlow.

27. Ludlow's diaries.

28. Yellow, but not maroon, is one of a number of colours on the Tibetan flag, which was designed in the 1913–20 period though incorporating earlier elements.

29. There is a considerable literature concerning the question of Tibetan identity. See, for example, F.J. Korom, (ed.), *Constructing Tibetan Culture: Contemporary Perspectives* (Quebec: World Heritage Press,

1997); P. Christiaan Klieger, *Tibetan Nationalism (The Role of Patronage in the Accomplishment of a National Identity)* (Berkeley, CA: Folklore Institute, 1992).

30. Ludlow's diaries.

31. Reports of the Gould mission may be found in OIOC L/P&S/12/4197.

32. The adoption of Western clothing by individuals during the modernization process is of course a significant indicator of that individual's adoption of Western modes of thought. But in their efforts to foster Tibetan nationalism the British otherwise favoured the Tibetans retaining their traditional clothing; for the practical reasons noted, football uniform was an exception to that policy.

33. The community divisions here are reminiscent of the model of those Indian imperial cricket tournaments in which teams composed of Europeans, Hindus, Muslims and Parsees competed.

34. OIOC L/P&S/12/4193, Lhasa Mission Report, 1936–37; L/P&S/12/4193-4467, Lhasa Mission diary entries of May and August 1939.

35. OIOC L/P&S/12/4197, Gould to India, 30 April 1937; L/P&S/12/4201, Lhassa Mission diary entry of 20 Aug. 1944.

36. OIOC, L/P&S/12/4193, Lhasa Mission Diary entry of 14 Dec. 1938; contemporary margin note.

37. Snellgrove and Richardson, *A Cultural History*, p.265. Such edicts were religious injunctions rather than laws in the Western sense. But in this case, unlike the earlier ban on cigarette smoking, the injunction was effective.

38. See Linhui, 'Tibetan Sports', 2–4.

39. See for various examples, R.D. Schwartz, *Circle of Protest: Political Ritual in the Tibetan Uprising* (London: Hurst, 1994).

6

The Corporates and the Game: Football in India and the Conflicts of the 1990s

MARIO RODRIGUES

INTRODUCTION

The 1990s have been the decade of the corporations in Indian football. Philips and Coca-Cola, both large multinational companies, sponsored the National League. Major Indian firms such as Zee TV and the United Breweries Group (UB) made important investments either in specific clubs or in sponsoring Indian leagues or competitions. Zee TV actually took over Churchill Brothers of Goa in 2000–01, while the UB group sponsored Mohun Bagan, East Bengal, Mohammedan Sporting and the Federation Cup. In doing this they had immediate impacts, as certain sectors of the game became professional, a national league was organized for the first time and Indian clubs began to look to the global football market for players.

This chapter will examine Indian football in the decade of the corporations and assess the impact of commercialization, professionalization and globalization. The game has been run on a regional basis since the British period and has remained a bastion of amateur administrators dominated by the interests of the major football states and of important individuals able to run the Indian game as a personal fiefdom. This background has meant that the modern forces brought by the corporations have certainly not swept through Indian football as they have in other countries. Indeed, it is this resistance on the part of the traditional structures and organizations within Indian football to modernizing forces brought by the 1990s that will continue to shape the game into the new millennium.

INDIAN FOOTBALL STRUCTURES BEFORE THE 1990s

With the foundation of the Indian Football Association (IFA) in Calcutta in the 1890s, the British established the regional pattern of football organization that still continues to exist.[1] The IFA was, in fact, purely an association for the government of the sport in Bengal, and more particularly Calcutta, and it was followed by similar associations in the other regions of India. The All India Football Federation (AIFF) now comprises 31 state associations, including the

Railways and Services Boards, each of which has the aim of managing the local game.

The pattern of regionalism in the game was reflected in the competitions that were organized. Leagues, where conducted, were organized by the regional associations for their member teams and there was no national league until 1996–97. Similarly, all-India cup competitions were organized locally and teams from outside the region participated by invitation only. However in 1941–42 the national championship for the Santosh Trophy was kicked off by the AIFF at Calcutta. This competition was contested by selections representing each state association and was hosted by the associations.

These competitions were not supported through overt corporate sponsorship as such but rather by patronage by interested organizations or benevolent individuals. For example, the prestigious, century-old football tournament the Durand Cup was conducted by the Army. Maharajas and princes were more likely to show interest in games such as polo and cricket (cricket teams were maintained by the rulers of, for example, Patiala, Indore, Gwalior, Baroda and Nawanagar) and the Ranji Trophy, India's national cricket championship, was donated by the Maharaja of Patiala. However, India's first attempt at a national football competition was supported by the Raja of Santosh and teams compete to this day for the trophy in his name.

As Indian sport and football were largely amateur there was little prize money on offer and corporate sponsorship was piecemeal and rather limited. Football could sustain itself without much corporate sponsorship because gate earnings were high and organizational expenses and players' fees were low. According to the Mumbai football official Parvez Ziauddin,[2] whose late father Khalifa Ziauddin had been president of the AIFF and also a senior vice-president of the Asian Football Confederation (AFC), major corporate sponsors came on to the scene only from the 1980s onwards. One of the pioneers was Hindustan Lever, an affiliate of the Unilever Group. It used the Rovers Cup competition organized in Mumbai by the Western India FA to promote its 'Lifebuoy' soap. However, by the 1990s the company had decided to withdraw its football sponsorship and instead opted for rural marketing as a better way to find buyers of its products. The multinational India Tobacco Company has now taken over the sponsorship of the Rovers Cup in order to promote its 'Bristol' brand of cigarettes. In the centenary year of the competition in 2000–01 the teams therefore competed for the 'Bristol' Rovers Cup.

FIFA, PHILIPS AND THE IMPACT OF THE NATIONAL LEAGUE

In the mid 1990s a delegation from FIFA visited India to assess football's development, organization and potential. It concluded that the game was ripe for professionalization and it issued recommendations as to how this process might be started. Chief among these recommendations was the organization of a

National Football League with substantial prize money to encourage club participation.

Philips India Ltd, a subsidiary of the Dutch electronics and lighting multinational, was approached by the Calcutta-based Leisure Sports Management (LSM) agency that was appointed by the AIFF to find sponsors. Philips is globally active in the game and had been a sponsor of the Chinese league as it began to reorganize in the 1990s. Indeed, the company had used football as a marketing vehicle in India earlier in the decade when its Dutch team PSV Eindhoven had toured India under the management of Bobby Robson. Philips agreed to sponsor the new league since it was attracted by the prospect of being associated with the beginning of the professionalization of the sport encouraged by FIFA. A spokesman for the company made it clear that there seemed to be sound commercial reasons for involvement, 'strategically it made sense to own a sport which would over time become more popular. At that point the entry cost for this exercise seemed a lot less than that of cricket sponsorship.'[3]

Philips paid approximately Rs20 million[4] in sponsorship for the first two seasons of the National Football League. The total prize money in the inaugural year was Rs7.2 million and the winner's cheque was worth Rs3.5 million of this alone.[5] Financial prizes were made in proportionately lesser amounts for the subsequent finishers and there were shares in gate receipts for the clubs, man-of-the-match awards for individual players, and so on. In the second year the winner's cheque was increased to Rs4 million.

Coca-Cola India, which took on sponsorship of the National League in the third season, increased the total sponsorship to approximately Rs15 million. In the fourth year the AIFF president Priya Ranjan Das Munshi claimed that Coca-Cola had further upped the total sponsorship to Rs18 million.[6] However, there are now doubts that the company was involved at all and it has been alleged that this claim was an attempt by the AIFF to conceal its loss of the National League's sponsor after only one year. The AIFF failed to find a sponsor for the fifth NFL competition, which belatedly kicked off after a temporary boycott by some of the premier clubs.[7]

The advent of the National League and the involvement of such high profile corporate groups as Philips and Coca-Cola immediately attracted attention to the game. Other corporate groups, sensing opportunities to get an early position in an emerging phenomenon, acted to get a stake in football. The most significant of these was the UB Group. This company had maintained a limited presence in football throughout the early 1990s. Its fermented beer, Kalyani Black Label, was associated with the sponsorship of the Federation Cup. The company through this brand also sponsored the shirts of FC Kochin after this club was founded in Kerala in 1997.

The UB Group's most sensational and controversial intervention came in time for the 1998–99 season. Dr Vijay Mallya, the chairman of the group, netted the country's leading clubs, Mohun Bagan and East Bengal of Calcutta. He did this by taking a 50 per cent stake in each in a sponsorship deal worth Rs27.5 million each. The two clubs are India's biggest and are the fiercest of rivals and the deal was akin to the same company coming to control AC and Inter Milan or Rangers and Celtic. There was further speculation that year that the company was attempting to buy stakes in either FC Kochin or in the Bengal Mumbai Football Club.[8] But Mallya sprang another surprise in 2000 by buying the third Calcutta club Mohammedan Sporting. UB and its affiliated companies now controlled India's largest and oldest clubs. Mallya explained that his companies, which are also sponsors of motor sports and horse racing, were looking for avenues to enhance their brand equity and opted for football since it has a large following in India and because cricket sponsorship was so expensive. He revealed that the group spends Rs40 million on football annually and now has plans to start women's teams with Mohun Bagan and East Bengal, for which additional allocations will have to be made.

The Bengal clubs were subsequently attached to the prominent brands in UB's stable. Mohun Bagan was linked to McDowell (McDowell manufactures several spirits such as whisky, rum, gin and vodka), East Bengal to 'Kingfisher' Beer and Mohammedan Sporting to Herbertsons, another group company which produces alcoholic drinks. This move prompted the AIFF president Priya Ranjan Das Munshi to allege that Mallya was in breach of FIFA statutes that stipulated that one sponsor may be associated with only one club. The response was that Mohun Bagan was contracted to McDowell, East Bengal to United Breweries and Mohammedan Sporting to Herbertsons and that these companies were 'separate legal entities' even if they did share a common chairman.[9] Each club's footballers were drafted in to endorsement campaigns for the brands. East Bengal stars Baichung Bhutia, Raman Vijayan, Carlton Chapman and Franky Barretto starred in TV promotions during the 1998 World Cup broadcasts as brand ambassadors for the popular 'Kingfisher' beer. This was once a brand promoted by the West Indian cricket team. Mohun Bagan players were also asked to do a similar advertisement for McDowell, but they reportedly refused, claiming that they were being paid only to play and not to advertise.

Another serious corporate player emerged in Mahindra & Mahindra, the giant Mumbai jeep and tractor manufacturing company. Mahindra had traditionally patronized sport by maintaining squads in several disciplines, comprising players who were given jobs within the company so that they might play for the corporation's teams. The Mahindras hockey team, for example, had been very successful and had produced several Olympians and internationals. Its football team had also briefly attained national acclaim under the former national coach Dereyk de Souza in the early 1990s. But in 1998–99 the Mahindras management opted to terminate its hockey and cricket operations and to concentrate on football. Again, this decision was driven by marketing logic. The company sought corporate promotion for its core products, the jeeps, 'football being a rugged game it is perfectly suited to the tough and sturdy Mahindra vehicles',[10] reasoned

Alan E. Durante, executive director and president of the automotive sector of the company.

This new corporate resolve helped Mahindras to taste immediate success. Among the tournaments that they won in the first season of the new regime was the prestigious Durand Cup, a first for a team from Mumbai. But in 1999–2000 the team faltered and in 2000–01 the company has had to show renewed commitment to the team. The club has rebranded itself as Mahindra United[11] and signed new players and a new coach Shabbir Ali, who guided the Goan club Salgaocar to the NFL title in 1998–99.

One novel feature of the Indian football scene as a result of the arrival of the corporates and commercial cash was the newly founded professional club. With the sudden and dramatic increases in prize money that came with the advent of the NFL, entrepreneurs saw a business opportunity in football. Investing in a club in order to win the prize appeared to be a sensible speculation, especially as at the outset it seemed as if prize money was set to continue increasing. This resulted in the birth of two new professional clubs. FC Kochin, the country's first completely professional club, was established in 1997–98. This was followed a year later by the Bengal Mumbai Football Club (BMFC), financed by Bengali businessmen who had their base in Mumbai.

FC Kochin attracted the UB Group as sponsors for their inaugural season and became associated with the 'Kalyani Black Label' beer brand. BMFC agreed to a three-year sponsorship deal with Gulf Oil India Ltd, a company that also sponsored the Mumbai super and first division leagues and took on the bill for a first division club. Officials of both clubs piously proclaimed their intentions to promote and professionalize the game. Both clubs went in for big budget teams, replete with star players procured at sizeable costs. Success was immediate as FC Kochin won the Durand Cup and BMFC the Rovers Cup and each won its respective regional league title.

CHANGING THE ROLES: PLAYERS AND PROFESSIONALIZATION IN THE 1990s

The professionalization of football had begun in the early 1980s and Mahindras was one of the teams that was involved from the start. Under the old system, talented players were encouraged to play for corporate clubs (those in both the private and the public sector) since they were provided with lifetime employment by the company. This meant that upon retirement from sport the player could look forward to a living for a lifetime on the company which would retrain the individual or use already existing talents to make him a useful employee. The new type of professional player, however, had no such security and was paid on a contract basis for only a season or two.

The professionalization of the game can be explained in two ways. The first factor behind the process was the influence of FIFA dictates that encouraged professionalism in the Asian game and that were the result of the same FIFA study which recommended the starting of the NFL. Perhaps more important was the downsizing of large industrial workforces in the 1980s and especially in the 1990s, which was an effect of the policies of liberalization in the Indian economy initiated by Rajiv Gandhi. This meant that companies were unable to find berths for retired players as easily as they had done in the past and thus it made sense to pay a little more to a professional player for a season or two rather than to take on the responsibility of his welfare for life. However, some public sector clubs still provide jobs to professional players. Teams such as Mumbai's Air-India and Kerala's State Bank of Travancore are good examples of clubs operating under the old corporate system, although they do now have professional players on their books.

In Calcutta a curious system prevailed. Footballers playing for the Big Three (Mohun Bagan, East Bengal and Mohammedan Sporting) received professional fees but were also placed in company jobs with large Calcutta firms. For example, one of India's most famous strikers and a former international captain and coach Shabbir Ali was posted with United Industrial Bank while playing for East Bengal and Mohammedan Sporting in Calcutta in the late 1970s and the early 1980s. He continues to be employed by the bank (now the Allahabad Bank) even though he has become a professional coach and currently works on the other side of the country in Mumbai, where he is coaching Mahindra United. His professional duties as a coach take up the morning, his work for the bank takes up the rest of the day and he enjoys leave from work to join the team for matches.

The decline of such systems meant that players on contracts became eager to earn as much money per season as possible. As corporates became involved in the game as owners and sponsors, players realized that more cash was in the system and began to make inflated wage demands. The earnings of professional footballers more than doubled during the boom of 1996–98 as the 12 to 15 leading clubs were forced to spend to keep up with each other. A lower-end professional could aspire to a sum of about Rs70,000–100,000 per annum. However, superstars such as Baichung Bhutia and I.M. Vijayan reportedly earned Rs2.5–3.0 million per annum (today the earnings of leading players have dwindled to a modest Rs1.0–1.5 million per annum). The personable Bhutia also attracted lucrative endorsement deals, making him India's first rupee soccer millionaire.

The Indian football boom also resulted in the game opening itself up to the global market in players. Foreign players had been a feature of the game in the 1980s and successes included the Nigerian Chima Okorie and the Iranian duo of Majid Bhaskar and Jamshed Nassiri. Since the mid-1990s, however, larger numbers of foreigners have been used and players have come from Nigeria, Ghana, Zimbabwe and Kenya in Africa as well as from Jordan, Uzbekistan, Nepal, Bangladesh and Thailand in Asia and from Brazil in South America. Few of these players have been outstanding successes. Many of them have been found substandard and are either sent back when they come for trials or grudgingly accommodated, since the clubs cannot afford better players. According to NFL stipulations, a club may register five foreigners for a season but only play four in a match.

At the start of the Indian football boom importing foreign players was seen as one way to combat the growing demands of Indian footballers. Anthony Bothello, an official with Dempo, the Goan corporate club, was happy to observe that 'Brazilians settle for much cheaper sums than our Indian footballers who quote ridiculously high prices.'[12] This is no longer the case. The Brazilian strikers Jose Ramirez Barretto and Joao Santos, currently with Mohun Bagan, now command sizeable fees of about Rs1.0 million per season.

The increased quantity of money in the system also meant that it was now possible to contemplate using foreign coaches. Dempo once employed a Brazilian Francisco Gonsalves, while another Goan club, Vasco da Gama, hired the Portuguese coach Xeca. George Blues and Danny McLennan, British former professional players, had stints with FC Kochin and Churchill Brothers, respectively, and currently Churchill Brothers have an Uzbeki coach Gregory Tsetvin. A coach with a leading club today commands Rs300,000–700,000 per annum.

CHANGING THE RULES: CONTROL, CLUBS AND COMPETITIONS

Change was forced on both the clubs and the competitions as a result of the new-found interest in football of the large corporations. Many clubs faced a challenge to their identity in the stipulation by their large sponsors that the corporation's name was to appear in the name of the club. Mohun Bagan became McDowell-Mohun Bagan, and this was quickly followed by Kingfisher-East Bengal, Gulf Oil-BMFC and Zee-Churchill Brothers. The case of FC Kochin showed the extremes to which this process could be taken. Having three different sponsors in three years meant that it experienced three name changes in the same period. In its first year the club was known as KBL-FC Kochin. The following year was non-alcoholic as the club took on the title Coca-Cola FCK. Finally the club played under the name Hi-Power FCK since it was sponsored by a computer firm. That supporters see these corporate intrusions as challenges to the identity of their clubs is shown by the fact that a member of Mohun Bagan Club has challenged the renaming of the club in the courts, a case in which an outcome was still awaited at the time this was being written.

The Calcutta clubs provide another example of the ways in which corporates began to meddle with the structures that they had bought into. UB declared that in the coming 2000–01 season all transfers between the two teams that it controlled in the city, Mohun Bagan and East Bengal, were banned unless a transfer fee of Rs1 million were paid. The intention of the company in imposing this stipulation was to stabilize relations between different parts of its business empire, despite the fact that these were fiercely competitive, rival football clubs with a history of poaching players from one another. It was certainly part of a wider programme of increasing control as UB then declared that it would fine players who absented themselves from club matches and it decided that it would station a full-time corporate manager in Calcutta to monitor football activities.[13]

UB did not entirely get its own way as there continued to be resistance to interference from within the club structure. The Mohun Bagan president Swapan Sadhan Bose criticized the company for interfering with the recruitment of players and said that its association was detrimental to the club's interests,

> We thought that getting sponsorship will bring in professionalism but to our dismay we find it is ruining the game. The UB Group must realize that sponsorship is not a run-of-the-mill business takeover but it is only a way of sponsoring the clubs to get mileage and publicity of their products.[14]

Eventually the company relented, partly due to criticism and partly due to fears that the transfer ban was in violation of both AIFF and FIFA guidelines.[15] For the 2000–01 season Mohun Bagan striker Dipendu Biswas was planning to move to East Bengal and had apparently already taken an advance from the club before UB imposed its ban. With such a high profile transfer at stake and East Bengal being unwilling to pay the transfer fine, UB backed down and let Biswas go without imposing the transfer fine as a special case.[16] Biswas is currently flourishing with East Bengal and the club has won the McDowell Cup, the local super league and the IFA Shield since his arrival.

The integrity of the competitions in Indian football was also severely compromised by the power that sponsorship brought large companies. The most notorious example of this came in the third season of the NFL. In the second season Mahindras and Churchill Brothers had been relegated. Yet, at the start of the following season, both clubs were reinstated in the top division. The AIFF authorities claimed at the start of the tournament that the tournament sponsor, Coca-Cola, had insisted on the presence of the two relegated teams. This seemed to be a clear case of corporate intervention rather than the results deciding the composition of a league.

However, it subsequently appeared that Mahindras were co-sponsors of the NFL that year. Their hoardings dominated the sidelines and the latest utility drive vehicle was displayed at stadiums where matches were played across the country. In other words, Mahindras secured their presence in the top flight tournament by coming up with the cash to sponsor the league. Companies unable or unwilling to make similar gestures found that relegation meant relegation. In the fourth season the AIFF announced that Air-India and Indian Bank, which were relegated in the previous season, would not be reinstated since the sponsor did not require their presence.[17]

Other competitions witnessed other types of intrusion on the part of the sponsors. The six-nation South Asian Football Federation Cup was held in Goa in 1999 and was sponsored by Coca-Cola. The teams therefore played for the SAFF Coca-Cola Cup. Indian officials found themselves coming into conflict with representatives of a company called Asian Football Confederation Marketing Ltd. The agency had been appointed by the Asian Football Confederation to oversee the marketing of its events and one of its responsibilities was to ensure that the sponsors received adequate exposure. However, the attempt to enhance the visibility of Coke resulted in a rather lopsided focus to maximize exposure for the brand rather than the SAFF Cup competition. Suddenly football officials found themselves competing with a group of agents and publicity men for the organization of the games. 'Event managers like AFC Marketing should not take over the administration of the game. They may have some good people with them, but a lot of them do not know much about football', an official, who preferred anonymity, complained to the author.

The preference for marketing agencies rather than football administrators in promoting the game has not been limited to the corporations involved in football. The AIFF and its president Priya Ranjan Das Munshi have recently opted for several such companies, despite their apparent lack of experience in sports management. The British-based company Sapphire Enterprises Ltd now functions as overseas marketing representative of the AIFF as well as for the Bangladeshi FA. This company, fronted by P.C. Rajprohit, organized India's football tour to England in July 2000 and claims to have future tours arranged for the Indian team in south-east Asia.

The company entered football when Rajprohit was taunted by an English friend who pointed out that India, which has a population of a billion, does not have a single footballer who was world-renowned. This prompted Rajprohit to prove the sceptics wrong and his first intervention was to help India's best footballer, Baichung Bhutia, to secure a contract with Bury FC in the English League. To facilitate this an exemption had to be made in British immigration legislation for professional footballers which allows players only from those countries who feature in the top 75 of FIFA's rankings.

Another example relates to the staging of the Millennium Super Soccer Cup. The AIFF president acted on his own initiative and again turned to a little known agency called Studio 2100. Held in January 2001 at a budget of reputedly Rs300–400 million and intended to feature 16 national teams from Asia, Africa and Latin America and Europe, this event was meant to bring Indian football to the attention of the world. A company with experience in film production, Studio 2100 staged some World Wrestling Federation events before it made its foray into international football,

> As a company, Studio 2100 has been considering the next step in our evolution for a few years. Sports provided with an ideal and natural growth stream – our managing director, a soccer fan, having lived in Calcutta, believed that soccer was a worthwhile game to sponsor. We then worked on designing a major event what would mark our entry into serious and big time sports management as an extension of our event management operation ... The federation weighed all the pros and cons of the ideas we had mooted over nearly 18 months before giving us the go ahead,

explained Henna Juneja of Studio 2100.[18] The tournament was widely regarded as a failure since many national teams withdrew and those that did attend sent junior or reserve squads. The financial losses have yet to be determined.

CORPORATE WITHDRAWAL AND THE CLUBS

The coming of the 2000–01 season saw a sudden deflation of corporate interest in football. The UB Group's attempt to impose downsized budgets on the Calcutta clubs was the most dramatic example of this. The grants to Mohun Bagan and East Bengal were reduced by nearly Rs10 million each. This meant that, from a peak of Rs27.5 million per club in the first year of acquisition, the UB contribution had fallen to Rs22.5 million for each club in the second year and by 2000–01 had shrunk to Rs12.5 million each, of which Rs10.5 million was earmarked for the recruitment of players. UB, however, later relented and announced an additional Rs2.5 million to be made available to each club for recruiting good foreign players. It also decreed that 20 per cent of the prize money won by the club would be distributed among the players.[19]

UB's budgetary reductions had much to do with the disappointing impact of their cash. Despite liberal funding, Mohun Bagan and East Bengal finished fourth and second respectively in the third NFL (1998–99). In the fourth season, East Bengal ended a lowly seventh while Mohun Bagan too had floundered initially until a belated addition of the quality foreign players, Stephen Abarowei, Jose Ramirez Barreto and the top scorer Igor Shivkirin, saw them put together a convincing winning run that gave them the title.[20]

Other corporate clubs that had once spent heavily on quality players also curtailed their budgets. For example, JCT Mills had the best foreign professionals and Indian stars such as Bhutia, Vijayan and Jo-Paul Ancheri when they won the inaugural NFL title. Since then, however, the club has not hired foreigners and has relied on local players from the Punjab, mainly because the business fortunes of the parent company have suffered, which has ruled out large payments to the club. This is a familiar picture in Indian football and in previous years teams associated with companies have disappeared as their corporate overseers encountered problems entirely unassociated with football. Mumbai-based mills such as Orkay had star players such as the internationals Bernard Pereira, Shekhar Bangera and Rosario Antao. But the club was closed in the 1990s as the company began to founder under the weight of obsolete technology.

In Goa, the recession in the powerful iron ore mining industry affected the football fortunes of the mining-driven corporate clubs such as Dempo, Salgaocar and Sesa Goa. The last of these simply scrapped its team and started a less expensive youth soccer academy three years ago. In 1999–2000 Goa's corporate clubs, Salgaocar and Dempo, took the revolutionary decision of seeking sponsorship to offset stiff annual outlays. But there was little serious interest because of the strong identification of the clubs with the parent company.

Another strategy adopted by these clubs was to demand transfer fees for their players even though the transfer fee system is largely unknown in India. Indeed, Dempo suffered most for the failure of its strategies for fighting economic over-commitment. The club experimented with a low-budget team of cheap, inexperienced players. As a result it finished last in the 12-team NFL and the club was relegated. This has led to a reversal of the strategy and Dempo is one of the few clubs to have spent money in attracting new players ready for the 2000–01 season.

The slump also affected the fortunes of the two new professional clubs FC Kochin and Bengal Mumbai FC. The large outlays required to establish the teams and to have them compete for the top prize money meant that short-term profits were not forthcoming. Problems with sponsorship further exacerbated the situation. The BMFC managing director Krishnendu Sen said that, although the club spent more than Rs10 million in the first year, it got back only Rs3 million out of the total Rs5 million sponsorship promised by Gulf Oil. This was because 'We couldn't fulfil our contractual obligations through no fault of our own. In the second year our budget was Rs7 million but we recovered only Rs2.3 million.'[21]

These budgetary shortfalls led to a severe payment crisis with the players that badly affected BMFC's image and resulted in problems in attracting new players. It finished eighth in the Mumbai super division league of 2000 and therefore was not invited to the NFL qualifiers in the following season. No big sponsor nor star player will associate with a club that is unlikely to feature on the national stage in the coming season. FC Kochin too is reportedly in poor shape. The financial stringency made it resort to various cost-cutting exercises, such as hiring only Indian players for most of last season.

Not that football in India has entirely lost its attraction for large corporations. In the summer of 2000 one of India's major media companies, Zee TV, bought a majority stake in Churchill Brothers,[22] a team founded by one of Goa's most controversial business families. Zee's entry into football is reportedly linked to its proposal to start a fully-fledged sports channel and to its failure to secure cricket telecast rights from the ICC or the BBCI.[23] Goan soccer received a further boost when the Chowgule group, traditionally associated with Goan cricket, decided to use Vasco Sports Club as a vehicle for promoting its 'Arlem' beer. Vasco Sports Club was promoted to the NFL for the 2000–01 season.[24]

CORPORATE WITHDRAWAL AND THE COMPETITIONS

The second thoughts about football that were evident among the corporations also extended to their sponsorship of competitions within the sport. In the 2000–01 season three major tournaments, the Federation Cup, the Santosh Trophy and the National Football League, had no main sponsors.[25] The withdrawal of UB's funding of the Federation Cup has meant that it has not been played in three years and the company has been reported as intending to withdraw from the regional McDowell Cup that it established to be played out between the Calcutta clubs.

Bharat Petroleum Corporation Ltd had sponsored the Santosh Trophy for six years in a row. It appears that poor relations with the AIFF caused them to quit football in disgust in 1999. This meant that in 1999–2000 this prestigious interstate championship was conducted in Kerala without a title sponsor.[26] Priya Ranjan Das Munshi, the AIFF president, had promised to finalize a deal with Indian Oil for title sponsorship as well as signing up Coca-Cola and BPL Mobile as co-sponsors. Not only did these not happen but he intervened to stop the organizing football body, the Thrissur District Football Association, from completing a deal with a foreign network for TV coverage and with a local company for in-stadium advertising rights. Only a sell-out final featuring the hosts Kerala helped the organizers to avoid financial disaster and break even. O.K. Devassy, general convenor of the tournament, concluded that 'I am sure that no District Football Association in Kerala would take up the responsibility to conduct the Santosh Trophy in the coming years.'[27]

The NFL also faced the new season without a sponsor. Philips withdrew after the first two seasons. Its successor, Coca-Cola, raised the financial outlay in the third year to Rs15 million. In the fourth year (1999–2000) the AIFF president announced that Coca-Cola had reconfirmed its sponsorship with an increased commitment of Rs18 million.[28] The problem with this claim is that there is little evidence that Coca-Cola in fact paid anything in this season. The company itself would not confirm that it had signed any such deal and the AIFF was unable to produce any evidence of a deal with Coca-Cola which led to open speculation in the press that Coca-Cola had not sponsored the tournament at all.[29] A senior football official who requested anonymity confirmed privately to the author that Coca-Cola had not paid a single rupee and had in effect received a full tournament's publicity for nothing. Coca-Cola's comments on the matter were sought but without success. It has now been alleged that the NFL and other domestic tournaments were funded by the AIFF from the FIFA grant of $1 million that was intended to establish youth development programmes, others say it was funded from the Doordarshan payment for telecast rights of domestic tournaments.[30] The affair has now ended up in court. Ranjit Gupta, an official of the football association in charge of Bengal, has leveled charges of grave financial mismanagement against the AIFF and has lodged a case against the Federation while demanding a Central Bureau of Investigation inquiry into its affairs.[31]

The reasons for corporate withdrawal were sometimes specific to the particular company's fortunes. Coca-Cola's loss of interest in Indian football can be put down to its poor record in India, as well as its tangles with Indian footballing politics. The company has incurred a massive loss in its decade-old Indian operations and recently had to write off $400 million. This represented about 50 per cent of the company's investment in the country to April 2000.[32]

The company also had the misfortune to find itself on the wrong side of Churchill Alemao in Goa. Having invested in a new bottling plant in the state, the company was reportedly approached to sponsor Churchill Brothers FC. Coca-Cola declined, allegedly because the club had demanded a ridiculously exorbitant amount. Churchill Alemao, then serving as minister of industry in Goa but who was also co-founder of the club that bore his name, subsequently announced that the water for the new plant was to be cut off. He justified this decision on the grounds that that the plant was guzzling this precious commodity to the detriment of other less privileged customers. The Goan media had a field day speculating that this was retribution for the company's reluctance to sponsor the club.

There are, however, more general reasons as to why companies began to withdraw support for the football competitions. The first of these was a perceived lack of publicity in return for the outlays required. Babu Mather, former general secretary of FC Kochin, concluded that,

> Mallya [chairman of UB] backed out as sponsor because he didn't get enough mileage. Same with Coke. There's no other reason. Sponsors are least bothered whether it is cricket or football. They want mileage and will adopt the sport or activity that gives them most mileage.[33]

Philips certainly withdrew from the NFL because of poor returns. 'The experience was not favourable. What was promised in terms of exposure in the media did not happen ... The money spent was not commensurate with the outcome. So we felt that the long-term strategic intent of Philips would not be achieved', explained a Philips representative.[34] The company returned to using cricket as a marketing vehicle by co-sponsoring three international events in 2000. This decision is easily explained, 'Cricket is a ready recipe that works. As a sport/industry it is well managed and very well organized in India and abroad. It is a great media event and keeping everything else aside, this alone makes tremendous marketing sense.'[35]

The main reason that companies complained about poor publicity returns for their sponsorship of football was the inadequate television coverage of the game. Most sponsors wanted programmes on the cable-distributed, satellite channel ESPN-STAR Sports rather than the 'slipshod coverage'[36] provided by the terrestrial and government-owned Doordarshan channel. The latter is perceived to be a rather lumbering organization staffed by bureaucrats while ESPN-STAR uses the latest production techniques and is favoured by the wealthier classes. Vivek Singh of Procam Sports, a marketing agency, was certainly of the view that Doordashan was unlikely to be an effective means of promoting football and the companies that chose to associate with it, 'Who is going to make stars of Indian footballers? Not Doordarshan, of course. Without stars there is no charm in the game, without charm no sponsors and without sponsors no progress.'[37]

Unfortunately, the AIFF had signed a deal with ESPN-STAR to show the NFL and other important tournaments on the cable channel. But it changed its mind on the deal and handed the rights back to Doordarshan. This alleged breach of contract by the AIFF infuriated corporates and especially Philips whose sponsorship was linked to coverage on the channel.

This example points to the second factor that served to dampen corporate enthusiasm for football. This was the lackadaisical functioning of the AIFF. The perception that football was poorly organized and that its administrators were difficult to deal with is seen as a major reason why corporations quickly lost interest in Indian football. A number of clubs have openly criticized the Federation for its poor organization and the impact that this has on attempts to involve private companies. Babu Mather of FC Kochin complained that

> Sponsors are not coming forward because the Federation is least bothered about the development of the game ... They should have a professional marketing department and not contract with all and sundry marketing agents. Cricket, chess and tennis get enough sponsors. Why can't football which has such a large following? Things are far from encouraging for clubs like us, Churchill Brothers, Tollygunge Agragami, BMFC, etc.[38]

Krishnendu Sen, managing director of BMFC, is also critical of the AIFF's functioning,

> We lost Rs1.5 million in sponsorship money due to not being able to play in five major tournaments per year, mainly due to poor scheduling by the AIFF and discriminatory policies of some organizers ... Why should sponsors spend so much money when everything is so uncertain?[39]

BMFC were forced to miss the Sikkim Gold Cup in 1999–2000 because the AIFF had scheduled the Rovers Cup around the same time.

Sen pointed out that any attempt to implement modern systems in the planning of a football club were difficult due to the antiquated functioning of the AIFF,

> At the outset we wanted to be a self-dependent club, like those in Europe, without having to go to sponsors and donors with a begging bowl and folded hands. We planned to become self-financing and have our own ground, clubhouse, academy, etc. But we couldn't fulfil our objectives. We had new ideas but had to work within the old system which is rotten. Top corporates have told me they will not touch football because the AIFF continues to function the way it does.[40]

Company representatives similarly point to the poor performance of the AIFF. A company executive with a former sponsor of Indian football commented that,

> I don't want to do anything with the AIFF. As long as they mismanage their affairs no corporate will want to associate with them. But let's put it positively. If they improve their act they should have no difficulty in roping sponsors since football is a great game and has a lot of potential.[41]

Not that poor administration and mismanagement were features of the AIFF alone. Regional associations also showed themselves unable to meet the professional expectations of the companies that offered them sponsorship. The Western India FA lost the sponsorship for the local leagues because of financial irregularities. Vivek Singh, a director of the sports event firm Procam Sports Private Ltd which secured this sponsorship contract, lamented that 'Our Bombay experience is the microcosm of Indian football. Our clients, Gulf Oil, were completely disillusioned with the controversies that kept erupting from time to time and we had to do a lot of fire-fighting to pacify them.'[42]

The third reason for corporates to turn their backs on Indian football was the lure of cricket as a publicity vehicle in a country where the sport seems to dominate all others. Krishnendu Sen of FC Kochin recounted that, 'India Tobacco told me that if we have the budget we will sponsor cricket because returns there are definite.'[43] An embattled AIFF president Priya Ranjan Das Munshi raised the bogey of the game at an AIFF conference in Delhi in early 2000, 'Cricket is eating into football and is proving to be a hindrance to our progress. I have written to FIFA asking for help to bring football back to its glory.'[44] Das Munshi went on to claim at the same meeting that he had a sponsor for the Federation Cup (ultimately untrue), but that he would not divulge the name as he feared that cricket would snatch the deal away.

That cricket seems to dominate all other sport in India was emphatically confirmed by a *New GenerAsians* Cartoon Network market survey conducted across the Asia-Pacific rim between October and December 1999 by the marketing consultants A.C. Neilsen. The survey of children's social habits and preferences sampled 7,700 children aged between 7 and 18 in 29 cities and 12 countries in the region (Australia, New Zealand, China, Hong Kong, Taiwan,

TABLE 1
FAVOURITE SPORTS IN THE ASIA-PACIFIC REGION

Country	Boys	Girls
Australia	Australian rules football	netball
China	football	badminton
Hong Kong	football	badminton
India	cricket	badminton
Indonesia	football	jogging
Japan	football	badminton
Malaysia	football	badminton
New Zealand	rugby	netball
Philippines	basketball	volleyball
Singapore	basketball	swimming
South Korea	football	swimming
Taiwan	basketball	badminton
Thailand	football	swimming/badminton
Vietnam	football	badminton

Note: Tables 1, 2 and 3 draw on information from the Cartoon Network *New GenerAsians* survey.

Japan, Malaysia, Singapore, South Korea, Thailand, Vietnam and India) including over 2,045 youngsters in ten major cities of India. The basic requirement was home ownership of a colour TV, but a black and white one sufficed for India.

According to the survey, football is the most popular sport for boys in most countries of south-east Asia (see Table 1), as it is in West Asia and the Gulf.

Furthermore, footballers are the favourite sports personalities in several nations (Table 2). Asked to comment on the popularity of soccer in east Asian and south-east Asian countries Michael Church, editor of the Hong Kong-based *Football Asia*, explained,

> Football has a long tradition in places like Hong Kong, Malaysia, Indonesia (formerly the Dutch East Indies), Asia's first representatives at the World Cup in 1934. The game has caught the people's imagination. It's actually a surprise that basketball did so well in Singapore in the survey as football is very obviously the nation's favourite sport. Teams such as Manchester United, Liverpool and Arsenal have massive followings there, just as they have in Malaysia, Indonesia and Thailand. English football is broadcast live all over the region while in places like Thailand and the Manchester United magazine is published in the local language. The appetite for football is virtually insatiable.[45]

TABLE 2
FAVOURITE SPORTS PERSONALITIES IN THE ASIA-PACIFIC REGION

Country	Of Boys	Of Girls
Australia	Michael Jordan	Cathy Freeeman/Michael Jordan
China	Michael Jordan	Michael Jordan
Hong Kong	Ronaldo/Michael Jordan	David Beckham
India	Sachin Tendulkar	Sachin Tendulkar
Indonesia	David Beckham/Ronaldo	Susi Susanti
Japan	Hidetoshi Nakata	Hidetoshi Nakata
Malaysia	David Beckham	David Beckham
New Zealand	Jonah Lomuh	Jonah Lomuh
Philippines	Michael Jordan	Michael Jordan
Singapore	David Beckham	David Beckham
South Korea	Chan Park-Ho	Chan Park-Ho
Taiwan	Michael Jordan	Michael Jordan
Thailand	David Beckham	Sicco Kiatsak
Vietnam	Hong Son/Yunh Duc	Hong Sun

Football has become the major game for children in most Asian nations for a number of reasons. In countries such as Japan, Korea and China local associations have made a concerted effort to develop the game at that level in order to nurture their young players so that they shall succeed in the coming years. They have also developed heroes; Nakata in Japan is an obvious example, as are the Chinese players in Europe such as Fan Zhiyi at Crystal Palace and Yang Chen at Eintracht Frankfurt in Germany. The establishment of well-marketed professional leagues, such as the J-League in Japan, has also helped.[46]

In contrast, the Cartoon Network survey revealed that 82 per cent of the Indian boys quizzed said that cricket was their favourite sport. Football came a very distant second with just 3 per cent. For girls though, badminton was the first choice. Moreover, the favourite toy for Indian boys is a cricket bat and ball and Sachin Tendulkar is the most popular sports personality for both boys and girls, followed by the cricketers Saurav Ganguly, Ajay Jadeja, Rahul Dravid and Mohammed Azharuddin (Table 3).

TABLE 3
FAVOURITE SPORTS PERSONALITIES IN INDIA

Position	Of Boys	Of Girls
1	Sachin Tendulkar	Sachin Tendulkar
2	Saurav Ganguly	Saurav Ganguly
3	Ajay Jadeja	Ajay Jadeja
4	Rahul Dravid	Rahul Dravid
5	Mohammed Azharuddin	Mohammed Azharuddin

Cricket has even made inroads in Calcutta, the home of Indian football. Press reports highlight the sagging popularity of football in Calcutta[47] and of veteran footballers sending their children to cricket camps.[48] Goa too has seen cricket making inroads and posters of Tendulkar have displaced many of those of Beckham, Romario and Ronaldo in the beach shacks.[49] But the grass-roots reality, however, is not as bleak as the Cartoon Network survey suggests. The gap in participation at the school level in these two activities is narrow in Indian regions that have traditionally played football (Table 4).

TABLE 4
APPROXIMATE NUMBER OF SCHOOLS PLAYING CRICKET AND FOOTBALL AT
SELECTED CENTRES

Venue	Cricket	Football
Bangalore	129	70–80
Calcutta	48	20–30
Chennai	58	20–25
Delhi	15–40	50–55
Goa	234	215
Kochi	20–24	8
Mumbai	145	120

Sources: Bangalore: S. Vishwanath (*Deccan Herald*) and S. Sreekumar (*Times of India*); Calcutta: S. Sundar Ghosh (*The Statesman*); Chennai: S.R. Suryanarayan (*The Hindu*); Delhi: R. Sharma (*The Statesman*) and J. Basu (*Hindustan Times*); Goa: A..M. Mergulhao (*Herald*); Kochi: A. Vinod (*The Hindu*); Mumbai: Mumbai Schools Sports Association.

The reputation of cricket in India has recently suffered a considerable fall due to a series of exposures about match-fixing involving both internationals and Indians. The South African captain Hansie Cronje was exposed by the Delhi police as having been involved in match-fixing during the Proteas tour of India in early 2000. The Central Bureau of Investigation subsequently implicated Mohammed Azharuddin, Ajay Jadeja, Ajay Sharma and Manoj Prabhakar in the scandal and they received appropriate bans depending upon the extent of their involvement. The scandal has affected the marketability of cricket in India[50] and its attraction for potential sponsors.

Indeed, the author's own experience of covering sport in India suggests that cricket does not have an uncontested hold on the people. Having regularly attended domestic first-class cricket matches in western India in recent years, it seems that the game has virtually no following at this level. Many domestic first-class games, both of the limited and the non-limited over variety, which feature top players barely manage to draw 200 spectators. This is the case even in Mumbai, the home of Indian cricket. Cricket fever erupts only during international events and this because it is mainly media driven (however, Test Match attendances are also dwindling and only one-day internationals draw guaranteed crowds).

On the other hand, top club-level football matches are a big draw and clashes between the major clubs, say Salgaocar vs. Mohun Bagan in either Goa or Calcutta, or East Bengal vs. FC Kochin in Kerala, easily draw a minimum 15,000 spectators (see Tables 5 and 6; compare with Table 7). 'It is now becoming more and more obvious that domestic football is more popular than domestic cricket. One only has to visit the stadiums in Calcutta, Goa, Kerala and other cities where regional and national-level tournaments are held to realize this',[51] observed the Mahindras official Alan Durante. India currently holds the world record for the attendance at a football match between local teams as 131,783 fans packed the Salt Lake Stadium in Calcutta for the Federation Cup semi-final between Mohun Bagan and East Bengal on 13 July 1997.

To stress the gap between the pulling power of domestic football and of domestic cricket it is possible to compare the 1999–2000 national football and cricket finals (see Table 7), both featuring the host teams in action. The Santosh Trophy final between Maharashtra and Kerala at Trichur (Kerala) drew 40,000 with a few thousand stranded outside because the stadium was full.[52] The best attendance during the five-day Ranji Trophy final between Mumbai and Hyderabad at Mumbai was about 12,000 on the third day (see Table 8).[53] This was largely due to the fact that Tendulkar was expected to bat. As soon as he was out a large section of the crowd threw missiles on to the pitch and departed in frustration.

TABLE 5
ATTENDANCES AT SELECT NATIONAL FOOTBALL LEAGUE MATCHES, 1999–2000

Venue	Match	Attendance (000)
Bangalore	ITI vs. F C Kochin	15
Bangalore	ITI vs. Mohun Bagan	10
Calcutta	East Bengal vs. Mohun Bagan	50
Calcutta	Mohun Bagan vs. JCT Mills	45
Calcutta	Mohun Bagan vs. Churchill Brothers	45
Calcutta	Mohun Bagan vs. Salgaocar	40
Ludhiana	BSF vs. Mohun Bagan	5
Ludhiana	JCT Mills vs. Churchill Brothers	2
Ludhiana	JCT Mills vs. Mahindras	2
Margao	Salgaocar vs. Churchill Brothers	20
Margao	Churchill Brothers vs. East Bengal	25
Margao	Churchill Brothers vs. Mohun Bagan	25
Margao	Salgaocar vs. Mohun Bagan	25
Mumbai	Mahindras vs. Mohun Bagan	3.5
Mumbai	Mahindras vs. BSF	3
Kochi	FC Kochin vs. Churchill Brothers	35
Kochi	FC Kochin vs. Mahindras	25
Kochi	FC Kochin vs. Mahindras	25
Thiruvananthapuram	SBT vs. BSF	9
Thiruvananthapuram	SBT vs. East Bengal	7.5

Notes: NFL match attendance figures provided by Alberto Colaco, Chairman, NFL; ITI: Indian Telephone Industries; SBT: State Bank of Travancore; BSF: Border Security Force; JCT Mills: Jagatjit Cotton & Textile Mills

TABLE 6
ATTENDANCES AT SELECT FOOTBALL MATCHES, EARLY 2000–01

Venue	Match	Period	Teams	Attendance (000)
Pondicherry	Millennium Cup final	June 2000	SBT vs. Salgaocar	7–8[1]
Calcutta	McDowell Cup final	July 2000	Mohun Bagan vs. East Bengal	45[2]
Calcutta	Super League Derby	Sept. 2000	Mohun Bagan vs. East Bengal	80[3]
Calcutta	IFA Shield final	Sept. 2000	Mohun Bagan vs. East Bengal	78[4]
Mumbai	Super League Derby	Oct. 2000	Mahindra United vs. Air-India	2.5–3[5]
Sikkim	Governor's Gold Cup final	Oct. 2000	Mohun Bagan vs. Air-India	12–15[6]
New Delhi	Durand Cup final	Nov. 2000	Mahindra United vs. Mohun Bagan	15–20[7]

Notes: 1. S.R. Suryanarayan (*The Hindu & Sportstar*); 2. S. Sundar Ghosh (*The Statesman*, 1 July 2000); 3. *The Statesman*, 3 Sept. 2000; 4. *Hindustan Times*, 17 Sept. 2000; 5. Estimate by two reporters present; 6. Bimal Ghosh (Air-India coach); 7. Harish Rao (Mahindra United manager)

TABLE 7

FIRST-CLASS CRICKET ATTENDANCES AT SELECTED CENTRES, 1999–2000

Centre	Match	Type of Match	Daily Attendance
Mumbai	Mumbai vs. Maharashtra	Ranji Trophy zonal league	250–300
Mumbai	Mumbai vs. Saurashtra	Ranji Trophy zonal league	250–300
Mumbai	Mumbai vs. Rajasthan	Ranji Trophy super league	200
Mumbai	Mumbai vs. Tamil Nadu	Ranji Trophy semi-final	5,000*
Mumbai (one-day)	West Zone vs. Central Zone 500–600	Deodhar Trophy	
Mumbai	Mumbai vs. Maharashtra and Mumbai vs. Saurashtra	Ranji Trophy zonal One-day matches	300–350 per match
Chennai	All matches	Ranji Trophy	200–300
Chennai	All matches	Duleep Trophy	>1,000
Kozhikode	Kerala vs. Hyderabad	Ranji Trophy zonal one-day	8,000†
Kozhikode	Kerala vs. Hyderabad	Ranji Trophy zonal league	5,000†
Kerala (general)	Other one-day matches		2,000–3,000
Kerala (general)	Other Ranji Trophy, Duleep Trophy matches		1,000
Goa	All matches	Ranji, Duleep Trophy	50–60
Delhi	All matches	Ranji, Duleep Trophy, etc.	50–60
Bangalore	Matches featuring top teams		5,000–6,000
Bangalore	Matches featuring lesser teams		1,000–2,000

Sources: Mumbai: Prof. R. Shetty (joint honorary secretary, Mumbai Cricket Association); Bangalore: Brijesh Patel (honorary secretary, Karnataka Cricket Association) and Kaushik (*Deccan Herald*); Chennai: Ashok Kumbhat (honorary secretary, Tamil Nadu Cricket Association); Kerala: A. Vinod (*The Hindu* & *Sportstar*); Goa: Michael Siqueira (*Press Trust of India*); Delhi: John Cheeran (*Times Online*) and Manoj Vatsyayana (*Hindustan Times*)

* 10–12,000 when Tendulkar batted.

† These matches drew good crowds because of the presence of Mohammed Azharuddin, Hyderabad skipper, who became an anti-establishment hero of sorts during this period because the public perceived that he was being unfairly being kept out of the Indian team by the sports' authorities.

TABLE 8

ATTENDANCES AT FINALS OF NATIONAL CRICKET AND FOOTBALL CHAMPIONSHIPS

Venue	Opponents	Match	Attendance (000)
Mumbai	Mumbai vs. Hyderabad	Ranji Trophy (five-day match)	6 per day (10–12 when Tendulkar was batting)
Thrissur	Kerala vs. Maharashtra	Santosh Trophy	40 (2–3 outside due to full house)

Sources: Mumbai: Prof. R. Shetty (joint honorary secretary, Mumbai Cricket Association); Thrissur: A. Vinod (*The Hindu* & *Sportstar*)

CONCLUSION

The interest of large corporations in Indian football brought about immediate change as well as speeding up processes that had been transforming the game since the 1980s. Change came as clubs altered their names, acquired new owners with unfamiliar agendas and spent lavishly on new players. New clubs were founded to vie with the older institutions in competitions that now offered substantial prize moneys, but which were run by marketing firms rather than football administrators. The process of turning players into contracted professionals gathered pace and the Indian game became a more attractive market place in which footballers from around the world could sell themselves.

Yet despite these impacts the processes of change have met with a number of obstacles. The first of these is the AIFF, the body responsible for governing the game. An amateur body run by an Indian parliamentarian for the past 12 years, this organization is seen by many as responsible for the failure of corporate confidence in football that has hit Indian football finances in the new millennium. The second obstacle is the enduring appeal of cricket in India, which means that for the time being football's attraction to corporations looking for effective ways of promoting their products will remain limited.

Not that these obstacles necessarily mean that change in football in India will grind to a halt after the activity of the 1990s. As regards corporate money, it seems that once football administrators are able to demonstrate a capacity to effectively and transparently organize tournaments, private companies will show renewed interest in the sport. After good experiences in Goa and Kerala, where sponsorship of regional leagues was successful owing to good administration, Vivek Singh, of the marketing agency Procam Sports, claimed that there was no dearth of sponsors looking for well-managed events and good organizers,

> Corporates are hungry for big platforms and events which can capture the mind. They want the euphoria to last for some time. But sponsors now want below the line benefits (promotions, contests, etc.) and are not merely satisfied with above the line (media coverage) benefits.[54]

As regards the popularity of the game itself in India, this seems set to continue to grow from its solid historical base. Peter Velappan, Malaysian general secretary of the Asian Football Confederation, commented during a visit to Delhi that, 'India has a one billion population and 90 per cent of the population is still passionate about football. There is no reason why there cannot be a turnaround.'[55]

Quite simply then, football in India at the end of the 2000 season found itself caught in an uneasy state between the forces of the old and the new. The game was subjected in the 1990s to the processes of commercialization, professionalization and modernization, but the impact of these has been retarded and reshaped by the traditional pressures of bureaucratic and political interests and by cricket's enduring power. The next ten years promise to see football in India continuing to be caught in this conflict between the old and the new.

NOTES

1. For further details see P. Dimeo in this volume.
2. Private conversation with Parvez Ziauddin.
3. Email communication from Philips India Ltd spokesman.
4. In the region of £300,000. Although the rate of conversion has fluctuated, £1 has been worth about Rs60 throughout the 1990s and into the twenty-first century.
5. Sponsorship and prize money figures provided by Alberto Colaco, chairman, National Football League, in a private communication, 17 May 2000.
6. 'AIFF Makes Fresh Promises', *The Statesman*, 9 Dec. 1999.
7. This is discussed in more detail below.
8. S. Warrier, 'Mallya Bidding for Stakes in BMFC, FC Kochin', *The Times of India*, 22 Aug. 1999. The UB Group *did* sponsor FC Kochin in 2001
9. The answer was given in response to a question from the author at the press conference on 6 Dec. 2000.
10. Fax communication by Alan Durante in response to queries from the author. Durante enthused that this would help to raise all-round standards of organizing, executing and planning and would thus be able to popularize football following the Western mode of development. This in turn would attract more of the younger generation to the game because of better emoluments and amenities, and increase and improve the player base.
11. S. Warrier, 'Mahindras Are United Now', *The Times of India*, 4 May 2000.
12. M. Rodrigues, 'A First for Goan Football', *The Statesman (Mid-Week)*; report on the start of the professional league in Goa, 5 May 1999.
13. S. Sundar Ghosh, 'A Historic New for Maidan Soccer', *The Statesman*, 7 May 2000.
14. Press Trust of India report, 'Mohun Bagan Critical of Sponsors' Interference', *The Statesman*, 15 April 2000.
15. S. Sundar Ghosh, 'Electoral Politics Sole Concern', *The Statesman*, 20 May 2000.
16. 'Free Way for Biswas', *The Statesman*, 11 June 2000.
17. M. Rodrigues, 'Mere Sideshows!', *Mid-Week (The Statesman)*, 22 Dec. 1999.
18. From an interview with Henna Juneja released by the company's public relations agency on 28 Nov. 2000.
19. S. Sundar Ghosh, 'A Historic New for Maidan Soccer', *The Statesman*, 7 May 2000.
20. 'Blatter Lauds Mohun Bagan', *The Statesman*, 12 May 2000.
21. Telephone conversation with Krishnendu Sen.
22. 'Churchill Bros Tie Up with Zee Sports Ltd', *Herald*, 13 July 2000.
23. 'Zee Gets into Goan Soccer', *The Statesman*, 29 June 2000.
24. 'Arlem Group to Sponsor Vasco Sports Club', *Herald*, 9 July 2000.
25. M. Rodrigues, 'No Title Sponsor for Top Soccer Meets', *The Statesman*, 16 June 2000.
26. R. Menon, 'No Title Sponsors for Santosh Trophy', *Indian Express*, 6 April 2000.
27. A. Vinod, 'An "Official" Goof Up', *The Sportstar Magazine*, 5 May 2000.
28. 'AIFF Makes Fresh Promises', *The Statesman*, 9 Dec. 1999.
29. A. Biswas, 'Money for Kicks', *Outlook*, 24 April 2000.
30. S. Sunder Ghosh, 'Mighty Ones Fall, Minnows Rise', *The Statesman*, 7 June 2000.
31. R. Battacharjee, 'Gupta Seeks CBI Inquiry into AIFF Dealings', *The Times of India*, 8 June 2000.
32. Press Trust of India report, 'Coca-Cola Writes Down $400m Worth Assets in India', *The Times of India*, 6 April 2000.
33. Telephone conversation with the Babu Mather.
34. Email communication from a Philips India Ltd spokesman.
35. Ibid.
36. Telephone conversation with the Babu Mather.
37. Telephone conversation with Vivek Singh.
38. Telephone conversation with the Babu Mather.
39. Telephone conversation with Krishnendu Sen.
40. Ibid.
41. Telephone with an executive of a corporation that was until recently a major sponsor of football; the informant requested anonymity.
42. Interview with Vivek Singh.
43. Telephone conversation with Krishnendu Sen.

44. S. Warrier, 'High Drama at AIFF AGM', *The Times of India*, 11 Feb. 2000.
45. Email communication from Michael Church, editor, *Football Asia*.
46. Ibid.
47. United News of India report, 'Soccer Popularity in Calcutta Sagging', *Herald*, 18 Aug. 2000.
48. Kashinath, 'Lineage Goes Haywire!', *The Statesman (Midweek)*, 2 Feb. 2000.
49. R. da Cunha, 'We Like Cricket, Men', *Bombay Times*, 31 March 2000.
50. A.R. Verman, 'Scandal Doesn't Sell Cricket', *The Statesman*, 6 Sept. 2000.
51. Fax communication by Alan Durante in response to queries by the author.
52. Match attendance figures for the Santosh Trophy final provided by A. Vinod, who covered the tournament for *The Hindu/The Sportstar*.
53. Match attendance figures for the Ranji Trophy final provided by Prof. Ratnakar Shetty, joint honorary secretary of the Mumbai Cricket Association.
54. Conversation with Vivek Singh.
55. 'AFC Names Uzbek Coach for India', *The Statesman*, 6 March 2000.

7

'There are such talents in India':
Future Footballers of India – Problems
and Possibilities

BILL ADAMS

I've gone through this trade without much football schooling. Nobody taught me how to pass or how to trap a ball.

Baichung Bhutia[1]

Baichung Bhutia, India's captain during the tour of the UK in July 2000 and south Asian football's first major export to the professional leagues of Europe, learnt to play football without the benefit of modern coaching. This is a common story for players across India. Sukhdev Arwade, who was the Golden Boot winner in the Goan League in the 1998–99, recalled that he picked up the game simply through playing with his friends. From them he learnt the skills of the trade and picked up the motivation to succeed, 'my friends [in Curtorim] always provoked and insulted me because of my technique and said I would never rise to become a good player ... then I had a reason to play and practise football hard.'[2]

Of course, the process of learning the game from friends as a youngster and of developing skills throughout adolescence is not unique to the players mentioned and these experiences are no doubt common to those who play football the world over. This study will argue, however, that the development of young footballers and the emergence of talent are particularly difficult in India because of a number of obstacles peculiar to the society and the infrastructure of the country. It will also argue that certain examples and models are available in India that suggest that these obstacles are not insurmountable. Indeed, these examples and models point to the fact that it should be possible to develop structures that would encourage mass participation in football in India's cities and its villages while also serving the interests of the most talented young players.

CHILDHOOD IN INDIA

Children and the Labour Force

All Indians, regardless of income, greatly value education and almost all want at least their male children to be educated (98 per cent of parents declared such ambitions in the 1999 Public Report on Basic Education).[3] However, a significant minority of children receive no education at all and most attend school only for a very limited period before dropping out. The average Indian adult has spent less than 2.4 years in education[4] during his or her lifetime, and both the 1991 census and the National Family Health Survey of 1992–93 found that less than 30 per cent of all adults had completed eight years of schooling.[5] At this time a third of all children between the ages of six and 14 were out of school[6] and it has been calculated that 70 per cent of children may be considered as not having spent a childhood in school.[7]

This situation is not likely to change in the near future. Despite the rhetoric of the Independence period, there seems to have been little political will to broaden the base of education. Recent government statements have begun to change the focus towards simply achieving literacy rather than providing education across the country. However, that in itself is not without problems since in many areas simply being able to read and write your own name merits a classification as literate. It seems that for many Indians childhood will continue to be unaffected by education and educational institutions in coming years.

Children are, however, active members of the Indian workforce. It has been estimated that up to 10 per cent of India's children might be considered to be members of the full-time workforce,[8] and that the remainder of those outside education work an average 4.2 hours per day.[9] There is a danger nevertheless in over-exaggerating the nature of child labour in India and in representing the burden of work on Indian children of low-income groups as being one that excludes them from participation in leisure or educational activities.

> Available data on labour force participation [from the Census, the national sample survey, the PROBE survey and related sources] clearly indicate that only a small minority of children are full-time labourers. Second, these statements misrepresent the nature of the work performed by child labourers. The vast majority of child labourers work as family labourers in the home or in the fields, not as wage labourers.[10]

It seems that those not at school have much time which could be used in leisure or educational pursuits. The leisure time of such children actually compares favourably with that of their colleagues who receive some form of education since it has been estimated that even those in school work on average about two hours a day on top of the time that they spend on their studies.[11] It is the case then that many Indian children are actively engaged in the labour force, but it would be wrong to assume that the majority of these are full-time workers and that they have no leisure time.

Shortage of space for recreation is a difficulty faced by Indian children outside education. In the last 15 years the changing patterns in the rural and urban economies have resulted in an increased exodus to the cities from rural areas. Delhi, for example, has grown by 80 per cent in the last decade and is predicted to continue to expand at a faster rate in the next ten years. Land is at a premium in all the cities and a lack of plots for building is particularly acute in Delhi and Mumbai, where land prices are among the highest in the world and the authorities have an almost constant programme of razing unauthorized buildings. More and more young people are growing up in cities that are marked by this unprecedented demand for land. City-centre plots are contested between the builders of luxury housing and facilities for the urban elites and those new arrivals in the cities unable to afford established housing who therefore opt to settle with their fellow immigrants in the makeshift *jhuggis*. Huge areas of the cities have been taken over by poor people from the rural areas and slum clusters can be found in almost every area of the city. For example, the land adjoining the Nehru Stadium in Delhi contains one such cluster that houses several thousand rural poor, mostly from the villages of Bihar and the United Provinces. Quite simply, in these cities where land is so much in demand for housing and business premises there is little priority given to space for recreation.

Where sites are consciously developed to provide leisure space these areas are reserved for middle-class activities. Free spaces are beautified in order to provide routes for the promenading and socializing of well-to-do families. Throughout all the cities this policy is followed to a greater or lesser extent. For example, the 15 small parks of the Defence Colony in Delhi were subject to a 'beautification drive' in 1999. As such, flower beds, 'ornamental' features, and walk ways for the elderly replaced green open spaces where children could play.

Indeed, those sports facilities that are available are maintained by the elite classes for their own use. The largest and best football pitch in Delhi is to be found at the Siri Fort Sports Complex, where the fees prohibit all but the wealthy middle classes from using it. The irony is that these people rarely use the pitch except for the occasional week-long tournament and it has not been used consistently for years. This is despite the fact that the Delhi FA has only two pitches available to it on which to organize its leagues and cup tournaments in the entire city.[12]

In short, the place of low-income and low-status children in Indian society means that it is difficult for them to actively engage with football. They have little or no long-term contact with educational institutions, which means that they are unlikely to have learnt the sport at school or to have been encouraged to participate in a representative team. Most of these children are engaged in work, although the burden of this on their lives must not be exaggerated since few can be counted as full-time labourers. Instead, most help their families or communities in the day-to-day chores of running households and small holdings in such capacities as errand-runner, child-minder, goat- and cow-herder or stop-gap labouring assistant. While the average Indian child spends a little over four hours a day on such duties, he or she is expected to be the most flexible member of the household labour force and thus has an unplanned and *ad hoc* schedule. Indian children from the lower-income and lower-status groups therefore do have large amounts of spare time, but they do not have access to organized play. In the cities it is also increasingly difficult for Indian children to find places to spend this leisure time as land is gobbled up for the housing of the poor or for the recreation of the rich.

The poverty of these children is another major factor. Unskilled labourers in the cities earn in the region of Rs30 to Rs50 per day and far less in the rural areas and small towns.[13] A cheap football would cost in the region of Rs120. Football can flourish even in the most deprived of areas as long as there is the space and time to kick about an inexpensive ball. In many circumstances, however, Indian children outside education are deprived of many or of all of these things.

Children and the Schools System

Those children who do attend schools in India are far from a uniform mass enjoying a common experience of education. Outside the elite network of schools that charge sizeable fees for an education based on English public school models, the quality of the service on offer varies wildly from school to school. The Public Report on Basic Education estimated that the average number of children per class in India is almost 50. It concluded that up to 80 per cent of teachers in the Indian education system are untrained.

When considering the facilities at the schools at the lower end of the educational range the report found significant shortcomings. Of the government-supported schools 59 per cent did not have a playground. For privately-funded schools the figure was even higher, numbering almost 70 per cent. In short, the report found that children attending schools outside the elite sector were often in institutions where teachers were not trained in the most rudimentary of subjects, let alone qualified to teach sporting subjects. The lack of trained supervisors was not the only obstacle to the schools acting as a focus for developing an interest in sport. The fact that the majority of schools at this level lacked access to the space in which to encourage participation in physical activities and in games meant that the opportunity for children to learn the rules and techniques of modern sports through their educational institution was severely limited by lack of suitable resources.

Children at the tiny number of elite schools do not face all of these obstacles. Often set in extensive grounds, many of the elite residential schools offer a vision of rolling playing fields and an organized sports curriculum. The Assam School, for example, has almost 500 acres of grounds around the school buildings and marks out five football pitches for its 500 students. Yet these schools also have a number of features that serve to discourage either a broad interest in football among their students or the development of talent among their more promising members.

The origins of the schools in the period of British rule and their development as centres designed to train obedient Indians to help to run the empire in south

Asia continue to exert an influence in post-Independence India.[14] These schools were based on the public schools of Britain and were Christian, militaristic and distinguishable by their discipline. The regime of these institutions was based on the prefect system and the time devoted to physical education (PE). The culture of physical education placed much emphasis on response to orders and personal fitness. Through marching and the system of stationary exercises included under the label 'drill' children were taught to follow orders without question. Great emphasis was also placed on endurance. The aim was to produce physically fit men able to take on many different and challenging physical activities. Boxing, football, cricket, hockey, athletics, gymnastics, swimming and 'drill' all found their way into the physical education syllabus of these schools. A very full calendar was therefore introduced to accommodate all of these diverse sports which sought to produce children prepared to undergo diverse physical rigours on the orders of their superiors. The objective was the amateur all-rounder rather than the specialized sportsman. Fitness, discipline and obedience were required for the running of an empire in Asia rather than any specialist sports skills or specific knowledge.

The elite schools of independent India continue to regard sports in ways that would not have been unfamiliar to the British of a century ago. The all-rounder is still seen as more desirable than the skilled specialist. Football is only one of many sports at such schools and has to continue to find a place in the school calendar alongside other activities such as cricket, boxing, squash, shooting, athletics, swimming and hockey. This means that, while football may be allocated seven months of the year in the British school sports schedule, it ends up occupying less than six weeks of the Indian schoolboy's annual cycle. This six weeks is typically spent selecting and preparing a team for a tournament, after which it is disbanded and similar efforts are then made to begin choosing one for the next activity on the sports calendar.

These schools also continue to allot much of the time devoted to PE to preparation for the annual prestige events such as Founder's Day and Prize Day. To promote separateness and elitism, the British introduced these public displays of pomp and ceremony and these have been retained by the elite schools. Such days were not simply the culmination of academic or sporting calendars. They were events designed to display the virtues of organization and discipline inculcated at the schools. Their objective was, and still is, to impress parents and to assert the authority of the school on the locals. All are an excuse for pomp and ceremony marked by well-drilled march pasts and salutes. For these to succeed in impressing they need to be well-rehearsed and meticulously executed. This means that large amounts of the time allocated to PE are used in preparation for the special days of the school year. In addition to the time spent on these activities, the schools also allow for the numerous religious and national holidays and days of national celebration in India. The combination of days allocated to the preparations for ceremonial events and the frequent days off means that even the periods devoted to one sporting activity are often fragmented and disrupted.

As a range of sports are included on the school schedule in the year there is a lack of specifically trained coaches for any one sport. There is no teacher-training programme in India that includes a specialized football-teaching module. Until recently Doon School, among the most prestigious in India, allowed its football training to be taken by one of the biology teachers. This is a common problem across the elite school sector, although a few schools, such as Sherwood School in Nanital, have always had a specialist football teacher and have recently begun to use Sports Authority of India (SAI) coaches in their programmes. Although a significant development, this is not without its problems since SAI coaches lack up-to-date coaching knowledge and are hampered by an out-of-date coaching curriculum.

The PE curriculum is also a problem faced by teachers and pupils involved in football coaching at the elite schools. The PE syllabus and almost all of the teaching in Indian schools would not be out of place in the schools of the British system of the 1930s. For instance, according to the Indian Council for Secondary Education (ICSE), one of the examination boards responsible for testing sports achievement in schools, those taking football as an optional sport under the PE programme in 2002 will need to demonstrate an understanding of the 'Two Back System/Three Back System' and must also show a knowledge of what the ICSE call 'tactics of defence and attachment' [*sic*].[15] The language of the 'two back system' and the tactics of 'attachment' recall an era of pre-Second World War international football and indicate the need for a thorough revision of the football curriculum in schools to be complemented by a system of syllabus maintenance to reflect developments in the modern game.[16]

Unlike other countries, India does not have any organization to cater specifically for school or youth football development and this has led to many other anomalies. Often football teachers are unaware of rule changes within the sport. For example, in 1998 the author went to a prestigious residential public school to organize workshops for teachers responsible for football training there. The teachers asked for the latest copy of the laws of the game because, even though they knew that there was a change in the off-side rule during the 1990s, they did not know what it was. Without access to the internet or updated literature and with no organization responsible for informing them most schools and teachers have to rely on anecdotal sources.

Even where sport is taken seriously by schools there are hurdles to the proper development of football among young players. The culture of the elite schools is such that success in competition is seen as a reflection on the status of the school and the need to win is often placed above all other considerations. For instance, it is common in the most prestigious nationwide, schoolboy football competition, the Subruto Cup, for the finalists to cheat by including players who are many years past school age. In 1999 the tournament was won by Mamta Modern School despite the fact that the team had lost a number of players during the tournament since they had been disqualified by the organizers for being over age. Disqualification of over-age players is a regular occurrence and almost every year the organizers disqualify members of the winning school squad for being too old, and yet these same teams continue to enter and reach the final stages. When one of the organizers was asked why it was that teams that had cheated were allowed back in the competition year after year, he stated that if all the teams that resorted to such practices were disqualified there would not be enough entrants left for a competition. Even in friendly local school matches such practices are not uncommon and reputable schools have numerous stories about other institutions fielding over-aged players and indulging in blatant gamesmanship, often to the detriment of small and vulnerable children.[17]

Elsewhere though sport is not taken so seriously and many schools see periods allotted in the timetable to physical activities as privileges to be withdrawn from errant pupils rather than as educational opportunities for the students. Indeed, when it comes to the serious business of examinations the allocation of school time to any type of formal PE and of leisure time to personal sporting activities is seen as frivolous luxury to be seriously curtailed in the drive for sustained success. In part this is understandable, given the ferocious competition for college places. Entry marks for a good university average 85 per cent and above and competition is so fierce that it is not unusual for tens of thousands to apply for a few hundred places. This problem faces all prestigious colleges and is particularly acute with those that have good reputations such as St. Stephen's in Delhi, the National Institute of Fashion Technology (NIFT), the National Institute of Design (NID) and all the five internationally-renowned Indian Institutes of Technology (IITs).[18] Children start serious study for college places at the beginning of class 9, when most children are 14 years old, and almost all sporting activities are restricted from that age on. At the Delhi Super Soccer Academy (SSA) the impact of this is obvious since during class 9 attendance begins to drop off. In class 10 there is little or no attendance while in class 11 (when there is a break in the examinations for Indian children) groups turning up to train reach the sizes of pre-class 9 levels. But in class 12 no one comes. The neglect of late childhood physical activity will continue as numbers studying for classes 10 and 12 continue to rise and university places on offer do not keep up with the increasing demand for tertiary-level education.[19]

Quite simply, the Indian education system presents a range of obstacles to the development of both mass participation and individual talent in football. Students at lower ranking institutions face a lack of trained staff and adequate facilities. As was mentioned earlier, they are also expected to work with their families in the household or in business outside school hours and this naturally limits the time that they can devote to non-work activities. Finally, the demands of pursuing success in examinations during their teenage years means that space in the student's schedule for recreation is more likely to be devoted to rest than to developing football skills.

Elite institutions do not suffer from a lack of facilities and consciously include football in their fragmented sports curricula. But the lack of specialist football coaches and of training programmes to develop such staff, together with the jumbled PE calendar, mean that football receives little sustained attention at elite schools. The culture of many such institutions also militates against a concerted effort to develop footballers as such schools either simply regard sport as fun to be withheld as a punishment or they feel that immediate victory in competitions is so important that they resort to underhanded schemes to ensure a win rather than focus on the long-term development of good teams. Of course, the students of the elite schools must also succeed in their examinations so they come to find that the time available in the formative period of their teenage years is more wisely spent in revision than in football practice. In short, the development of football among India's youth faces a number of significant obstacles associated with the lifestyles and educational institutions of India.

INSTITUTIONS AS OBSTACLES

Appearing bitter about the facilities at the Sports Authority of India Eastern Regional Centre, the venue of the coaching camp, the Uzbeki coach said, 'I am not at all satisfied with the arrangements. It has been a painful experience.'[20]

Thirty-nine-year-old Islam Akhmedov of Uzbekistan was on his first assignment as coach of India's youth team when he made these comments. His criticisms point to another set of obstacles in the way of youth football in India, that of the problems associated with the agencies that ought to be responsible for its development.

The most obvious problem with these is that there is a proliferation of bodies that might have responsibility for football schemes and talent development for young Indians. In India the All India Football Federation (AIFF) is nominally in charge of the game in the country but youth football on a national level is traditionally supervised by another institution, the Sports Authority of India (SAI). This body controls most of the venues in India and is also responsible for training and certifying football coaches in the country. The Central Education Ministry, however, is responsible for the PE syllabus taught in schools and through this controls what students ought to know about football. Matters are further complicated by the role of state governments in determining sports/football education policies in their separate jurisdictions and by the State Soccer Associations that organize competitions and sponsorship for youth schemes in their own regions.

There might have been a positive side to these arrangements if the several bodies had a predilection for working together. However, this is not the case. For example in 2001 the SAI has at its head a minister of the ruling political party, while the AIFF has been dominated by the opposition and its chief whip Priya Ranjan Das Munshi for over a decade. In 1999, when FIFA came to inject cash into youth football development in India, it naturally turned to the AIFF as its Indian affiliate. FIFA gave $250,000 to the organization, which, in the circumstances, was a flawed decision. In India the AIFF has no direct control over the training, placement or deployment of youth football coaches that are, in fact, under the control of the SAI. Also, the AIFF has no control over the teaching or training of young football players in schools or for state-level representative teams. Thus the AIFF has neither the capabilities nor the affiliates to enable it to devise and execute a national football development policy. However, the AIFF did not allocate funds from the FIFA donation to bodies that did have access to youth football. Exactly what did happen to the money remains the subject of some controversy and of a court case brought by the secretary of the Calcutta affiliate of the AIFF. This alleges corruption and misappropriation of funds by the AIFF president. In response to calls for a youth development policy, some members of the AIFF have advocated a system of regional academies and the employment of local coaches. The problems with the academy system are discussed below, but it certainly seems to be the case that the proliferation of bodies with some responsibility for youth football and the lack of exchange between these bodies mean that it is difficult to target resources and reform effectively.

The nature of these bodies is also a problem. The AIFF might stand as an example here since the problems with lack of accountability and poor strategic planning are well documented.[21] Indeed, such are the problems with this body that in 2000 the leading clubs formed the Indian Premier Football Association (IPFA) to challenge the power of the AIFF, citing financial mismanagement as their reasons for doing so. Islam Akhmedov, the Uzbeki coach mentioned above, was part of the Asian Football Confederation's (AFC) most recent attempt to force reform on the AIFF. Originally appointed in early 1999 to train the senior team, it was announced by the AIFF within days of his appointment that, contrary to their previous statement, he would train the junior Indian football teams and not the senior squad. This was despite the fact that Akhmedov was recommended by the AFC, which had said the AIFF had agreed not to interfere with his functioning.[22] Peter Velappan of the AFC subsequently revealed that it had asked the AIFF to centralize key activities in New Delhi by appointing professionals to handle administration and communications, technical development and the management of the national teams. It had insisted that AIFF finances should be audited to leave no room for any suspicion.[23] The AFC also expressed concern over the National Football League that Velappan viewed as in 'dire need of help'. Hence the AIFF has a poor reputation both within India and in the international football community for its handling of the game.

Not that the national football bodies in India are the only sources of frustration in the administration of the game. The author's own experiences of having teams excluded from the Delhi Soccer League show that the state associations also often have other objectives than simply the advancement of the game. In September 1999 the author was approached by a group of Delhi businessmen to set up and to coach a team in the Delhi league. They would provide financing and Bishop Cotton School Old Boys would supply the administration. Former players from the school would form the nucleus of the team and a leading international sports company would supply all the kit. The author wrote to the Delhi Soccer Association (DSA) in September 1999 seeking admission to the league. On 13 October the Association responded. It said that the proposed team could not be considered as the DSA did not have enough pitches for existing members. There were, in fact, only two pitches for use by the Delhi League. It stated that, in view of this lack of pitches, the applications of at least ten clubs had not been accepted. On 15 October the author responded by pointing out that the new team could bring a pitch with it and that the author had the use of three other pitches and could find yet others for any other team that needed one. Nearly six months later on 31 March 2000 the DSA responded by refusing the offer of pitches and by adding the club to the queue already awaiting admission,

> Thanks for the help and cooperation extended by you for securing the playing fields for the activities of the Delhi Soccer Association. In this connection, I would like to inform you that the policy of the Association is to act independently without involving outside Agencies.[24]

The Greater Delhi region has a population in excess of that of the Netherlands. The Delhi Soccer League has only 20 existing teams in two divisions (though some cannot field 11 players in each match throughout the season). The 'season' lasts less than a month. Despite at least 20 pitches being available in the city, the DSA uses only two pitches for the Delhi League. Both are SAI pitches. One of these (in the warm-up area of the Nehru Stadium) is too small to conform to the laws of the game and is subsequently marked out wrongly since the penalty areas have been shrunk to fit. Quite simply, the vested interests of the existing football clubs and their power over the DSA means that new teams and new facilities are never allowed to challenge them.

The stranglehold of the DSA and the existing clubs on the game at the state level provides a disincentive for young players to continue with the game beyond their childhood experiences. As most of the existing clubs are linked to institutions such as the police or to other government departments, players find it difficult to get into teams unless they are willing to take jobs with these institutions. Clubs that are simply football teams with no government organization behind them are rare so that there are few opportunities for the young player simply looking to play football. 'What is the point of taking up soccer in school if my child cannot find a team to play for after schooling is finished?' was a question one Super Soccer Academy parent asked when talking about this issue.

In short, the development of youth football faces obstacles from the football organizations that operate in India. The first problem is that of the proliferation of these bodies so that internal efforts are disjointed and lack coordination and external attempts to rejuvenate the system founder on the question of which organization to support. The second is the nature of the bodies themselves, which are often accused of being inefficient and plagued by agendas that have little to do with the development of football.

DEVELOPMENT POSSIBILITIES: MODELS AND EXAMPLES

Football Academies

> There are such talents in India, there are some very good players ... the frustration is that we've got lots of interest in football, but nobody in India is really bothering to do anything with it.
>
> Baichung Bhutia[25]

There is an increasing awareness within the Indian game that the existing systems are not succeeding and that alternatives might usefully be considered. For those who wish to respond to Baichung's complaint and who plan to try to do something about India's future footballers the question remains of how to go about developing the game.

One model available is that of regional academies. The AIFF and the AFC recently announced in a series of press releases that they were considering the development of a system of regional academies that will be set up to act as magnets for, and as the means of developing, talented young footballers. There has been some speculation that these might be similar to the Tata Football Academy (TFA). However, others have suggested that they will be similar to those attached to professional clubs in the United Kingdom and elsewhere in Europe. Whichever one is considered both models will need to be considerably modified to achieve any substantial success. When considering the establishment of regional academies it is worthwhile examining the success and shortcomings of the TFA.

The Tata Football Academy is a residential academy situated in Jamshedpur. It was conceived in 1983 and inaugurated in 1987. The objective of the institution is 'to provide the mainstream of national football with a perennial pool of young footballers trained and orientated to international standards'.[26] As such, promising youngsters aged about 14 are recruited from selected tournaments and trained for four years. After graduation it is hoped that they will seek a career in professional football. The TFA not only provides football training but also all-round developmental opportunities with facilities for formal education and vocational training, 'The fully residential programme includes special features such as free board and lodging, a handsome monthly stipend, free playing kits, free summer and winter clothing, ceremonial kits, comprehensive medical care, free education, a group insurance scheme and other benefits.'[27]

The Academy boasts a swimming pool, gymnasium, conference facilities and all the amenities associated with a modern football training institution. Selected TFA cadets are regularly sent to major international institutions such as the Sports University of Cologne and foreign coaches are invited to the Academy. Capital costs were around Rs9 crores and the Academy has an annual budget of Rs60 lakhs.[28]

The TFA initially achieved a modicum of success and many clubs were quick to sign up TFA graduates. However, in recent years the promising youngsters of the TFA have failed to outshine those who had not benefited from this great expenditure. Cost cutting at the TFA has resulted in staff cuts and the remaining coaches find it necessary to perform two or more functions. Despite its best efforts, the Academy has been plagued with numerous over-aged applicants seeking the relative luxury of the institution and the lucrative contracts which come from graduation as a promising 18-year-old.

Though the Tata Football Academy was a valiant effort it has not achieved the breakthrough success that was hoped for. Incorporating the most senior coaches in India, it has failed to produce any truly outstanding players. In the process it has swallowed up massive amounts of Tata finance (estimated at over £1 million). Assuming that the proposed regional academies cost comparable amounts it is necessary to consider whether this is likely to be a sensible use of important financing.

Regional centres dealing with those selected as the most talented youngsters are not a new idea in India. For years the SAI has been choosing the 'best young players' and giving them weekly coaching at their stadiums and centres throughout India but with little impact. New academies would simply suffer from the existing problems of Indian football that have limited the SAI scheme and have, to a certain extent, dogged the Tata Academy. These problems lie in two main areas. The first is the player base from which academies and training schemes can select their recruits. In areas outside the main football playing areas of West Bengal, Goa, Kerala and to a lesser extent the north-east, there is not a large pool of talented children from which the academies would be able to recruit annually because football is not regularly played as part of local culture. In areas where football has a popular following clubs are already going into schools, identifying promising children and giving them professional coaching.

The second major impediment in these areas is a lack of coaches with up-to-date knowledge and the necessary motivational and communication skills. New academies in these areas, unless exceptionally well-funded and able to acquire foreign staff, would end up by relying on the existing coaches that are already working with youngsters. Many of these coaches are not highly educated, they have poor teaching and planning skills and few have been subject to programmes of on-going training and assessment. Thus there is nothing to allay the suspicion that such academies would simply be old wine in expensive new bottles, with the same badly prepared staff teaching outdated tactics to another crop of technically poor students.

Such regional academies as are being contemplated do, however, suit the style of Indian sports politics because grandiose, high capital schemes provide good publicity. Less ostentatious, small-scale, long-term projects do not give immediate photo opportunities. The danger is that the foundation of high cost regional academies is driven by political considerations rather than those of India's football future.

The Delhi Super Soccer Academy

The Delhi-based Super Soccer Academy is a possible model for developing youth football. Established in 1998, it was intended to be a self-financing, low cost operation. The primary aim of the SSA is to develop modern football in India. Having started with one coach and one assistant, the intention is that in each year it will be possible to double the number of coaches. Now in its third year, the Academy employs four young coaches all of whom have been trained in modern coaching and teaching methodologies. The coaching syllabus is based on the English FA's model and uses the English FA Soccer Star Assessment Scheme. Coaching strategies used include the use of videos and multi-media materials supplied from Britain and Holland. Recently the Academy linked up with a local school where it is integrating a football development syllabus from Australia into the curriculum. Each year, through participating schools, summer camps and weekend classes, it has held regular coaching sessions for approximately 500 children.

The SSA does not select on the basis of talent, nor does it accept sponsorship from corporate bodies, preferring to maintain its independence. Instead it seeks partnership relationships with organizations working to promote the introduction of modern football into India. It has good relations with several corporate and educational organizations in India,[29] in Britain and in Australia. From the start it was made clear that the SSA intended to succeed by distancing itself from existing bureaucratic football associations and organizations. Experience has proved this to be an important strategy, and organizations that have made it sponsorship or partnership offers have expressly stated that the distance of the SSA from India's football bodies is a reason for their involvement.

The SSA was founded to provide football coaching and training for boys and girls between seven and 18 years old and to run training courses, workshops and seminars for school sports teachers. It was set up to be self-financing and profit is not the motive since all revenue is reinvested in football development. Instead of a purpose-built establishment costing many thousands of rupees it uses the grounds of existing public schools. The SSA has developed three main strategies.

For the children of the rich the SSA holds school-based soccer camps in Delhi at weekends, after school hours and during the holidays. Run in the same way as similar football coaching academies in Britain, such as the Bobby Charlton Academy, the coaching sessions are paid for by the students. Since they bear the cost of the coaching, the school saves money in terms of the salaries of coaches and the cost of coaching aids. Also, participating schools are eligible for free places for their sports teachers at the training workshops given by the SSA each year. These are designed to complement the work of the SSA and cover topics such as the teaching of football skills, coaching skills for sports teachers and the integrating of football into the curriculum. Of course, only students from prestigious schools can afford the fees for this after-school coaching.

The second initiative that the SSA has set up is the Summer Camp at Saat-tal and at Mukteshwar in the Himalayas. These are run in partnership with Wildrift Adventure Camps. These camps are highly successful and in the third year of operation the SSA had to turn applicants away because demand far outstripped the number of places (over 90 per cent of those who go on the camps sign up for the following year). The camps take place every May and numbers are restricted to 28 children per camp. Each camp provides three hours of football every day and a range of other activities that include swimming, fishing, volleyball, forest treks and educational workshops. The camps are attended by wealthy school students between the ages of seven and 16 who pay fees for the experience.

However, the camps are also intended to promote football among the youth of the local villages. For instance, at Saat-tal[30] the SSA has built a full-size pitch complete with regulation-size goals. The pitch is in a natural stadium formed by a dried-up glacial lake and is surrounded by steep banks of pine forest. To build and maintain the pitch the SSA used local labour and every day during the camp free coaching workshops were held for the local youth. Those attending in this capacity join in the games with the fee-paying children. At the end of the camps the SSA is careful to donate sets of football balls so that the local youths can continue to play until the next summer. In 2000 two children left behind their football boots for the local children.[31] In this way the SSA has provided resources and coaching for football for both rich and poor, urban and rural, and has broken down social barriers and provided employment for local youths.

The third initiative that the SSA has undertaken is the provision of consultancy advice to educational organizations wishing to develop and update their football coaching systems. The SSA are working closely with Schoolnet India Ltd to devise syllabuses and promote modern PE throughout India. The SSA is retained by the Bishop Cotton School, Simla, to train both its staff and its pupils. This involves a month-long camp every summer, while for the rest of the year a football newsletter, hand-outs and lesson plans are provided to update and develop the staff responsible for soccer education at the school. This contract is now in its third year and the school has won the Bhupinder Singh Memorial Trophy for the last two years. The school senior team has now graduated to playing college and Army sides. For the Shri Ram School, Delhi, the SSA has entered into an agreement to upgrade and reorganize the whole of the institution's PE syllabus. With the help of Australian educationalists, the Academy is introducing aspects of the Australian PE curriculum into the school.[32]

This includes the whole of the Australian soccer development programme that runs all the way through the school from age six to 18.

The problems of the SSA have tended to come when it has tried to find places for its graduate players in existing football organizations in India. In the first year of its existence two young players were identified as having exceptional ability. These boys were turning up for weekly coaching every Saturday but there was no opportunity for them to play regular football throughout the year since they came from a small school without a team. The SSA contacted the SAI and applied for places for the players on a SAI coaching scheme. The letter and its follow up were ignored. A third letter to the senior bureaucrat in charge elicited a standardized response which ignored the specific request and simply stated that the SAI ran coaching schemes for all sports including football. The two boys never received an assessment let alone extra coaching or exposure. However, in the summer of 2000 the two were taken to Bradford City FC in Britain. They were given a trial and encouragingly told to come back the following year. The boys were then given the opportunity to trial in the USA. Included in a batch of a hundred trialists for the Colorado State team (under 14s) both were among the four eventually accepted. As a result of this they spent the summer training and playing in Colorado. That it is easier to arrange trials of promising young Indian players from the SSA in the USA and Britain than it is in Delhi highlights some of the problems discussed above regarding the football institutions of India.

CONCLUSIONS

The obstacles in the way of developing football among the young of India are numerous and have been detailed here. Indian children have a range of demands on their time and find themselves in places and situations where sport is a luxury. Even where they are able to find the time and the space to play games, it seems that the organizations that could be responsible for encouraging them to learn and to love football are failing them. Lifestyles and existing football agencies limit the access that children have to football and football coaching.

It must be made clear, however, that despite the demands on the time and attention of Indian children it is not impossible to attract them to organized games and to have them enthusiastically engage with sport in general and with football in particular. For example, since the foundation of the SSA three other after-school football coaching organizations have been established. There is also the case of the American School in Delhi. This has formed a Soccer Little League where games are designed to be enjoyable for children and where one objective is to involve the parents in sport and to encourage them to engage their children in football. Over 500 children participate. At a different social level, Reebok sponsor an event every year to encourage the lower income groups of the city to come together in sport. On successive Sundays over several weeks of the year the lower income groups congregate at the Nehru Stadium in Delhi to take part in a range of athletic races and sporting activities. Heats are held and the eventual winners receive small cash prizes (Rs300). The events are very popular with hundreds of people participating. The SSA's summer camps at Saat-tal and Mukteshwar demonstrate that a desire to participate is not limited to the metropolitan areas and that young people in the small towns and villages can be just as enthusiastic about football.

These schemes and the experiences of the author at the SSA demonstrate two important points about the youth of India and the future of football. The first is that, despite the range of other calls on their time, young Indians do enjoy engaging in sport and that football in particular has popular appeal. Greater efforts to promote it would secure mass participation in the sport. The second point is that Baichung Bhutia is correct when suggesting that there are some exceptionally talented young players in India and that the country has its fair share of potential professional players. In short, the development of youth football schemes in India would promise to produce both the widespread playing of the game and a crop of exceptional players for the professional leagues.

As has been stated, one key obstacle to the development of football participation among children is the failure of the existing football organizations. As these have proved resistant to any type of reform, a new agency has been set up which will specifically deal with youth football. This organization, the Indian Youth Soccer Association (IYSA), will address itself to the different types of childhood experience in India and will work with the three youth constituencies identified here. These are the children out of school but not in full-time employment, children in government/low-status private schools and finally those in elite educational institutions. The objectives of the organization are to encourage participation in football among Indian youth, to regulate existing youth football and to promote and develop opportunities for competitive school football.

At each level the IYSA will establish appropriate organizations and provide equipment and support. At the elite level this might include organizing and officiating at youth tournaments to eradicate such malpractices as the playing of older players in age-group teams. At government school level this will involve helping parents to gain experience in establishing after-school clubs and organizing local mini-leagues. For non-school children regular football fairs might be held to attract attention to the sport and to encourage people to establish non-school-based teams for entry into the mini-leagues.[33]

The IYSA is seeking affiliation to the AIFF but will be independent of it and its regional affiliates in terms of management and operation. Its executive committee is made up of high profile representatives of the corporate sector and progressive sports-orientated educationalists. The administrative functions will be the responsibility of professional, qualified managers with expertise in modern administrative systems. To ensure the non-politicization of the organization, the IYSA is being funded primarily through corporate sponsorship rather than government grants. Politicians and bureaucrats will not be allowed to hold office even in an honorary capacity. The registration of the organization as a charitable trust has been completed and it was due to be operational by the end of 2000.

It may well be the case that there are many obstacles in the way of young Indians of whatever class or caste who want to learn football and enjoy playing it. But while there is the desire to learn and there is that ability to play, and as there are more and more people willing to plan ways around the difficulties, it is possible to imagine these obstacles being overcome and a range of new opportunities presenting themselves to the future footballers of India.

NOTES

The title is taken from A. Vinod, 'A Case of Indifference to the Actual Cause', *The Hindu*, 8 April 2000.

1. A. Vinod, 'A Case of Indifference to the Actual Cause', *The Hindu*, 8 April 2000. A copy of the article may be found at www.indianfootball.com
2. For details see J. Mills in this volume.
3. The PROBE TEAM in Association with the Centre for Development Economics, *The Public Report on Basic Education in India* (New Delhi: Oxford University Press, 1999), p.14, Chart 2.7.
4. Ibid., p.16, Chart 2.9.
5. Ibid., p.9.
6. Ibid.
7. Ibid.
8. Ibid., p.16 Chart 2.8.
9. Ibid., p.16. Chart 2.9
10. Ibid., p.16.
11. Ibid.
12. The author of this article had an application to enter a team in the Delhi League rejected owing to a shortage of pitches.
13. The approximate conversion rate is Rs60 to £1.
14. For an indicative example of these schools and their impact see J.A. Mangan in this volume.
15. *Indian School Certificate Examination, Regulations and Syllabus* (New Delhi: Indian Council for Secondary Education, 1999), p.194.
16. The author has been approached by the ICSE to advise on updating the football curriculum.
17. The author, for his first game in India, took a team of 10 and 11-year-olds to play a prestigious school in Delhi. The other team were all nearly 6 ft tall and some sported moustaches. Bribing the referee, excluding the other team's supporters/parents and selecting opposition teams that are sure to be beaten are common practices.
18. There are five IITs in India. and these have a combined annual intake of 2,500 students. Over a million people make initial approaches to these colleges and hundreds of thousands make application for these places.
19. College places that required 62 per cent at class 12 around 20 years ago now require an average pass of 83 per cent or more (for instance, Lady Shri Ram College, Delhi. Eng. Lit.). Each year all the colleges publish their cut-off marks and each year they rise. St. Steven's College Delhi, where I have coached football, had a cut-off mark of 90 per cent for all their honour courses in 1999.
20. Press Trust of India (PTI), 'Akhhmadov Confident of Winning Qualifiers', *The Times of India*, 26 May 2000.
21. See for example M. Rodrigues, in this volume; Vinod, 'A Case of Indifference'.
22. Reported by Arunava Chaudhuri in 'News for the Day', www.indianfootball.com, 7 March 2000.
23. Report by Aruanava Chaudhuri, 'News of the Day', www.indianfootball.com, 9 March 2000.
24. Quoted from a letter to me from DSA Honorary Secretary, Syed Nasir Ali, 31 March 2000. Subsequent to my application, and realizing that new members would not be allowed into the League, I moved on. Sadly, so has the financing and administrative support for a new club.
25. Vinod, 'A Case of Indifference'.
26. Tata Football Academy Brochure, 'Out of Small Wonders We Make Great Stars' (Jamshedpur: TFA), p.9.

27. Ibid., p.10.
28. One crore is equal to 10,000, one lakh is equal to 100,000.
29. For instance, with the ICSE, Schoolnet Ltd, such schools as Bishop Cotton and Shri Ram, educational organizations such as TEACH, commercial organizations such as Wildrift, Clintus and Reebok, and with football clubs such as Simla Young Ones.
30. The Hindi word 'saat' means 'seven'; 'tal' means 'lake'.
31. The local youths are very poor, many of them play barefoot. The first year our football posts disappeared, they had been taken for firewood. Subsequently we built our goalposts of water pipes. These are inexpensive, of an ideal circumference and are available in many villages in the mountains.
32. The author is an adviser/trainer for a Delhi-based organization called TEACH. This exists to further educational development through links/exchanges with teachers in other countries. It has exchanges with teachers/principals from Western Australia. A PE expert named Rachel Marwick from Western Australia is supplying the author with the required advice, curricula information and lesson plans. Other advice and background material are forthcoming from the Australian High Commission in Delhi which has a scheme to introduce elements of Australian fitness training into the Indian system free of charge.
33. An India Youth Soccer Association website is being constructed. In the interim the author will supply full details of the organization on request.

8

Talent Identification and Development in Indian Football

JOHN HAMMOND

INTRODUCTION

This study aims to present a number of systems by which the identification and development of talent within Indian football might be promoted. The contribution by Bill Adams showed that there were a number of obstacles in the way of the development of young footballing talent and it began to explore engagement with football through the school system and a broad organizational base. The model suggested here is aimed at football development beyond this 'grass-roots' level and has as its main objective the production of elite players for the professional game and the Indian national team.

The study is significant since it is in many ways a response to the problems identified by delegates at the conference 'Football India: the Past, Present and Future', held in July 2000 at University College Northampton. A number of those present were concerned with the lack of an overall strategy in Indian football and with the rather piecemeal and localized nature of development. Suggestions, including the greater involvement of foreign coaches from the non-resident Indian diaspora and the foundation of football academies, seemed limited by the reliance on the poor quality of the systems which fed these elite levels in the first place. The development of football academies and the experience of foreign coaches may be beneficial but only if set at the end of a programme that successfully and consistently identifies, nurtures and develops talent throughout the age groups to be fed into these institutions and programmes.

The model outlined here draws upon the author's experience of coaching in Australia. Indian football now shares many characteristics with Australian football in the 1970s, when the sporting authorities there implemented a successful talent identification and development programme. Clearly India will have many differences from the Australian context, but the study aims to provide an example showing that countries where football is not the national sport and where organizational coherence is initially limited can implement a centrally planned programme that in the long term can produce talented individuals and a national team capable of success.

The study is organized into five main sections. The first gives some background information about the experience of the author to provide both a context for this model and a sense of the author's experiences. The second is a short description of Australian soccer development and history[1] which describes how the sport there developed from a game played by migrants to the present day, when the Australian national team enjoys considerable success. Education of coaches and coach development is a vital part of progress in any sport and the third section addresses these aspects, with particular reference to the lessons that can be learned by Indian football administrators from the Australian experience. Equally important, if not more so, is player development in terms of both talent identification and talent development; these issues are discussed in the fourth and the fifth sections.

CONTEXT

The author's knowledge of the Australian model for coach and player development comes from 25 years of experience in Australian soccer development from the early 1970s to the late 1990s. That experience included coaching, coach education and sports administration. In terms of coaching, the author was coach or manager to Western Australian teams competing in national championships on six occasions. During the mid 1980s he acted as coordinator of the Western Australian Institute of Sport Soccer squad for three years, which was directly linked to the Australian Institute of Sport. In 1985 he also acted as a national selector for the junior squad that toured China in 1986. In addition, he was a staff coach with the Australian Soccer Federation (ASF) from 1975 until 1998 and instructed on more than 200 coaching courses at Levels 1, 2 and 3.[2]

AUSTRALIAN SOCCER

Australia's first international match was played against New Zealand in 1922 at Dunedin, a match that New Zealand won 3–1. This defeat indicated the weaknesses in Australian soccer and it was not until after the Second World War that some international recognition was achieved. The nation's greatest football successes have been in the Olympic arena. Sydney 2000 was the fifth time that Australia had participated in the football tournament in the Olympic Games. The first of these came in 1956 in Melbourne, where they qualified as host nation. After defeating Japan 2–0 in the opening round, the Australians found the Indians too hard to handle in the next round and lost 4–2. The result of that encounter is significant since it is shows that the Indian football team were superior to Australia at that stage. Since then, however, Australians have made significant advances, whereas the Indian team have failed to capitalize on their post-war successes.[3]

The highlight of Australia's successes on the international stage was the qualification for the 1974 World Cup finals. This is the only time that the team achieved this feat. This success came before the implementation of a soccer development strategy. A 0–0 draw with Chile was followed by defeats by the strong European teams of West Germany (0–3) and East Germany (0–2). West Germany were the tournament hosts and the eventual winners and so this defeat was far from a disgrace.

The next time Australia qualified for the Olympics was over 30 years after Melbourne, when they got through to the Seoul Olympics in 1988. Australia caused one of the biggest shocks of the tournament by beating the favourites Yugoslavia. A further victory over Nigeria ensured that they qualified for the quarter-finals, at which stage they were beaten by 0–3 by the Soviet Union.

Australia's involvement in the Olympics continued, but a change in the format for the 1992 Barcelona Games meant that only players under 23 years of age were eligible to play. Australia caused another sensation by beating Holland in the qualifying rounds, thanks to a Ned Zelic goal. By this time it had become commonplace that top Australian-born players such as Zelic were playing for European clubs. In Barcelona the team went on to distinguish themselves by reaching the semi-finals and narrowly missed a bronze medal after losing 0–1 to Ghana. For the 1996 Atlanta Olympics the format changed again, this time to allow three over-age players to join the squad. Having overcome Canada to qualify, Australia faced a difficult group which included France and Spain. Needing to beat Spain to qualify for the next phase, the 'Olyroos' let a two–goal advantage slip and lost to the highly regarded Spanish team.

Australia's path to the 2000 Olympics was, as in 1956, made easier by virtue of being host nation with automatic qualification. With most of the team now plying their trade with top sides in Europe, the chances of winning a medal seemed high, despite a draw in a taxing group. However, a combination of poor form and injuries to top players saw the team have their worst showing in Olympic finals for some time.

THE DOMESTIC COMPETITION

The National Soccer League (NSL), which was established in 1977 by a consortium of clubs based in the southern and the eastern states (Adelaide, Melbourne, Sydney, Newcastle and Brisbane), currently numbers 16 teams. It was set up to enhance the level of play in domestic competition which, until then, had been focused at state level and which was often dominated by the bigger clubs. Currently, the League includes teams from Perth, Adelaide, the eastern seaboard cities (where nine teams are based) and from New Zealand, home to one of the League's newest clubs, the Football Kingz.[4] The NSL has proved immensely popular, for instance, Perth Glory and Northern Spirit (Sydney) both attract crowds of over 20,000. Meanwhile South Melbourne, a club that has recently won two consecutive league championships, represented the Oceania region at the inaugural FIFA World Club Championship held in 1999 in Rio de Janeiro.

Such players as Mark Bosnich, Mark Viduka, Ned Zelic, Paul Okon, Kevin Muscat and Stan Lazaridis, who are all established players in European teams, all started in the NSL. It is expected that the next generation of players, including Brett Emerton, Danny Milosevic, Simon Colosimo and Jacob Burns, will emulate their more experienced international team-mates. The establishment of the nation-wide NSL, alongside a proper development system at all age levels, has had a profound effect. In the previous domestic competitions, relatively few Australian-born players were able to make the transition to top-level European football. Clearly there has been a significant rise in the quality of players coming through the Australian system.

The 1999–2000 NSL season has left many with glorious memories, including a record-breaking crowd for the Grand Final, between the Wollongong Wolves and Perth Glory in Perth, of over 30,000. This proved a fitting climax to a season of record-breaking attendance for the competition as a whole, with over 1.2 million spectators watching games during the regular season. Highlights also included guest appearances from former overseas internationals, including Ian Rush and Peter Beardsley, the passing of the NSL's highest goal tally by the former Adelaide City and Socceroo striker Damian Mori, and the emergence of successful, regionally-based teams led by the Wollongong Wolves.

With the recently forged partnership between the NSL and the International Entertainment Corporation (IEC), which encompasses sponsorship and marketing rights for the NSL, there will be an investment of some $A21 million (about £8 million) into the game over the next seven years. This level of sponsorship has never been seen in Australian soccer before and indicates the sustained growth of the sport. While soccer will always expect to play second fiddle to Australian Rules (in Perth, Melbourne and Adelaide) and Rugby League (in Sydney and Brisbane), it has cornered a substantial niche market in its attraction for migrant communities from Europe and Asia. It is now firmly in second place around the country to the main football code in each state with respect to spectator appeal, and its participation rates are higher than for any other winter sport except netball.[5]

The foresight of that investment coupled with improved playing standards, which demonstrated the talent on offer in last season's Grand Final, and an expected post-Olympic boost as some of the world's finest footballing nations display the world game on Australian soil, sees the game well placed to climb to new heights in the coming years. Undoubtedly, these are the consequences of a coherent long-term planning strategy which began with the establishment of the National League, and continued as the League expanded geographically from Western Australia and across the Tasman Sea to New Zealand. It focused on all the levels and provided a balanced approach to football development. It has led to a situation where a coherent strategy is being developed between the game's administration, the clubs and the sponsors. These types of relationship can flourish in an environment of good organization, efficient use of resources and collective developmental goals. Strategic purpose is combined with pragmatic management. India, by comparison, has faced problems in this respect despite the fact that, as with Australia, there has been considerable commercial interest in sponsoring the game.[6]

Indeed, a comparison with India is important as there are a number of similarities between the game in Australia and that in India. The histories of league organization in Australia and that in India bear comparison. Until the 1996 National Football League was created, Indian football was organized regionally, with the states hosting their own leagues, and the only national competition being at state level. Before the establishment of the Australian NSL, the domestic competition was similarly based on the states, with only Melbourne and Sydney having a competition that could have been considered equal to the lower leagues in Europe at the time, for example, the then fourth division of the English Football League. The players in the national team were usually drawn from these dominant cities and, in fact, the Indian national team continues to be dominated by members of teams from Calcutta and Goa.

Furthermore, football in India has a number of competitors for the attention of sports players as does the game in Australia. Field hockey has a long tradition in Indian culture, although its attraction is less than that of the rival football codes in Australia. Cricket has huge appeal in both countries, but the seasonal nature of cricket and football sees them coexisting around the world in relative harmony. In short, football in India and Australia do resemble one another in various ways and at various points in their separate development. The question remains then as to why the game in Australia is currently thriving whereas the present and future of Indian football are so troubled.

COACHING AND COACH DEVELOPMENT

The tendency to view overseas coaches as more accomplished than those already in the system is evident in most countries where football is regarded as developing. This should be resisted as a wholesale solution to the improvement of coaching in India and, indeed, the experience of importing coaches to India has not been especially good.[7] Australian soccer suffered from the influx of 'football mercenaries' in the 1960s and the 1970s brought about by affluent club presidents keen for a quick-fix for their club. While a flurry of publicity surrounded appointments such as those of Tommy Docherty or Ferenc Puskas as national league coaches in the 1980s, their influence on the development of Australian soccer was minimal. The same could not be said for the money they would have made on what was essentially a working holiday. An illustration of the lasting strength of the propensity to view the overseas coach as automatically better was the appointment of Terry Venables as national coach. He was employed for 18 months in this capacity even though his predecessor had acquitted himself admirably in the role. Venables did not even live in Australia during that time and he took more than double the previous coach's annual salary (at around \$A400,000 or £160,000), despite failing in the bid to get the team to the World Cup finals in 1998.

While Docherty and Venables could be viewed as soccer mercenaries who left behind no lasting contribution, the employment of foreign professional coach educators by the governing bodies of soccer did give the game a legacy of structured development which formed the basis of today's arrangements. The lesson to be drawn is that a well-thought-out role for foreign coaches, based on the long-term development of the foundations of soccer development, will bring a greater reward than the bringing in of a high profile national team manager. Such an approach also proves to be considerably cheaper.

The influence of professional coach educators from Britain imported to run 'The National Soccer Coaching Scheme' is a case in point. The establishment of the national scheme was led by Eric Worthington, who was appointed as National Director of Coaching in 1973 direct from Britain. The scheme became a catalyst for Australian coach education and player development and an exemplar for other sports in the country. The then Australian Soccer Federation was responsible for Worthington's appointment and the scheme was funded by commercial sponsorship and government sports grants. A former professional footballer with Watford, Worthington was an FA staff coach and senior lecturer in physical education at the University of Loughborough. Soon after, the state soccer federations followed the ASF's example by appointing their own full-time directors of coaching who were also funded through sponsorship and/or government grants. These state directors of coaching, also with educational qualifications and FA coaching credentials, were, in the main, committed to life in Australia and therefore the effect of their appointments was long lasting. Before the 'Worthington Scheme', individual states ran accreditation courses through their associations, but this was piecemeal and somewhat nepotistic. The new system was not based on personality but on a sound administrative, developmental and educational structure that could be implemented and adapted within the ever-changing environment of modern sport.

The objective of Worthington's coaching scheme was that it should generate a cohort of well-versed coaches who could continue the promotion and development of the game and who would base their work on sound organizational methods. Clearly the practical measures designed to achieve this were a success. By generating an appropriate number of qualified coaches at all levels the scheme could be self-perpetuating in that future coach educators would come from the ranks of those achieving the most senior of the qualification levels. For instance, the scheme produced Jim Selby who is the present National Coaching and Development Manager. He is a product of the coach education scheme that was set up by Worthington and succeeded him as the head of Australia's coach education programme.

However, coaching and coach education have, in turn, changed with the development of a national coaching network for all sports in Australia since the inception of the Worthington Scheme. Selby responded to these changes by enhancing the soccer coaching education system to consider the needs of beginner coaches and changes in coaching methods. Selby says that, 'after carrying out extensive research all over Australia with junior league coaches, club and federation secretaries, all the way through to directors of coaching',[8] he came to the conclusion that the established system was too top-heavy for both players and coaches. Rather than focus on the elite level, the new system caters more for the broader base of the sport in that 98 per cent of Australian soccer players are not in the elite category and therefore a similar proportion of coaches will be operating at the grass-roots level. Consequently the coaching scheme needs to reflect this and to cater for coaches who may be dealing with the less talented players, even though they may still be keen to improve through good coaching.

Selby claims that the new scheme has been such a success that the Oceania Federation is also considering adopting it to encourage more people to become involved at all levels. Although figures for new participation in football since the scheme was launched are not available yet, there has been a significant rise in the number of enquiries from coaches and the number of juniors participating is also continuing to rise sharply. He also suggests that previous pass rates on some coaching courses were too low because the delivery was too demanding of coaches' time. The new system lets coaches plan their education and accreditation schedule into more manageable segments. Selby adds that, as a result, there is a much higher return rate of coaches to complete the next level of qualification and that this is encouraging because there is a growing need for coaches, especially at a junior level.[9] Soccer as a sport is growing quickly in Australia, the total number of juniors playing has increased from just 250,000 to about 480,000 and it is necessary to establish an equivalent growth in the number of trained coaches.

Selby's initiative has been adopted by both Soccer Australia (formerly the ASF) and the state federations. It represents the first real change to the coaching scheme since 1973. It is designed to make football more enjoyable for players and coaches of all levels. In essence, it has changed the accreditation system for coaches by providing more manageable pathways to the next level of qualification, which encourages a higher return rate. This development means that the system set up by Eric Worthington, which was based on the English FA's coaching scheme of the day, has now evolved into an Australian system that has adapted to the needs of Australian soccer and to Australian conditions.

With the success of the 2000 Olympic Games and of its international football competition, which proved extremely popular, the high profile start to the new year's NSL and a number of players now signed to prestigious European clubs, Australian interest in soccer is clearly growing. It is important to understand the relationship of the different levels of development. The success of Australia at the top levels is not essential in building a grass-roots of support for football in the country. India might learn from this. The balance must be struck between the often contradictory objectives of youth talent development, increasing the game's popularity, making the sport attractive to sponsors and the media, creating a cadre of top-class players who can join elite foreign clubs, and making the national team a success. The 2000 Olympics may have been a disappointment for the 'Olyroos', and the 'Socceroos' may not have yet qualified for another World Cup, but the sport is popular and many talented players are emerging. Obviously the popularity of players such as Harry Kewell and Mark Viduka will create excellent role models for Australian youngsters. However, making the game easier and more enjoyable at a lower level is equally important.[10] It is this that the recent changes in the coaching scheme aims to achieve, so that the popularity of the sport developed through the media exposure of Australia's best soccer products may be matched by the enjoyment that the ordinary player will get from participating in it.

These developments within Australia indicate that 'home-grown' coaches should be produced as soon as possible. This experience should affect the development of an Indian coaching scheme so that the standards of Indian football coaching can be established to suit the local conditions and also be perpetuated. A properly planned and implemented education scheme to develop qualified coaches is essential in that process. In addition, the early development of 'staff coaches' to provide instruction is vital to the success of such a scheme. This produces something of a dilemma if there are not already coaches in place who can act as instructors. To bridge this immediate gap in the early stages instruction could come from FIFA coaching development courses which are provided almost free of charge to countries where soccer is still developing.

As indicated earlier, once the staff coaches (or coach educators) are in place the coaching scheme can flourish and be supported from within, provided that some supporting infrastructure is established for guidance in the early years for inexperienced coach instructors. This would probably be facilitated by the appointment of a national and some regional directors of coaching in a similar way to that in Australia. These people would need to be full-time appointments and be remunerated appropriately, as would other professionals in India. The Australian experience saw the state directors of coaching receive salaries similar to those of the best paid schoolteachers and the national director of coaching similar to those of middle management in the public service. All the positions were also supported with expense allowances for the extensive travel which was required in these positions.

COACHING LEVELS

Any coach education scheme should be cognisant of players' needs in terms of coaching methods and approaches. It should provide a spectrum of coaches from the junior club coach or school team coach through to those who aspire to become professional coaches. It is generally accepted that at least three levels of qualification or licence should be established. Each level provides a prerequisite for the next, that is, any given level is dependent on the knowledge and skills gained at the lower level. In addition, the length of the courses that need to be attended to reach a certain level is incremental, for example, level one may be 12 to 18 hours in duration, whereas level three could be a week-long course.

In terms of content and objective, obviously each level has a particular focus and target group. These are outlined below.

Level One, sometimes known as the foundation or preliminary level, is for coaches of juniors and for teachers. It should focus on fun and participation through soccer and should also include some basic understanding of the growing child. Courses at this level should be no longer than 18 hours in total and assessment should be low key and achievable. The syllabus would include instruction about the technical aspects of passing, heading, receiving the ball, dribbling and tackling, as well as basic approaches to coaching and the organizing of young players in worthwhile experiences that enhance those techniques.

Level Two is for those who may be coaching senior amateur and/or representative teams. It should focus on the coaching of sound technical skills and expanding the knowledge of basic techniques to more sophisticated forms, such as volleying or screening the ball when in possession. The course should provide an introduction to the principles of team play and aim to help players to make the right decision in different contexts during a game. It should also provide a fundamental understanding of sport science as well as the management of the injured player. This intermediate level qualification may be split into two or three stages, as in the new Australian system, but would last for around 30 to 40 hours in total. There should be a more formal assessment to examine and extend the coaches' knowledge and skills.

Level Three should be aimed at professional and elite development, and should focus on enhancing technical skill, tactics and strategy. It should total around 10 to 12 days of full-time attendance, once again in segments where appropriate, and its assessment should be rigorous and demanding. The syllabus would focus on the coaching of group and team skills and would provide the participant with the knowledge required of a professional or national-level coach. The all-round management of a group of players or a club could also be included in this third tier, but the final content and outcomes for the course should be a natural progression from level two and developed for the Indian setting.

Funding to support courses could come from sponsorship, from within the game itself and/or from government sporting grants. However, it would usually be expected that participants should also pay a fee to attend the course, which would cover the cost of administration, notes or course texts and the production of certificates. The length of the course and the status of the coaching level attained should be reflected in the cost of enrolment. Conversely, there is an argument that advocates that the initial courses should be offered as cheaply as possible in order to encourage volunteer coaches to attend. This issue should be discussed by the coaching directors when setting up a coaching scheme. Clearly, the Indian situation would differ. Many coaches would be unable to fund their own coaching education. Funding from the football authorities or from clubs should be in place to encourage widespread participation.

TALENT IDENTIFICATION

Skilful players can be identified by experienced and objective observers who watch them in training sessions and matches. More often than not, educated football coaches are best suited to this task. Those with less experience of the technical aspects of football, even keen fans, do not make the best judges of a player's technical ability. In addition, those with close personal connections with potential players are usually too involved with the situation to make an objective judgement. However, real comparisons can only be made in the competitive situation where there is some consistency in the standards of both teams so that players of similar ability may be matched against each other. It is easy to catch the eye of the inexperienced observer if a player is playing well below his standard and dominating a game.

One way of ensuring that players find their level is to establish a hierarchy of zones and regions, based on geographical and soccer populations. Each of these ought to produce representative teams. These teams then play annually in competitive 'talent ID' competitions that provide the opportunity for systematic observation by regional and national coaches.[11] In Australia Harry Kewell, the current Leeds United striker, was identified through this system.

A model of this type of system can be seen in Figure 1. Players are first selected to represent their geographical zones and play in a championship, which satisfies two needs. The first is for competition against teams of a similar standard and the second is the opportunity for the talent scouts to view players in competitive football. To this end, geographical zoning can be the starting point, but the playing population base is also vital.

Given that teams who represent a similar sized playing population are likely to be relatively evenly matched then the player catchment for zones should reflect this. As the players progress from one level to the next, they will get closer to being more evenly matched with their team-mates and opponents. Although there may be fluctuations in using this principle at lower levels, at the regional level players are more likely to be of a similar standard. Therefore at national championship level the national squad may be selected with some confidence that the best players are on show in a competitive environment. This is an opportunity that talented players often lack in a developing soccer nation. In addition, the more evenly matched the players are the easier it is for the talent identification process to be sure that players are being adequately tested as they display their skills.

A cautionary note should be made here with regard to the investment required to establish a talent identification scheme like this. In Australia the scheme works because there is governmental support for elite sport and at the

FIGURE 1
TALENT IDENTIFICATION – THE REGIONAL MODEL

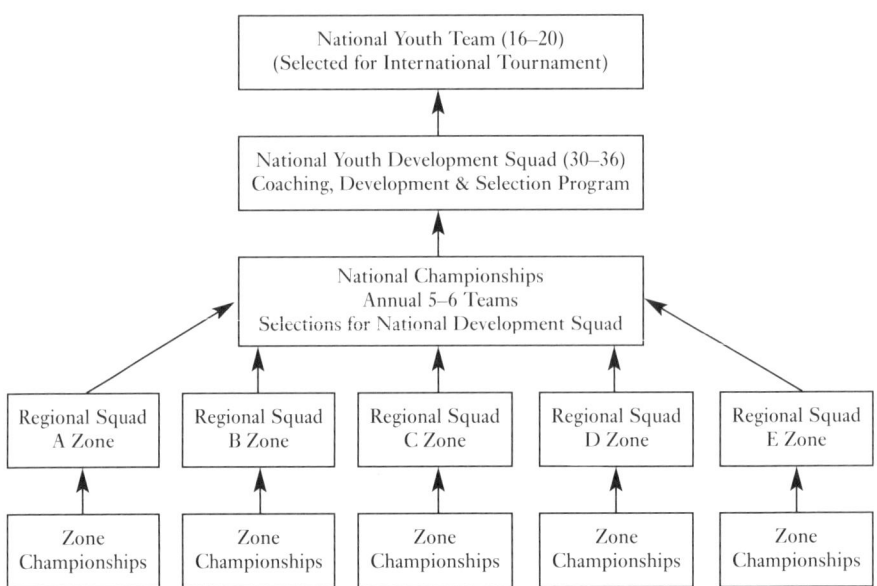

lower and the middle representative level there is considerable local community and parental support for aspiring young footballers. The relatively affluent socio-economic climate in Australia facilitates this supportive atmosphere so the talent scheme will work. In India there is a different socio-economic base and the issue of resourcing such a scheme would be a major factor in its adoption.

The use of a talent identification model such as this depends almost solely on systematic observation of the players at each level. While such observation can be taught to a certain extent, there will always be some subjectivity, as with any human judgements. Therefore aids to the identification of success on the field would make the process that much more objective. For instance, the simple noting of statistics may be used in match analysis, focusing on individual players, and in recording aspects of the game such as passes completed, shots at goal and tackles made.[12] More sophisticated methods can also be adopted, such as notational analysis,[13] using computers and video footage to record players' achievements and to highlight important attributes. However, in the absence of sophisticated talent identification systems, the trained observer, in the form of an experienced coach, is best suited for the task. But the identification of talented players in itself is only part of the process and talent development should also be planned for and implemented systematically.

TALENT DEVELOPMENT

Talent identification and development are inextricably linked and any programme should be designed with this in mind. For instance, the opportunity for players to receive more advanced coaching with regional or national squads would accompany their identification and selection at each level. Therefore a number of principles concerning the selection of players for the next stage may be seen as guiding both talent identification and the development process.

Players should be sorted on skill first[14] at the lower levels of identification. Emphasis on physical stature and prowess may see highly skilled individuals being overlooked. The maturation process for young players is such that there could be up to four years difference in skeletal maturity in players of the same age. Consequently, the late developer may appear to be physically incapable of coping with the higher level of soccer, yet inclusion in development squads with some protection in competitive situations may be more appropriate. The game is littered with players who were able to dominate matches at junior level because of their size but, in fact, had poor levels of skill. These children are usually overtaken by their more skilled peers after the growth spurt occurs during the teenage years.

Once sorted on the basis of skill then other issues come into play, depending on the level of the development programme. Certainly, despite being highly skilled, a player whose physical stature gives him a distinct disadvantage may need to be protected in the competitive situation to avoid injury and the demotivating effects of not being able to compete. However, late maturers can be included in development squads and introduced into the competitive situation more gradually.

Conversely, the eventual body size and body type may be particularly important for certain positions. Goalkeepers need to be taller than their colleagues and to have the build to withstand some physical contact with the more robust forwards. Central defenders are often required to be dominant in the air and so taller players also have an advantage in that position. Although there are notable exceptions to these rough profiles, typical physiques have been identified for specialist positions in team games.[15]

Assuming that physical maturation has neared its conclusion, levels of physical fitness, power and strength may be used to select regional and national squads. Certainly, those physical capacities that are more inherent and less likely to respond significantly to training, such as speed, can be used in the selection. Even capacities that can be greatly enhanced by training, such as endurance, can be used to exclude players temporarily, with advice about programmes that would bring them to the necessary levels for high level performance.

AN ACADEMY MODEL FOR TALENT DEVELOPMENT

The effect of the programmes of the Australian Institute of Sport (AIS) that have produced so many world-class athletes would be familiar to most sporting enthusiasts. In soccer, 201 players have passed through the AIS soccer programme from 1981 until 1998.[16] Ninety-seven have become Australian youth internationals, 36 have played for the Australian Olympic team and 28 for the full national side.[17] Many AIS players have pursued successful overseas careers in the sport, including Frank Farina, Ned Zelic, Danny Milosevic, Mark Viduka and Alistair Edwards.

An 'academy' model for talent development may be seen in Figure 2. The model proposed here follows similar principles and organization to the Australian talent development system. Used in conjunction with the talent identification system recommended here, this academy-style development programme starts at the local level with preferably weekly programmes for players still at school through to full-time programmes for elite players aged between 16 and 19.

FIGURE 2
TALENT DEVELOPMENT – THE REGIONAL MODEL

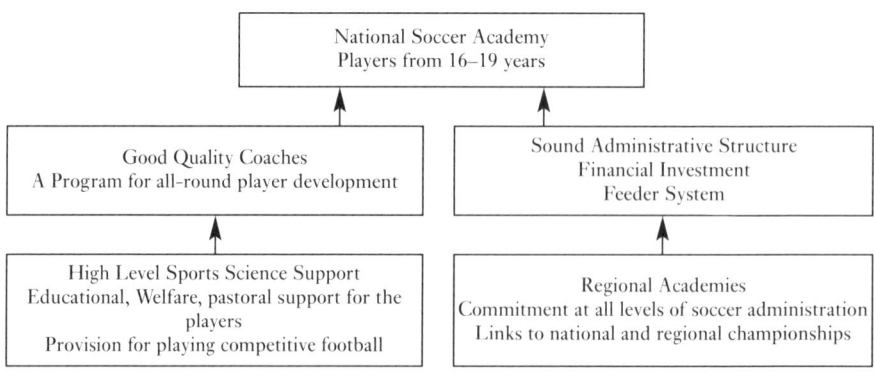

Essentially, the academy has as its pinnacle the national academy, supported by those elements identified in Figure 2 at the second tier, those of coaching (left) and sound administrative structures (right). In the third tier are identified other elements of required support, such sports science and the educational structure described in the left-hand box. The lowest right-hand box outlines the role of the feeder regional academies as an integral part of this hierarchical system.

These suggestions assume a level of support for the players that is probably not in place in India today. However, in order for this type of programme to work it must provide first-class coaching input, contemporary sport science support and an educational programme that ensures that the players gain a balanced development in all walks of life. Of course, in Australia life is very different from that in India, so the system should be modified to suit the economic and cultural environment without watering down the quality and principles of the programmes. As previously discussed, the issue of financial resources is one that sees Indian sports development differently from the situation in most Western countries. However, another model from Australia outside the sporting sphere could provide a solution to this dilemma for the potential government funding of sports development. The higher education model sees graduates who earn above a certain salary level paying back tuition fees to the government through extra taxation. This concept could be adopted for sporting scholarship holders in Indian academies. That is, those that make it through the support of scholarships into professional sport would be contracted to repay a percentage of their earnings back to the institute. This means that eventually the institute would be self-funding. Reputable sporting institutes would also attract sponsorship money and, considering India's population base as well as previous football sponsorship deals in the country,[18] this would not be impossible.

CONCLUSION

The model proposed here has assumed that the goal is to develop soccer in India for native-born footballers, both for those with the potential to play in the national team and for those engaged with the game at lower levels. The views expressed here may be interpreted by some as naïve or too simple because players of Indian origin born overseas have not been mentioned. This has been deliberate in order to reinforce the notion of self-sufficiency for Indian soccer and in some ways to attempt not to muddy the waters. However, in reality the global movement of soccer players cannot be ignored, especially as Indians form such large populations of expatriates throughout the world.

While the advantage of a player with playing experience in top European or South American football competition is indisputable, the long-term effect might be exactly the same as was experienced in Australia and in the USA three or four decades ago. Both of these countries, as developing soccer nations, suffered from the 'football mercenaries' mentioned earlier who were usually players at the end of sometimes not very illustrious careers. India should do without the colonization of the game by foreigners. Equally, the boosting of the national team with European-based Indians may be an attractive strategic, short-term solution to lifting the profile, but it could also be counterproductive in the long term. Any moves along these lines should be part of a well-thought-out strategy that eventually leads to Indian-born players dominating the national team and assisting longer-term development programmes.

Conversely, the soccer authorities may become anxious that their talent identification scheme, in coming to fruition, may see a mass exodus of Indian-born players to the 'big money' opportunities available in Europe. This, while being almost inevitable, is an advantage in the longer term. The experience gained by these players in high level competition will be a great benefit to the national team and to domestic competitions. This is because most of the players will return at the end of their careers to Indian clubs and bolster the quality of play as well as nurturing younger players around them. In addition, many will end as coaches in India and further improve the quality of football in that way. This is happening already in Australia, with players such as Farina, who have spent time in the European leagues and have returned to play or coach in the national league. Over the next few years the Australian NSL could be further bolstered by the return, from Europe, of players such as Mark Bosnich, Mark Viduka and Stan Lazaridis. Given time and good planning, this could be the situation for Indian football in ten years.

In summary, the model of talent identification and development is transferable to India in principle. It will require adjustment to suit the specific social and economic needs of the country. More importantly, it will require adjustment to suit the specific issues relating to Indian football culture. It has to be well organized and well supported, with financial and structural resources coming from the state, from the football authorities, from clubs and from business. The partnerships that develop need to be based on trust and a common vision. If India is to succeed on the international stage, it will need a new culture of cooperation. The financiers, architects, and the builders will all have to work together. The model proposed here is their blueprint.

NOTES

1. The term 'soccer' is used to differentiate association football from Australian rules football. In Australia the game was marginalized by giving it the name soccer so that the dominant games of rugby or Australian rules maintained the 'Australian identity', despite more recent multi-culturalism in Australian society; P. Moore, 'Soccer and the Politics of Culture in Western Australia', in N. Dyck (ed.), *Games, Sports and Cultures* (Oxford: Berg, 2000), pp.117–34.
2. Coaching courses in Australia are designed at different levels, level 1 is for coaches of juniors and teachers with level 3 being aimed more at professional coaches. Staff coaches are recognized instructors who run the courses.
3. For more details see N. Kapadia in this volume.
4. To take advantage of including the strongest New Zealand club and consequently giving the league an international dimension as well as improving Australasian football in general.
5. Active Australia, *Physical Activity Patterns*, www.sportnet.com.au/activeaustralia/national, accessed Feb. 2001.
6. See M. Rodrigues in this volume.
7. See N. Kapadia in this volume.
8. J. Selby, *New Coaching Scheme a Huge Success*, www.socceraustralia.com.au/development/news.sps, accessed Feb. 2001.
9. Ibid.
10. Ibid. Kewell and Viduka are high profile players in the English Premier League with Leeds United who would command a place in any international team.
11. Based upon the Australian system.
12. M. Hughes, 'Notation Analysis in Sport', in G. Atkinson and T. Reilly (eds), *Science and Football II* (Netherlands: E & F Spon, 1993), pp.151–9.

13. A. Borrie, C. Palmer, D. Whitby, L. Burwitz and L. Broomhead, 'The Use of Notational Analysis in Support of the Coach', in G. Atkinson and T. Reilly (eds), *Sport, Leisure and Ergonomics* (Netherlands: E & F Spon, 1995), pp.248–53.

14. A cautionary note about computer systems which purport to identify sporting talent through inputting a series of physical characteristics is needed at this juncture. These systems merely select an appropriate physique, which may be acceptable for rowing or cycling but will not be useful in team games such as soccer because of the highly specialized skills required.

15. J. Bloomfield, T. Ackland and B. Elliott, *Applied Biomechanics in Sport* (Melbourne: Blackwell, 1994), p.7

16. More recent data are not available, but the annual intake usually sees between 12 and 20 scholarship holders at any one time.

17. Australian Institute of Sport, *Facts on Line – Soccer*, www.ausport.gov.au/aissoc.html, accessed Feb. 2001.

18. See M. Rodrigues in this volume.

Conclusion: Soccer in South Asia – Past, Present and Future

PAUL DIMEO and JAMES MILLS

FOOTBALL AND SOCIETY IN SOUTH ASIA

This volume has begun to identify a range of themes and conclusions in the history and sociology of soccer in south Asia. Chief among these is the key observation that, while the game was introduced by the British, football was almost immediately adopted and adapted by a number of different Indian communities and groups. In short, a number of the writers here have shown how the game was a tool of empire at various times and places. However, they have also been concerned to show that the game quickly became a site for the contestation of colonial power and representations and for the development and playing out of a number of different identities and processes.

It has been among our main objectives to show how and where football has been shaped by these developing identities and processes but it is also important to show that the game has been central to their emergence. Indeed, the authors would place football alongside cricket in Appadurai's estimation of the sport as a unique medium for the development of the forces of Indian history, combining as it does the esoteric elements of masculinity and metaphor with the mobilizational elements of spectacle, physical expression and competition.[1] The imagined identity and the historical process are suddenly given physical immediacy and a bodily impact in sport, and it may well be this that explains the emergence of organized games as a global social force in the twentieth century and the place of football in south Asian history and society over the last hundred years.

The editors are acutely aware, however, that there is much ground that has not been covered since the research remains to be done. If the work aimed in the first place to provide information on south Asian football and a point of access to the analytical frameworks that have been used to date for exploring the game, it had as a final objective the identification of questions that have yet to be answered. Most of the rest of this concluding chapter will be devoted to outlining important research areas for the future.

AN ANALYTICAL FRAMEWORK

It is our suggestion that the development of football in south Asia can be organized into five distinct phases, each of which has its own unique set of relationships, symbols and events. These phases are not entirely independent of each other since earlier phases always leave their legacies. However, the phases outlined serve to mark out the processes of change as well as to suggest ways of approaching future research:

1. Colonial exclusion and pedagogy, 1860–1911
2. Anti-colonialism and religious communalism, 1912–47
3. Nationhood and internal state and ethnic division, 1948–62
4. Problems of organization, popularity and standards, 1963–95
5. Modernization, revival and the involvement of the south Asian diaspora, 1996–2001

These phases have their own specific characteristics, as illustrated through the histories and analyses of this volume.

The first phase involved British colonial groups bringing football to India and establishing the organizations, the methods, the styles, and the morals through which the sport should be played to reflect the demands of the Empire. It was initially dominated by British officials and administrators, by the pedagogues of the Anglo-Indian colleges, by the officers and men of the Army and by the resident civilians employed in colonial trade and religion. The reasoning behind the introduction of the game was imperial since the game was, on the one hand, a means of drawing the colonized nearer to the ideals of the British male and, on the other, a way of keeping the Indian at arm's length. In this the game reflected and articulated the wider paradoxes of imperial rule in India at the end of the nineteenth century. This is much the same in the case of Indian responses. The urge to reject British systems and the desire to take the colonizer on and beat him at his own game are contradictory responses that are nevertheless born of the same emotion to resist, and, indeed, the adoption of the British ways because they are seen as part of a more successful culture is a further contradiction.

These paradoxes and contradictions, together with the diverse experiences of football in Kashmir, Tibet, Bengal and Goa, alert analysts to the complexities of sport in colonial India. These experiences may sometimes have common features, such as the application of football as a moral tool, but analyses risk confusion if conceptual frameworks are imposed or if similarities are emphasized without due respect to historical detail. Earlier investigations of this period in the history of Indian football have been important in identifying the area of study as significant, but a much broader and more sophisticated approach is now required. Tyndale-Biscoe and his like were not the only colonizers playing football with the locals and those unlike him need to be identified, in the trades teams, on the visiting ships and in the lower ranks of the Army. Their agendas, the styles of football that they taught and the meaning of the game that they transmitted will have had as much impact as that of the school-masters and missionaries, and yet these topics remain unexplored. The diversity of the British vectors of football in India is an important topic for future research.

Similarly then, the diversity of Indian responses in this first phase needs to be a central research issue for the future. Many Bengali cultural nationalists refused the temptations of British sports, seeing in them a more damaging cultural imperialism, despite the obvious joys of beating their masters at their own game in moments such as the 1911 Mohun Bagan victory. Even in Bengal, the place where football has traditionally been most popular, local people were divided as to the political consequences of taking up the sport.

Analyses should not focus only on the top-class clubs that developed enormous popularity and achieved these significant victories. There were many leagues throughout India for schools and for the less talented that played a part in bringing people to football. By concentrating only on the elite sportsmen it is easy to ignore less prominent participants who, nevertheless, had their lives affected by the game. It also means that it is possible to miss the structures in both Indian society and British colonialism that ensured that certain players did become elite sportsmen while others, despite their talents or commitment, remained nothing more than regulars in the local kick-about.

One way forward with such research is to broaden the geographical extent of the studies available. A start has been made on the football histories of a number of regions in this volume, but there is little research on other areas. Football is now played across India and yet its introduction in somewhere such as Assam through the tea planters and their associations was different from the first games of football played by sailors in Bombay. The study of Tibet here also reminds the historian that little contemporary proof of a regional interest in soccer is not necessarily evidence that the game was never significant there. The failure of the game to catch on in some areas is surely as important as its success elsewhere.

The second phase (1912–47) began with British attempts to undermine Bengali nationalism by shifting the capital of British India to Delhi. Indian football clubs grew in confidence and demanded full and equal access to the competitions originally created for the exclusive use of British clubs. Yet there remained clear signs that certain British ideologies were still important in Indian football in this period. Discourses of racial inferiority, for example, were implicitly accepted by many Indians who agreed that the lessons learnt from the game were a means for improving their 'race' and assisted the progression towards national independence.

Moreover, the amateur ethic seems to have persisted in India in a period when the sport in Britain was being challenged by the emergence of working-class players who demanded payment and by businessmen who saw the economic potential of such a popular sport. This was a period in British football, and also elsewhere in Europe, when the amateur ethic and the traditional authority of the gentlemen of the elite schools who perpetuated it were largely displaced. India shared with Britain large attendances at football matches and strong identifications with clubs, and yet the commercial activities that grew out of these in the latter were not replicated in the former.

The foundation of the All India Football Federation (AIFF) in 1937 underlines this point. At first sight it seems to point to a modernizing process as the regional nature of the game was brought under a national umbrella. However, further scrutiny shows that the organization was governed by amateurs and bureaucrats. The reasons for the survival of the amateur ethos in the Indian game, a colonial legacy that is all too familiar to observers of football in the country to this day, are important.

The period was one in which organizational changes were made in the wake of the initiative taken by the clubs. Mohammedan Sporting's policy of scouting talented Muslim players from across the country ushered in a system of player migration that was national in scope. The horizons of football began to broaden and the leading clubs assumed political meaning on a national, rather than just a Bengali, level. Kapadia and Dimeo in this volume have begun to highlight the incorporation of the successes of clubs such as Mohun Bagan and Mohammedan Sporting into political rhetoric in the period. But the precise relationship between footballing achievements and the emergence of new identities and political positions is still uncertain. Football may simply have been an occasion for expressing already existing divisions, but it may have actually caused these or acted as an occasion for a physical experience of what up to that point had been simply a metaphor or idea.

The third phase (1948–62) represents a time in which India used football to represent its new status as a nation to a global audience. The achievements of Indian national teams in the Olympics and the Asian Games and the invitation to the World Cup of 1950 are unexplored windows on to the experience of nationhood and national identities. One of the more interesting questions here is the extent to which sport became a language in which to express independence and the extent to which the desire to be heard led to the Indian game's being homogenized to international standards. Certainly, more effort was made to conform to and engage with global sporting culture since playing without boots was banned, the time for matches was extended to 90 minutes and tactics developed in line with the more common formations such as the 4–4–2 system. Foreign coaches were employed and the Englishman George Ainsley would have taken India to the World Cup in 1950 if the AIFF had accepted the invitation. Moreover, the Swedish team Helsingborg toured Bengal and India undertook several tours to other parts of Asia. During the period Indian teams were praised by several major figures in international football, including Sir Stanley Rous and Dr Willy Meisl. There was much activity then in this period and, at first sight, it seemed as if the future of Indian football was full of potential. Successes had dried up by the middle of the 1960s, however, and quite why this period of promise petered out is entirely unexplained.

Two other developments during this period were vital. First, there was the liberation of Goa in 1961 that brought into India a state passionately committed to football and where the game had a unique history. Secondly, Mohammedan

Sporting's success dwindled but the rivalry between Mohun Bagan and East Bengal blossomed. Fired by the ethnic divisions in Calcutta after the arrival in the city of immigrants from the former East Bengal (that became East Pakistan in 1947 and Bangladesh in 1971), the rivalry has come to dominate Indian football. Both developments saw football take a central place in the emergence and articulation of new and important identities as Goans used the game to express their distinctiveness from other Indians and the communities of Calcutta made clear their histories through their football allegiances. The question, once again, is to what extent soccer contributed to these identities and divisions or simply mirrored them.

The fourth period (1963–95) seems to have been largely characterized by demise. The promise of the post-Independence period faded. The manner in which the AIFF conducted its business remained obscured by a lack of public accountability and accusations of corruption have persisted, although no proof of wrongdoing has been produced. The structures and objectives of this organization remain an important research topic as it continues to dominate the Indian game under the shadowy rule of Priya Ranjan Das Munshi.

Several other factors contributed to the sport's general depression. The international achievements of south Asian nations in other sports such as cricket and hockey and the attraction of these tended to focus attention on activities other than football. The short-term importance of local rivalries such as the Mohun Bagan–East Bengal contest drew attention from longer term and broader patterns of development. The 1980 Eden Gardens tragedy in which 16 fans died during a riot at a match between Mohun Bagan and East Bengal made the game look disreputable and dangerous.

The economic and the political situations also played their part in the stagnation of Indian football. The politics of the period and the economic protectionism that was practised meant that India was inward looking and isolated in a period when football was becoming the global sport. A devalued currency, restrictions on moving money in and out of national boundaries and the inability to match the pay for foreign players and coaches meant that Indian football failed to engage with developments in the game and, as a result, tactics became outdated and coaching techniques moribund.

Much more information is needed about this period, about why south Asian football appears to have become becalmed after the signs of activity in previous decades. There seems to be a strong connection between a retreat from football globalization and India's political and economic isolationism in this period. Yet the focus away from international success and the importance attached to winning derby games and interstate trophies may reflect the wider fragmentation of India's national identity under pressure from regionalism and communalism over the last 20 years. The relationship between society and football in this period needs to be examined far more closely.

The final period (1996–2001) starts with the FIFA-instigated establishment of the Indian National Football League (NFL), an ambitious project that suggested new ambitions. This was a deliberate attempt to raise the standards of the game and to construct a national competition on the lines of foreign models of organization. Yet, despite the initial media and corporate interest, the NFL appears to be faltering and the processes of commercialization and professionalization that the NFL was intended to kick-start have foundered.

The AIFF appears to be taking much of the blame for this. The secretary of the West Bengal FA, Ranjit Gupta, recently challenged in court the AIFF president to open the organization's accounts for public inspection. Moreover, in December 2000 nine of India's top clubs, led by the owner of United Breweries, Vijay Mallya, launched a break-away football organization as a confrontational challenge to the AIFF. This led to the temporary suspension of the NFL. Clearly, the management of football in India is in trouble. Further investigation of such developments would obviously contribute to a sense of football's current state and events for development. Meanwhile, the lack of research into contemporary football cultures and administration in the other nations of south Asia is an obvious gap in knowledge.

While the National League faces several crises, other aspects of south Asian football are more positive. The financial contribution made by large corporations indicates their awareness of the sport's popularity and promise. Large sponsorship deals, such as United Breweries' interest in Bengal's top clubs, suggest the commercial viability of football. Yet this also raises the difficult question of vested interests posed by UB's attempts to buy control of a number of major clubs.

In Goa, by contrast, the traditional close alliance of companies and clubs means that supporters do not imagine that the clubs are representative of their interests and identities. The only successful club that represents a community is Vasco da Gama, as it has its own stadium whereas all the other clubs share the government-owned Fatorda Stadium in Margao. This creates an unusual situation in which large crowds attend matches without demonstrating any of the partisanship found in almost every other football setting in the world. It also opens up questions of how the game can develop without an element of supporter loyalty.

Thus there are important comparative issues in contemporary south Asian football that need to be drawn out through sustained research. On the international level there have been a number of interesting developments. First, the South Asian Football Federation Cup was established in 1993 from the South Asian Federation Games. Secondly, Baichung Bhutia became the first south Asian to play professional football in Europe. This signalled the existence and quality of Indian football to a sceptical global audience. Thirdly, India and Bangladesh played tour matches in England in July 2000. The matches attracted reasonable crowds, largely from the south Asian communities living in England. Finally, the internet has been used as a means of publicizing south Asian football and bringing together interested members of the global, south Asian diaspora.

There is a current availability of information and contact that did not exist five years ago. One of the main web sites is indianfootball.com, run by the Indian-German student Arunava Chaudhuri, but clubs are beginning to construct their own sites for information and exchange.

These several developments are evidence of the renewed integration of Indian football with the global game. They also point to the emerging importance of the south Asian diaspora in the future of the game. FC Kochin was established by non-resident Indians, the websites are run by Indians living in North America and Europe, the national coach of the Indian team on tour in England spoke admiringly of English Asian footballers and declared that 'the AIFF should tap these unknown sources of talent as it may hasten the development of Indian football' and squad members declared that 'we are more popular in England than in Punjab'.[2] South Asian communities around the globe clearly have a growing interest and influence in football in India.

Exactly what the implications of this are will be an important research area. How football fans, players and administrators in India will receive these foreign interventions remains to be seen. Individuals socialized within Western societies may assume the superiority of models of progress familiar from the societies that they have grown up in. As such, the arrival of Westerners of south Asian origin in India could be a curious echo of centuries of colonial discourse and material intervention. Cultural and sporting change in this context will not necessarily be the easy 'transnational' mutuality that is assumed. Thus local and global differences remain central, not only to an understanding of contemporary football and its development, but also to the mechanisms through which globalization and the diaspora will affect south Asia in the new century.

A final development that has been entirely neglected in this volume due to the lack of current research is the relationship between women and football in south Asia. It is clear that women's football is something of a growth area and, despite the continuing social barriers facing women in their attempts to play football, the national team has had more success than the men's team in recent years. The meaning of football for the women involved and the obstacles in their way are important issues for future work.

In short, this volume is a significant first step in writing the histories, the sociology and the ethnographies of football in south Asia. It has brought together the existing scholars in the subject together with the most significant journalists and experienced coaches. It has attempted to provide information and analysis and, perhaps most important of all, it has started to identify the questions that still need to be asked. Identity, politics, organizational behaviour, gender and globalization are among the key issues that remain to be fully explored in south Asian football and its relationship with the histories and societies of the region.

Yet one final issue, barely touched upon here nor, indeed, in the wealth of other studies of sport and of football, is that of the aesthetics of the game.

Football is a spectacle,

> still we watch sports – to see who wins, who loses, who bears up or who doesn't. Mostly, we wait for a surpassing moment when the grave odds of life are reversed; when time is either stopped or transfigured. We love these transfigurations. Shining performances are privileges granted only a few times in a life, and we will put up with anything to see them.[3]

This is perhaps the most important issue of all: that of the question of the aesthetics of the game in south Asia. The region's cultures have their own visual traditions, their own concepts of story-telling and history, and a wide experience of public festivals and spectacles that combine crowds, performers and sacred spaces. The relationship between the football match and the football occasion and these other aspects promises to be a fertile source for exploring the way in which the aesthetics of sport become entangled with a society's wider understandings of beauty, of event and of performance. And, after all, in south Asia, as with the rest of the world, it is the incorporation of the game on the park into a wider cosmos of fantasies and identities through these moments of aesthetic ecstasy that makes football so important in so many lives.

NOTES

1. A. Appadurai, 'Playing with Modernity: The Decolonization of Indian Cricket', in C.A. Breckenridge (ed.), *Consuming Modernity: Public Culture in Contemporary India* (Minneapolis, MN: University of Minnesota Press, 1994).
2. N. Kapadia, 'P.K. Banerjee, Sukhwinder All Praise for the Back Four', *The Telegraph*, 31 July 2000.
3. F. Milburn, *Polo: The Emperor of Games* (New York, NY: Alfred Knopf, 1994), p.9.

Select Bibliography

J. Alter, *The Wrestler's Body: Identity and Ideology in North India* (Berkeley, CA: University of California Press, 1992)

J. Alter, '*Kabaddi*, a National Sport of India: The Internationalism of Nationalism and the Foreignness of Indianness', in N. Dyck (ed.), *Games, Sports and Cultures* (Oxford: Berg, 2000)

A. Appadurai, 'Playing with Modernity: The Decolonization of Indian Cricket', in C.A. Breckenridge (ed.), *Consuming Modernity: Public Culture in a South Asian World* (Minneapolis, MN: University of Minnesota Press, 1995)

S. Banerjee, *Cluber Naam Mohun Bagan* (Calcutta: Aparna Book Distribution Centre, 1998)

Sir C. Bell, *The People of Tibet* (Oxford: Oxford University Press, 1968) [first published 1928]

H. Bhabha, *The Location of Culture* (London: Routledge, 1994)

P. Bishop, *The Myth of Shangri-La: Tibet, Travel Writing and the Western Creation of Sacred Landscape* (London: Athlone Press, 1989)

M. Bose, *A Maidan View: The Magic of Indian Cricket* (London: Allen & Unwin, 1986)

M. Bose, *The History of Indian Cricket* (London: Andre Deutsch, 1990)

J.M. Brown, *Modern India: The Origins of an Asian Democracy* (Oxford: Oxford University Press, 2nd edn, 1994)

R. Cashman, *Patrons, Players and the Crowd: The Phenomenon of Indian Cricket* (Delhi: Longman, 1980)

I. Chowdury-Sengupta, 'The Effeminate and the Masculine: Nationalism and the Concept of Race in Colonial Bengal', in P. Robb (ed.), *The Concept of Race in South Asia* (Oxford: Oxford University Press, 1995)

S.B. Cook, *Colonial Encounters in the Age of High Imperialism* (New York, NY: HarperCollins, 1996)

A. de Mello, *Portrait of Indian Sport* (London: Macmillan, 1959)

P. Dimeo '"Team Loyalty Splits the City into Two": Football, Ethnicity and Rivalry in Calcutta', in G. Armstrong and R. Giulianotti (eds), *Fear and Loathing in World Football* (Oxford: Berg, 2001)

E. Docker, *History of Indian Cricket* (Delhi: Macmillan, 1977)

L. Gandhi, *Postcolonial Theory: A Critical Introduction* (New Delhi: Oxford University Press, 1999)

M. Ghoshal, *Kolkatta Football* (Calcutta: Jaya Ghoshal, 1988)

S.L. Ghosh (ed.), *Indian Football* (New Delhi: Shaheed Prakashan Press, 1975)

V. Ghosh, (ed.), *Limca Book of Records 2000* (New Delhi: VG Communications, 2000)

R. Giulianotti, *Football: A Sociology of the Global Game* (Oxford: Polity Press, 1999)

R. Guha (ed.), *Subaltern Studies I* (Delhi: Oxford University Press, 1982)

R. Guha, 'Cricket and Politics in Colonial India', *Past and Present*, 161 (1998)

A. Guttmann, *Games and Empires: Modern Sports and Cultural Imperialism* (New York, NY: Columbia University Press, 1994)

M. Harrison, *Climates and Constitutions Health, Race, Environment and British Imperialism in India, 1600–1850* (Delhi and Oxford: Oxford University Press, 1999)

E. Hobsbawm, *Nations and Nationalism since 1780* (Cambridge: Cambridge University Press, 1990)

C.L.R. James, *Beyond a Boundary* (London: Penguin, 1964)

N. Kapadia, 'Decline Of Hyderabad Football', *DCM Football Tournament Journal* (Delhi: DCM Football Tournament Society, 1986)

N. Kapadia, 'India in International Soccer – Olympics', *Durand Journal 1999* (Delhi: Durand Football Tournament Society, 1999)

F.J. Korom (ed.), *Constructing Tibetan Culture: Contemporary Perspectives* (Quebec: World Heritage Press, 1997)

D. Linhui, 'Tibetan Sports: Thirty Years of Development", in *China's Tibet*, 6 (1995)

D. Lopez, *Prisoners of Shangri-La: Tibetan Buddhism and the West* (Chicago, IL: University Press, 1998)

R.H. MacDonald, *The Language of Empire: Myths and Metaphors of Popular Imperialism, 1880–1918* (Manchester: Manchester University Press, 1994)

I. McDonald, 'Physiological Patriots? The Politics of Physical Nationalism and Hindu Nationalism in India', *International Review for the Sociology of Sport*, 34 (1999)

I. McDonald, 'Between Saleem and Shiva: The Politics of Cricket Nationalism in "Globalising India"', in J. Sugden and A. Bairner (eds), *Sport in Divided Societies* (Aachen: Meyer and Meyer, 1999)

J.A. Mangan, *Athleticism in the Victorian and Edwardian Public School: The Emergence and Consolidation of an Educational Ideology* (Cambridge: Cambridge University Press, 1981)

J.A. Mangan (ed.), *The Cultural Bond: Sport, Empire, Society* (London and Portland, OR: Frank Cass, 1992)

J.A. Mangan. *The Games Ethic and Imperialism: Aspects of the Diffusion of an Ideal* (London and Portland, OR: Frank Cass, 2000)

T. Mason, 'Football on the Maidan: Cultural Imperialism in Calcutta', *International Journal of the History of Sport*, 12, 1 (1990)

A. McKay, 'The Other "Great Game": Politics and Sport in Tibet, 1904–47', *International Journal of the History of Sport*, 11 (1994)

A. McKay, *Tibet and the British Raj: The Frontier Cadre 1904–47* (Richmond: Curzon Press, 1997)

J. Mills, *Madness, Cannabis and Colonialism: The 'Native Only' Lunatic Asylums of British India, 1857 to 1880* (Basingstoke: Macmillan, 2000)

J. Mills and P. Dimeo (eds), 'Sports in South Asia', special edition of *Contemporary South Asia*, 10, 2 (2001)

S. Mookerjee, 'Early Decades of Calcutta Football', *Economic Times: Calcutta 300* (Sept. 1989)

P. Moore, 'Soccer and the Politics of Culture in Western Australia', in N. Dyck (ed.), *Games Sports and Cultures*, (Oxford: Berg, 2000)

G. Moorhouse, *India Britannica* (London: Harvill Press, 1983)

A. Nandy, *The Tao of Cricket: On Games of Destiny and the Destiny of Games* (New York, NY: Oxford University Press: 1989)

M. Pearson, *The New Cambridge History of India, 1: The Portuguese in India* (Cambridge: Cambridge University Press, 1987)

T.L. Pennell, *Among the Wild Tribes of the Afghan Frontier* (London: Seeley, 1909)

R. Robinson, *Conversion, Continuity and Change: Lived Christianity in Southern Goa* (London: Sage, 1998)

J. Rosselli, 'The Self-Image of Effeteness: Physical Education and Nationalism in Nineteenth Century Bengal', *Past and Present*, 86 (1980)

A. Rubinoff, *The Construction of a Political Identity: Integration and Identity in Goa* (London: Sage, 1998)

R. Saha, *Ekadashe Surya* (Calcutta: Deepprakashan Publications, 1990)

O. Salazar, 'Goa and the Indian Union: the Portuguese View', *Foreign Affairs*, (April 1956)

J. Scott, *Weapons of the Weak* (London: Yale University Press, 1985)

T. Shakya, 'Tibet and the Occident: The Myth of Shangri-la', in *Tibetan Review*, 27 (1992) M. Sinha, *Colonial Masculinity: The 'Manly Englishman' and the 'Effeminate Bengali' in the Nineteenth Century* (Manchester: Manchester University Press, 1995)

T. Skorupski (ed.), *Adventures of a Tibetan Fighting Monk* (Bangkok: Tamarind Press, 1986)

C.E. Tyndale-Biscoe, *Kashmir in Light and Shade* (London: Seeley Service, 1922)

E.D. Tyndale-Biscoe, *Fifty Years against the Stream* (Mysore: Wesleyan Missionary Press, 1930)

J. Weir (ed.), *Drink, Religion and Scottish Football 1873–1900* (Renfrew: Stewart Davidson, 1992)

S. Wolpert, *A New History of India* (Oxford and New York, NY: Oxford University Press, 5th edn, 1997)

W. Yao, 'An Inquiry into Polo – Tibet's Contribution to Athletic Sports', in Shiro Ihara and Z. Yamaguchi (eds), *Tibetan Studies: Proceedings of the 5th Seminar of the International Association for Tibetan Studies* (Narita: Japan, 1989)

W. Yao, 'On the Origin of *sho* (Dice) and *sbag* (Domino): Exploration in the Amusement Culture of the Tibetan People', in E. Steinkellner (ed.), *Tibetan Studies: Proceedings of the 7th Seminar of the International Association for Tibetan Studies, Graz 1995*, Vol.2 (Wien: Verlag der Österreich-ischen Akademie der Wissenschaften, 1997)

Notes on Contributors

Bill Adams is Director of Coaching of the Super Soccer Academy, New Delhi, and a founding member of the India Youth Soccer Association. He was educated at the Universities of Oxford, Leeds, and Essex and has taught at several universities in the United Kingdom and at NIFT, New Delhi. He is the author of *The Five Lessons of Life* (Rider, 1999). He has been coaching soccer since 1976.

Paul Dimeo lectures in Sports Studies at University College Northampton. His PhD was completed at the University of Strathclyde in 2000, with the title 'Racism, Football and Cultural Difference: The Experience of Scottish Asians'. He has been researching aspects of the history and sociology of south Asian football since 1998, and has published a number of articles on this subject in academic journals and collected volumes.

John Hammond is Head of Sports Studies and Sports Science at Edgehill University College. Previously he taught physical education and sport studies at school, college and university level in Australia for 23 years. During that period he was a staff coach with the Australian Soccer Federation's National Coaching Scheme and coached five state teams in National Championships. He has presented papers at a number of international conferences and written for a variety of academic and professional publications.

Novy Kapadia has been a football analyst for Star Sports/ESPN since 1996, and has assumed the same role for the Indian state television channel Doordarshan. He has reported on several international sporting events since 1980 for All India Radio and for the BBC World Service. Since 1982 he has also been the Delhi- based sports correspondent of *The Telegraph*, an English daily newspaper and *Sportsworld* magazine. He has been the editor of the *Durand Football Journal*, India's only comprehensive statistical and information-based football journal, since 1983. He is also editor and a consultant for the Sports Section of the *Limca Book of Records*, India's equivalent of the *Guinness Book of Records*.

J.A. Mangan is Director of the International Research Centre for Sport, Socialisation and Society at the University of Strathclyde. He is the founder and general editor of the Frank Cass series Sport in the Global Society, and the founding and executive academic editor of the Cass journals *The International Journal of the History of Sport*; *Culture, Sport, Society*; *Soccer and Society*; and the *European Sports History Review*. His books *Athleticism in the Victorian and Edwardian Public Schools* and *The Games Ethic and Imperialism* have recently been reprinted by Frank Cass.

Alex McKay is an Indo-Tibetan historian, with a PhD in south Asian history from the School of Oriental and African Studies, London University (1995). He is the author of *Tibet and the British Raj: The Frontier Cadre 1904–1947* (Curzon Press, 1997) and editor of *Pilgrimage in Tibet* (Curzon Press, 1998), in addition to numerous academic articles. A research fellow at SOAS and the International Institute for Asian Studies in Leiden, he is currently editing a three-volume history of Tibet and researching the Indo-Tibetan pilgrimage to Mount Kailas.

James Mills is a lecturer in modern history at the University of Strathclyde. He is a social historian of India and the author of a range of publications on the history of medicine in south Asia. Chief among these is *Madness, Cannabis and Colonialism: The 'Native-Only' Lunatic Asylums of British India, 1857–1900* (Macmillan), published in 2000. He is currently writing a history of cannabis legislation in the United Kingdom with the funding of the ESRC.

Mario Rodrigues is a Mumbai-based journalist who has served with *The Daily*, *Blitz*, *The Independent*, *Bombay Times* and *The Statesman*. He has published on China and on Goan music, besides editing a volume on Indo-South African cricket. He has keenly followed Indian football for 24 years and written about it for 18. He was co-organizer of the India vs. Soviet Union charity football match at Mumbai in 1990, iand is the president of the city's United Athletes Sports Club.

Index

Soccer in South Asia

Empire, Nation, Diaspora

EDITORS: PAUL DIMEO and JAMES MILLS

While the importance of cricket in south Asian, especially Indian, culture has been widely studied, football's place in that society has been unjustly neglected. The game in India, the world's second most populous nation, is thriving.

This first major study of Indian football traces the history, achievements and prospects of the game both in south Asia and among expatriate Indian, Pakistani and Bangladeshi communities. It shows how football has been closely linked to the processes that have shaped the societies and histories of the region since the nineteenth century – colonialism, the rise of nationalism and communalism, and the establishment of nationhood – and looks at the recent state of the sport and the issues that most concern observers of football in India today. The academics, journalists, football coaches and administrators who contribute to this collection examine the impact of commercialization, professionalization and globalization, the strengths and weakness of the current Indian football administration, and they discuss how the game might be developed to make India a major force in world football. This book will be of interest to historians and sociologists of sport in general and of football in particular, to all academics who research or teach south Asian issues and to general readers with an interest in the global game and its development.

Paul Dimeo is Lecturer in Sports Studies at University College Northampton. He has published a range of articles on racism in Scottish football. He is researching the social history of football in south Asia.

James Mills is Lecturer in History at the University of Strathclyde. He has written articles and books on the social history of colonialism in south Asia. He is working on a history of drugs in India with the financial support of the Wellcome Trust and the ESRC.

Cover photograph: East Bengal's striker Bijen Singh is challenged by a Zee Churchill defender. Photograph by Mohammed Shafiq.